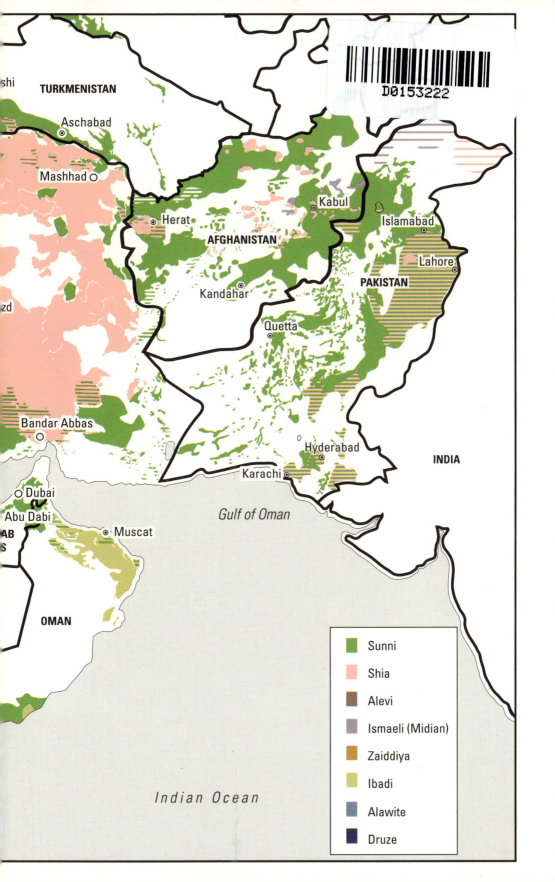

TURKMENISTAN

Aschabad

Mashhad

Herat

AFGHANISTAN

Kabul

Islamabad

Lahore

PAKISTAN

Kandahar

Quetta

Bandar Abbas

Hyderabad

INDIA

Karachi

Dubai

Abu Dabi

Muscat

Gulf of Oman

OMAN

Indian Ocean

🟩	Sunni
🟧	Shia
🟫	Alevi
🟪	Ismaeli (Midian)
🟧	Zaiddiya
🟨	Ibadi
🔵	Alawite
🔷	Druze

SUNNIS
AND
SHI'A

ENDSHEET: Map of the Near and Middle East

SUNNIS
A Political
AND
History
SHI'A
of Discord

Laurence Louër

Translated by Ethan Rundell

PRINCETON UNIVERSITY PRESS

PRINCETON AND OXFORD

Published by Princeton University Press
41 William Street, Princeton, New Jersey 08540
6 Oxford Street, Woodstock, Oxfordshire OX20 1TR

press.princeton.edu

Library of Congress Cataloging-in-Publication Data

Names: Louër, Laurence, author. | Rundell, Ethan S., translator.
Title: Sunnis and Shi'a : a political history of discord / Laurence Louër;
    translated by Ethan Rundell.
Other titles: Sunnites et Chiites. English
Identifiers: LCCN 2019027366 (print) | LCCN 201902 (ebook) |
    ISBN 9780691186610 (hardcover) | ISBN 9780691199641 (epub)
Subjects: LCSH: Shī'ah—Relations—Sunnites. | Sunnites—Relations—Shī'ah. |
    Islam—Doctrines. | Islam and politics.
Classification: LCC BP194.16 .L6813 2020 (print) | LCC BP194.16 (ebook) |
    DDC 297.8/042—dc23
LC record available at https://lccn.loc.gov/2019027366
LC ebook record available at https://lccn.loc.gov/2019027367

British Library Cataloging-in-Publication Data is available

Editorial: Fred Appel and Jenny Tan
Production Editorial: Debbie Tegarden
Text Design: Leslie Flis
Jacket/Cover Design: Layla Mac Rory
Production: Erin Suydam
Publicity: James Schneider and Kathryn Stevens
Copyeditor: Anita O'Brien

This book has been composed in Arno Pro

Printed on acid-free paper. ∞

Printed in the United States of America

10 9 8 7 6 5 4 3 2 1

CONTENTS

SUNNIS
AND
SHI'A

INTRODUCTION

Relations between Sunni and Shi'i Muslims are often said to be characterized by over a thousand years of uninterrupted war, the result of ancestral hatreds stemming from disagreements over the Prophet Muhammad's rightful successor. According to Sunnis, who today probably constitute as much as 90 percent of the world's Muslim population, Muhammad left no instructions as to who should succeed him when he died without a male heir in 632, leaving it up to his companions to determine who would best govern. By contrast, the Shi'a believe that Muhammad, directly inspired by God, designated his cousin and son-in-law Ali ibn Abi Talib as his successor. The latter would become the fourth caliph, and Shi'a hold that a lineage of Imams was born of his marriage with the Prophet's daughter, Fatima.

Yet the conflict between Sunnis and Shi'a was never just a mere quarrel over the prophet of Islam's succession. For it immediately raised essential questions as to the nature of legitimate political authority. What sort of qualities should be possessed by the Muslim head of state? Could he be an ordinary human being or should there be something of the divine about him? How was he to be chosen and, by extension, what was the most legitimate type of political regime?

Such were the questions raised by the protagonists of the time. They were ever on the mind of future generations, giving rise to political and religious doctrines as well as myths that continue to structure Sunni and Shi'i political imaginaries to this day. For Sunnis and especially Islamists, the "rightly guided caliphate" of Muhammad's first four successors represents a golden age of just government to which one must return. For the Shi'a, by contrast, the first three caliphs were no more than usurpers. In fighting unjust authority, the heroes of our time must in their eyes strive to emulate Hussein, the son of Imam Ali, who was killed by the army of Caliph Yazid in 680.

Over the centuries, these controversies were activated or deactivated depending on the political context. This is the central argument of the present book. Religious doctrines thus generally evolved in response to the political needs of dominant and dominated groups. They served as legitimating ideologies for political elites; rebels used them to oppose the powers that be; clerics wielded them to assert themselves vis-à-vis state power. In the course of these interactions, Sunnis and Shi'a were not always in open conflict. While Shi'ism in its various manifestations has long been the principal ideology of opposition to the established powers of the Middle East, the Twelver movement that today predominates gradually took shape around a project of doctrinal and political deradicalization that resulted in marginalizing the esoteric and revolutionary currents that were so central during the first centuries of Islam. Orchestrated by Shi'i religious scholars, this process made it possible to conceive of peaceful coexistence with the established powers and also established Shi'ism as a school of religious law that, in point of its conclusions, ultimately differed little from the canonical Sunni schools.

When the Safavids in 1501 moved to establish Shi'ism as the state religion over a territory roughly corresponding to that of contemporary Iran, however, the conflict was reactivated. By making what had been a communal religion into an official religion and using it as a tool for wielding influence beyond their frontiers, the Safavids created a lasting fault line in the Middle East, with the Sunni-Shi'a divide being superimposed in the collective imagination on a conflict between Iran and the rest of the Muslim world. This fault line still exists today: for many Sunnis, every Shi'a is necessarily Iranian or at least an agent in the service of Iran's expansionist intrigues. Many of the conflicts that are today tearing the region apart center on the conflictual relationship between Saudi Arabia and Iran, the two states claiming to embody and champion Sunni and Shi'a Islamism, respectively. Their rivalry intersects with and internationalizes what are at the outset independent local conflicts, introduces religious issues into political struggles, and hardens fluid denominational identities.

To understand the dynamics by which the conflicts between Sunnis and Shi'a are activated and deactivated, the present work takes a twofold approach. In the first part I offer a global political history of Sunnis and Shi'a from the beginning of the quarrel over succession until today. In doing so, I seek to explain the historical roots of contemporary conflicts, underscore historical continuities and ruptures, and cast light on dynamics of antagonism and points of convergence.

The second part offers an at once historical and sociological study of several national configurations in which the Sunni-Shi'a divide structures the political field. This brings to the fore the manner in which Sunni and Shi'a identities are articulated with other social, ethnic, linguistic, regional, economic, and status identities. It is this articulation, specific to each society, that explains why, though present in many Middle Eastern countries, the Sunni-Shi'a divide does or does not develop into more or less violent conflicts depending on the domestic and regional political contexts.

PART ONE

BETWEEN POLITICS AND RELIGION

Chapter 1

CALIPHATE AND IMAMATE

To the great questions regarding government and its relationship to God, those who were to become the "Sunnis" and "Shi'a" gave different answers. These, in turn, were for several centuries the object of continuous doctrinal elaboration. As a result, one cannot truly speak of "Sunnism" and "Shi'ism" before the tenth century. In terms of their doctrine, worship practices, and relationship to power, moreover, neither Sunnism nor Shi'ism constitutes a homogenous entity.

A Theocratic Caliphate (Seventh to Eighth Centuries)

The response offered by those who would become the "Sunnis"—literally, "those who follow the *sunna*," or the Prophet's tradition—to the question of succession and the exercise of power initially delineated an oligarchic political regime. For Muhammad's successor was chosen from among his companions (*sahaba*). The latter rapidly agreed to appoint Abu Bakr al-Siddiq (d. 634), one of the Prophet's closest companions and father of his favorite wife, Aisha, whom Muhammad tasked with leading prayer in his stead after he fell ill. Upon his death two years later, the companions chose Umar ibn al-Khattab (d. 644) to replace him, once again it seems without major difficulty. The latter was also a close companion of Muhammad, who had married one of his daughters.

While their early conversion to Islam, fidelity to the Prophet, and sincerity of faith were the cardinal virtues of these first two successors, they above all had to demonstrate qualities of leadership in a context marked by intensifying factional struggles and the possible disintegration of the community of believers assembled by the Prophet, particularly after the latter was repudiated by several Bedouin tribes in preference to their own prophets. Abu Bakr and Umar showed great political skill in combatting these centrifugal forces. They were also warlords who set about expanding the Muslim state, unifying the Arabian Peninsula, and extending their sovereignty northward to Syria, Egypt, and Iraq.

Muhammad's successors often simultaneously held several titles, all referring to a form of dual authority that was indissociably political and religious in nature: *khalifa, imam, amir al-mu'minin*, and *mahdi*. In some cases, the meaning of these terms and the practices associated with them profoundly changed over time. The term *khalifa*, for example, which we translate by "caliph" and which is today commonly used to refer to Muhammad's various successors at the head of the Muslim state, initially expressed the purely temporal idea of succession (the caliph is literally "he who is behind/comes after") as well as that of divine representation on earth. Indeed, the first caliphs had called themselves *khalifat Allah*, which may be rendered as either "God's caliph" or "God's deputy."[1] The term *imam* (literally, "he who proceeds") explicitly referred to the idea of religious guidance, while *Amir al-Mu'minin*, or "Commander of the Faithful," denoted a charismatic leader deriving his power from God and acting to ensure that His will be done on Earth.[2] The term *mahdi*—often translated by "messiah"—referred to the idea of a guide inspired by God.[3]

Though the subsequent history of the caliphate is, as we shall see, one of ever-growing differentiation between political and religious power, the first caliphs were thus also religious leaders and exercised a theocratic-type power. In particular, they played a central role in developing religious law, defining ritual, and settling on the text of the Koran. This last point is particularly important. The third caliph, Uthman ibn Affan (d. 656), took the initiative of establishing a written version of the Koran. In doing so, his aim was to supply a reference text that would stand as an authority in the particular context of the time—a time characterized by a mainly oral culture (Muhammad himself was illiterate) and the circulation of several versions of the sacred text. This was a matter of great importance to the caliphal powers: settling on an official text and eliminating competing versions, which were often associated with political factions and allowed the theocratic legitimacy of the caliph to be established. The text of the Koran was later canonized on the initiative of Caliph Abd al-Malik ibn Marwan (d. 705) in an effort to raise Islam to the level of other monotheistic religions by providing it with a sacred book and simultaneously assert its difference and superiority vis-à-vis these competing religions.[4]

Legitimist Dissidents: The Alids

The response offered by those who would become the Shi'a to the great questions raised by the power vacuum after Muhammad differed from that offered by the future Sunnis. While it contained a conception of political power that would increasingly diverge from that embodied by the caliphate, it was at first perfectly in keeping with the dominant conceptions of the caliphate as a theocratic power fusing political and religious authority. The term "Shi'a" comes from the Arabic *shi'a*, which means "party" or "partisans." In the context of the factional quarrels surrounding the succession of Muhammad, it refers to the "party of Ali" (*shi'at Ali*), or the "Alids." In contrast to those who would become the Sunnis, today's most prevalent current, who held that Muhammad had not left instructions for his succession, the Alids claimed it was impossible that the Prophet would have left Muslims without direction. According to them, shortly before his death and directly inspired by God, Muhammad appointed Ali ibn Abi Talib (d. 661) as his successor while stopping with his entourage in the oasis of Ghadir Khumm on his way back to Medina following his final pilgrimage to Mecca. Ali was the Prophet's young cousin and husband to his daughter Fatima. According to Shi'a tradition, he was the first man to convert to Islam (the Sunnis claim that status for Abu Bakr).

Ali's claim to succession and that of his partisans may be likened to a legitimist movement. For them, the succession should be open only to members of the Prophet's family, the *Ahl al-Bayt* (or "People of the House") of Muhammad. Given the importance of lineage in Arab societies, it may be conjectured that, should Muhammad have had one or more living sons (all his sons died in childhood), the legitimist movement would have focused on the claims of his male descendants. In their absence, the blood tie with the Prophet passed by way of his daughter Fatima. The partisans of Ali in effect claimed that, following the latter's death, the government of the Muslim state should be transmitted to his male descendants issuing from his union with Fatima.

It seems that, while he may have had some reservations, Ali did not truly seek to assert his claim when the first three caliphs were being selected. Historians often describe him as a man lacking political sense and thus ill-suited to exercising caliphal power. It was the quarrels that developed during the reign of Caliph Uthman that made Ali a unifying figure for many of the discontented.

Like Ali, Uthman was a son-in-law of the Prophet and one of the first to have embraced Islam. But he was also the representative par excellence of the Meccan aristocracy, the very group that had plotted to expel Muhammad from Mecca where he lived, forcing him to seek refuge in the neighboring town of Medina, and who only belatedly joined the Muslim community—according to their detractors, for purely opportunistic reasons. Furthermore, Uthman came to power at a time when the Muslim state was undergoing major transformations, a fact that created tension between the various categories of believers. The first two caliphs' conquests had considerably increased the state's territory, rapidly enriching a class of conquerors who resided far from the Medina caliphate and wished for greater independence vis-à-vis the central government.

In an effort to contain these centrifugal forces, Uthman in this context relied on the members of his clan, the Umayyads, putting them in key positions, sometimes to the detriment of actors who had won renown in the conquests such as Amr ibn al-As, the governor of Egypt whom Uthman dismissed from his duties. The growing discontent resulted in a series of revolts ending in political assassination: soldiers killed the caliph while he was reading the Koran at home.

Uthman's opponents proclaimed Ali as the new caliph. Though he had neither orchestrated nor even encouraged it, Ali soon appeared the principal beneficiary of Uthman's murder and was accused of not seeking to punish the guilty, particularly since he had kept some of them in his immediate entourage. Under these conditions, Ali's rise to power, far from appeasing the situation, witnessed a continued struggle between factions, the most powerful of which were strongly anchored in the various provinces of the empire. Among those opposing Ali were Muhammad's favorite wife, Aisha, whose soldiers he defeated at the Battle of the Camel (656), and, above all, the Umayyads, who demanded vengeance for the assassination of Uthman. Leading them was the powerful governor of Syria, Muawiya ibn Abi Sufyan (d. 680), a skilled politician with a powerful and disciplined army.

Having sought in vain to dismiss him from his functions, Ali decided to confront Muawiya in what remains one of the most painful episodes in the history of Islam: the Battle of Siffin (657), which took place on the banks of the Euphrates near the present-day city of Raqqa in Syria. After several days of fighting and negotiation, the two parties submitted themselves to arbitration: each side chose two wise men to determine who was in the right, Ali or Muawiya. It seems that they came down against the caliph, who was held responsible for failing to take action against Uthman's murderers. Yet nothing was resolved for all that. Ali did not relinquish the caliphate, and, even as he prepared his next military strike against Muawiya, at the Battle of Nahrawan (659) he decimated the ranks of those of his partisans who had opposed his decision to accept arbitration.

Denying any validity to human judgment, the latter held that Ali should have continued the battle, with its outcome to be determined by God himself. They left Ali's camp and for this reason came to be known as the Kharijites—literally, "the leavers" or "the withdrawers." Today Kharidjism—the third great current of Islam after Sunnism and Shi'ism—recognizes the legitimacy of only the first two caliphs. It is principally represented by Ibadism, whose followers reside in certain regions of Algeria (the Mzab) and, above all, Oman, where the Ibadites established a state in the eighth century and today constitute a majority of the population.

Following the Battle of Siffin, Muawiya for his part launched raids against Ali's strongholds, mainly located in what is today southern Iraq. In 660 his supporters officially proclaimed him caliph in Jerusalem. A few months later, in 661, Ali was assassinated by a Kharijite. The Battle of Siffin resulted in what Muslims call *fitna*—that is, schism or strife. It deeply divided the *Umma*, or community of believers. Ali's murder marked the end of what historians call the primitive caliphate, a period that, as we shall see, has provided Sunnis with a veritable golden age myth. After Ali's death, the Umayyads, who reigned from 660 to 750, and then the Abbasids, who held power between 750 and 1258, transformed the caliphate into a classic dynastic power. The towns of Mecca and Medina lost all political centrality, becoming mere places of pilgrimage, while Damascus and, later, Baghdad became centers of political power and doctrinal elaboration.

A Religious and Communal Imamate (661–874)

According to all religious currents deriving from the Alid group, Ali is at once the fourth caliph and the first in a lineage of Imams. Like the caliph in the early years of Islam, the Imam simultaneously exercises religious and political power. While, as we have seen, the caliphs were often called "imams" over the course of history, this term took on specific meaning in Shi'ism, becoming "the mainspring of all Shi'a doctrine."[5] According to the Shi'a, each prophet is accompanied by one or several Imams. While the prophet is responsible for transmitting the obvious meaning of God's message to as many people as possible, the Imams are tasked with revealing its hidden meaning to an elite by virtue of their intimate relationship with God. The Shi'a call this intimate relationship to the Divine *wilaya*. This polysemic term, the uses of which have, as we shall see, significantly evolved over time, was used by the Imams themselves to refer to their doctrine as an unveiling of secrets. It also refers to the notion of love of God and authority.

In Shi'ism, not surprisingly, the notion of the imamate is based on the idea that the world is divided between an exoteric apparent reality (*zahir*) and an esoteric hidden reality (*batin*). While the Shi'a adhere to the fundamental dogma of Islam according to which Muhammad is the last of the prophets sent by God (*khatimiyya*) and thus do not present the Imam properly speaking as a prophet (*nabi* or *rasul* in Arabic), the Imam nevertheless possesses all attributes of a prophet according to the classic terms of religious sociology: in personal contact with God, he reveals divine secrets, is exempt from sin, and has infallible judgment (*ma'sum*).

After Ali's caliphate, none of the Imams wielded state power. The eldest son of Ali and Fatima, Hassan al-Mujtaba (d. 670), succeeded his father as Imam and, realizing that the balance of power was clearly against him, reached an agreement with Muawiya whereby Hassan officially renounced his claims to the caliphate. Upon his death, his brother Hussein Sayyid al-Shuhada (d. 680) took over and, imitating Hassan, kept to Medina, far from political matters. Yet the death of Caliph Muawiya in 680 opened a window of opportunity. Under pressure from his father's supporters, who had gathered in the town of Kufa (contemporary southern Iraq) and assured him they possessed an army ready to serve him, Hussein was persuaded to lay claim to the caliphate. Accompanied by his family, he set out to join his troops ready to confront the new Umayyad caliph, Muawiya's son, Yazid ibn Muawiya (d. 683). Several kilometers from Kufa, he was intercepted by Yazid's troops. Abandoned by his supporters, who at the last moment thought better of it given the unfavorable balance of forces, Hussein was killed together with most of his entourage on the site of what subsequently became the town of Karbala, today one of the main sites of Shi'a pilgrimage.

Hussein's martyrdom is a central episode, as indicated by the fact that he is to this day commemorated by various rituals of mortification known as Ashura (in reference to the tenth day of the Muslim month of Muharram, when Hussein was killed and the ceremonies came to an end). It was rapidly transformed into a myth that continues to profoundly mark Shi'a identity to this day. This myth has been the object of several interpretations. The Alids initially held that Hussein, nicknamed the "prince of martyrs," had obeyed a divine commandment in voluntarily submitting to death, an understanding close to Christian conceptions of the death of Christ: Hussein was said to have offered himself in sacrifice in the aim of saving the true religion and unifying the community of "true Muslims."[6] In the contemporary period, the Karbala myth has been reinterpreted as the act of a man who chose death rather than submission to an unjust power, and he is treated as an exemplary figure by Shi'a Islamist movements.

At the same time, the Karbala episode marked a definitive renunciation of political power on the part of the descendants of Ali and Fatima. For after Hussein, none of the Imams openly laid claim to power. What is more, they regularly recommended that their followers not publicly display their convictions and even conceal them (*taqiyya* or *kitman*). Given these circumstances, the imamate above all assumed the form of a communitarian and religious authority. Apart from the particularly difficult task of disciplining and bringing together the various Alid factions, the Imams were also responsible for administering the everyday affairs of the faithful, something that included developing and spreading doctrine as well as collecting and redistributing taxes. The sixth Imam, Ja'far al-Sadiq (d. 765), played a central role in this respect.

Ja'far al-Sadiq performed his duties at a particularly troubled time that saw the Abbasids carry out a victorious revolution against the Umayyad government and install a new dynasty of caliphs. The Abbasids claimed to descend from an uncle of the Prophet named Abbas. They extensively drew on their kinship with Muhammad, presenting their movement as intended to bring together the entire family of the Prophet, the Hashemites. Ja'far al-Sadiq was on excellent terms with them, a fact that allowed him to recruit Alids to high positions in the Abbasid court[7] and thus in practice create an Alid pressure group within the caliph's entourage. As we shall see, this was to play a decisive role in the construction of Shi'a religion and community. One consequence of Ja'far al-Sadiq's rapprochement with the caliphate was that he became a well-regarded religious figure in Sunnism, respected even among the ulama for his religious learning.[8]

Continuing the work begun by his father, Muhammad al-Baqir (d. 743), the sixth Imam used this protected political perch to concentrate on doctrinal elaboration and, in particular, the development of Shi'a religious law—still known to this day as "Ja'fari" jurisprudence. Some clarification is called for here.

In Islam, religious exegesis is mainly a matter of deducing practical rules from divine law as it is revealed in the Koran. These rules are called *fiqh*, a term that is translated by "religious law." The term "Sharia," for its part, refers to revealed religious law, the meaning of which is not immediately given and which therefore requires exegesis, or what is known in Arabic as *ijtihad*—the "effort of interpretation." From this term derives that of *mujtahid*, which refers to Muslim religious scholars, also known as *faqih* (pl. *fuqaha*)—that is, "specialists of *fiqh*"—or "ulama," from the Arabic *alim* (pl. *ulama*), which literally means "scholar." In practice, therefore, Sharia amounts to *fiqh*, which results from the exegesis carried out by the ulama. The various currents of Islam differ among themselves as to the rules of law (*fiqh*). Since mankind is fallible, these differences are accepted as normal. They exist between the Sunnis and Shiʻa but also within Sunnism and Shiʻism.

In laying the foundations of Shiʻa religious law, Jaʻfar al-Sadiq was in truth part of a broader movement among religious scholars seeking to achieve a monopoly on religious authority. Among the ulama who were in the process of establishing what would become Sunnism, this phenomenon was accompanied by the emergence of various schools of religious jurisprudence, or *madhhab* (pl. *madhahib*). These initially consisted of communities of ulama who had reached agreement as to the rules of religious law and were involved in the theological debates of their time. These schools also rapidly became social and political movements. Generating processes of popular adherence, these movements took part in political struggles, with most of them associated to one degree or another with state authorities. In the Sunni world, four schools of jurisprudence survive to this day, each bearing the name of its respective founder and constituting an official dogma: Hanafism (after Abu Hanifa, d. 767); Malekism (after Malik ibn Anas, d. 796); Shafeism (after al-Shafiʻi, d. 820); and Hanbalism (after Ibn Hanbal, d. 855). It was in this context that Jaʻfar al-Sadiq directly contributed to joining the figure of the Imam with that of the religious scholar. Moreover, he took particular care to train disciples to serve as intermediaries with the broader society and played a decisive role in the construction and maintenance of relative communal unity among the Alids. A major difference with the Sunni ulama was the fact that the Imams claimed to be infallible on the grounds that they were directly inspired by God. In theory, therefore, their authority could not be challenged. This authority was transmitted from one Imam to the next. This is the notion of "divine nomination," or *nass*, the foundations of which were laid by Jaʻfar al-Sadiq's claim that each Imam chose his successor in direct conversation with God. In practice, Imams were always the sons of their predecessors, and, although official Shi'a doctrine denies this, from a sociological perspective this divinely inspired mode of succession closely resembles a dynastic form of government.

In regard to the construction of leadership, this conception of the imamate as an infallible, divinely inspired religious authority had the advantage of rendering it necessary independently of the actual exercise of political power. Even if the Imam was not the caliph, he was an indispensable point of reference and held a kind of authority. As a result, it was unnecessary for him to take part in revolutionary activities, which could even be useless or dangerous.[9]

Alid Radicalism

When one speaks of Shi'ism today, it is generally in reference to a doctrine that was simultaneously constructed in opposition to and in tandem with Sunnism but, perhaps above all, against a collection of currents and movements that, while historically deriving from the Alids, took distinct doctrinal and political paths. As a result, they have little to do with the Twelver Shi'ism (also called "imami") today practiced by the majority of Shi'a, which as we shall see corresponds to a form of orthodoxy that has its analogue in Sunnism. Some of these currents are to this day characterized by highly esoteric doctrines and—at least until the tenth century—political radicalism.

The Twelver Shi'a are so-called because they recognize a lineage of twelve Imams issuing from the union of Ali and Fatima. According to them, while still a child, the twelfth Imam, Muhammad al-Mahdi, was hidden by God from human view in order to protect him from the plots of the caliphs. Believed to be present on earth but in hiding, he will return at the end of time to establish the reign of justice and truth. He is thus a messiah, or *mahdi*. Twelver Shi'a call him "the hidden" or "the awaited" Imam. They distinguish between two phases in his occultation: the Minor and Major Occultations. During the former, which lasted from 874 to 941, the Imam continued to communicate with his faithful via representatives; in 941 the Major Occultation began, and humankind lost contact with the Imam.

Many historians doubt that the twelfth Imam ever existed. As we shall see, his occultation intervened at a time of profound crisis for the imamate, and it can be hypothesized that the doctrine of occultation served to sublimate what was a hopeless situation, doubtless marked by the extinction of Ali and Fatima's lineage as well as by the weakening of the Imam's legitimacy. It must be noted that the idea of occultation was far from new in Alid circles, where it was repeatedly used to revive or attempt to revive a politico-religious movement at risk of dying out. It can even be said that, from the eighth century, the phenomenon of occultation proliferated among politico-religious leaders. Thus the supporters of Muhammad ibn al-Hanafiyyah, son of Ali and a woman other than Fatima, declared him hidden at the time of his death. As we shall see, one of Imam Ja'far al-Sadiq's sons was for his part also said to have been hidden. Similarly, some Alids for a time held that Musa al-Kadhim (d. 799)—considered by Twelvers to be the seventh Imam—had not died but rather been hidden.[10]

These instances of occultation testify to the difficulty of uniting for the Alids. This was in particular reflected in frequent quarrels over succession, which in turn gave rise to radical politico-religious movements. While the Imams recognized by the future Twelvers withdrew from political life, these movements insisted on the necessity of continuing the armed struggle against the caliphs. Though some have disappeared, others survive to this day in the form of minority religious communities, some of which established states that lasted until the twentieth century.

One such group is the Zaydis, who took their name from Zayd ibn Ali (d. 740). Following the death of the fourth Imam, Ali Zayn al-Abidin, in 713, two factions emerged, each swearing allegiance to one of his sons: Zayd ibn Ali and Muhammad al-Baqir. While the supporters of Muhammad al-Baqir continued along the quietist path of nonconfrontation with the caliphal government, his brother's supporters launched a rapidly quashed uprising during which Zayd ibn Ali was killed. His supporters, the Zaydis, did not disappear for all that and even succeeded in founding states in the ninth century. A Zaydi imamate in present-day northern Yemen thus survived until 1962 (see chapter 10). The Zaydis believe that while the imamate must be restricted to the descendants of Hassan and Hussein, it must not be transmitted in hereditary fashion but rather passed on to a person who is not just versed in religious exegesis but also ready to lead the armed struggle against unjust powers.

Another quarrel over succession erupted following the death of the sixth Imam, Ja'far al-Sadiq, who had designated as successor his son, Isma'il ibn Ja'far. But Isma'il died before his father, sowing doubt among some of the Imam's followers, who wondered how a guide inspired by God could have made such a mistake. The crisis was only aggravated when the Imam's second son, Abdallah, died a few weeks after being named Imam. While the Twelvers recognized al-Sadiq's third son, Musa al-Kazim, as their seventh Imam, some of al-Sadiq's supporters were persuaded that Isma'il was not dead but had rather been hidden by God and had transmitted the imamate to his descendants. Isma'il's supporters, the Ismailis, were one of the most dangerous threats to the stability of the Abbasid caliphate, against which they carried out often very violent military actions. This was particularly true of a branch of the Ismailis known as the Qarmatians (after its founder, Hamdan Qarmat), who in the late ninth century rapidly extended their influence and ultimately founded a state in the region of Bahrain, which at the time referred to the Arabian coast of the Persian Gulf between Basra (present-day southern Iraq) and the Qatar Peninsula. From there, the Qarmatians expanded their influence to the southern part of the Arabian Peninsula, even launching raids against Mecca, where they seized the black stone embedded in its cubical sanctuary, the Ka'ba.

Other followers of Ismailism established themselves in the western reaches of the Muslim Empire, mainly in the region of present-day Tunisia, where they had much success among certain Berber tribes struggling against the central government. In the early tenth century, they succeeded in establishing a powerful state in this region under a dynasty claiming to descend from Ali and Fatima that was for this reason known as the Fatimids. From the Maghreb, the Fatimids, whose objective was purely and simply to bring down the Abbasid caliphate, conquered Egypt. It was there that, in 969, they founded Cairo, which became their new capital until their fall in 1171. Among other things, they built the mosque and university of al-Azhar there: today a center of Sunni orthodoxy, this site was initially conceived as an institution for Ismaili propaganda.

Despite its past power, Ismailism disappeared from Egypt, doubtless because the Fatimids did not pursue a policy of mass conversion, their doctrine remaining confined to ruling circles. Furthermore, the Fatimids never succeeded in producing a unified official Ismaili doctrine. Many variants thus persisted, often grafting themselves onto quarrels over succession. To this day, they sketch the contours of a particularly fragmented doctrinal and communal landscape.

One of the best-known religious groups originating in Ismailism are the Druze. They are today concentrated in the Near East (Lebanon, Syria, Israel), where they occupy an important position in the local political equilibrium. The Druze derive their name from Muhammad al-Darazi, the vizier (the equivalent of prime minister) of Fatimid caliph al-Hakim bi-Amr Allah, an unusual figure that some historians believe to have been mad and whose reign was marked by much violence. A few years before mysteriously disappearing in 1021 during a nighttime walk, he had been proclaimed divine by his supporters grouped around al-Darazi and a certain Hamza ibn Ali. The latter played a key role in transforming this current of Ismailism into a religion in its own right, its affiliation with Islam a matter of controversy. In a context in which many Ismailis continued to believe in the imminent appearance of a messiah (*mahdi*), Hamza ibn Ali and Muhammad al-Darazi declared that al-Hakim was not dead but had rather been hidden by God.[11]

Upon the death of the Fatimid caliph al-Mustansir in 1094, Ismailism was once again split by controversy, this time opposing supporters of the deceased caliph's rival sons, al-Musta'li and Nizar. The Nizaris were forced to flee and subsequently established themselves in Iran and the Indian subcontinent. They are remembered in legend as the group known as the "Assassins"—in reality, a Nizari emirate based in the fortress of Alamut on the banks of the Caspian Sea (present-day Iran) whose chiefs practiced political assassination against their enemies. The Nizaris nowadays recognize the authority of Aga Khan. For this worldly billionaire is also heir to a dynasty of Iranian Imams who were forced into exile after having rebelled against the Iranian Qajar kings in the nineteenth century. Following the fall of the Fatimids, the supporters of al-Musta'li for their part mainly found refuge in Yemen, from there spreading their doctrine to the Gujarat region of present-day northeastern India, principally among a merchant caste known as the Bohra. In the wake of other quarrels of succession, the Ismaili Bohra themselves split into several currents.

Before the massive spread of Ismailism and the Fatimid experience, the Shi'a community that remained faithful to Musa al-Kadhim and his descendants experienced another schism. This is worth noting as it helps us understand contemporary developments in Syria. During the lifetimes of Ali al-Hadi (d. 868) and Hassan al-Askari (d. 874)—the tenth and eleventh Imams, respectively, both of whom suffered from a significant legitimacy deficit—a certain Muhammad ibn Nusayr claimed that the latter had transmitted a new religious message to him and that the twelfth Imam—the vanished Imam—had chosen him as his successor. While most Shi'a rejected his claim and firmly condemned the esoteric doctrines he professed, ibn Nusayr succeeded in attracting a group of supporters who ultimately organized a separate religious community. Like the Druze, the Nusayri took refuge in mountainous zones in order to live their faith free from persecution and are today mainly concentrated in northern Syria.[12] Beginning with the French colonization of Lebanon and Syria, they have commonly been known as Alawites. It is from this population that the al-Assad family, which has ruled Syria since 1970, comes.

Chapter 2

RIVALRY AND CONVERGENCE

The proliferation of radical protest movements helped accelerate the crystallization of Sunni and Shi'i orthodoxies. By "orthodoxy," I am here simply referring to the advent of an "official Islam"[1] in the framework of close relations between government and institutionalized religion. Via a process of reciprocal emulation, the establishment of Sunni and Shi'i orthodoxies was as much a matter of political and religious rivalry as it was of convergence.

The End of the Theocratic Caliphate
(Ninth to Thirteenth Centuries)

Starting in the ninth century, the caliphate radically evolved in a way that gradually eliminated its theocratic dimension. In a context of growing social and bureaucratic complexity, the Abbasid caliphs increasingly delegated power to the ulama. The latter were responsible for administering day-to-day religious affairs, particularly in their capacity as judges (*cadi*), a role that covered many fields of action. These included the law and the administration of mortmain goods (*waqf*), a sort of pious foundation pursuing religious objectives and overseeing charity for the poor.[2] This delegation of power to the ulama favored the emergence of an institutionalized official religion and a distinct clergy claiming a monopoly on religious authority. Their claim was based on a specific knowledge of the hadith—the actions and words of the Prophet as they had been reported by a chain of reliable intermediaries—which the ulama used as the basis for Koranic exegesis and to elaborate religious law.

Claiming to be specialists of Koranic exegesis, the ulama endeavored to limit the caliphate to the exercise of political power. This did not take place without conflict. Caliph al-Ma'mun (d. 833) thus attempted to impose Mutazilite dogma on the ulama. These scholars and philosophers were a rationalist movement defending the idea of human free will vis-à-vis God's. They moreover claimed that the Koran was not eternal but rather had been created at a specific historical moment. After several years during which many refractory ulama were targeted by what some have described as an "inquisition" (*mihna*), the caliphal government was forced to abandon these efforts to impose its ideas. In keeping with the majority opinion among religious scholars, the eternal—and thus uncreated—nature of the Koran became a matter of official dogma.[3]

The reinvention of the caliphate was a direct consequence of the growing power of the ulama.[4] This process consisted of two aspects: settling on the great foundational myths of Sunnism, on the one hand, and developing a minimalist conception of the caliphate, on the other. Among these foundational myths was the sacralization of the companions of Muhammad. This resulted from the activity of ulama hadith collectors who wanted to put a symbolic end to factional quarrels by elevating all the companions, whatever their role in the *fitna*, to the rank of infallible transmitters of divine truth and at the same time provide a solid foundation for religious exegesis by holding up the possibility that the Prophet's words and actions were transmitted by irreproachable eye-witnesses. It is to be noted that this is a major point of divergence with the Shi'a, who hold that the companions orchestrated the usurpation of Ali's throne and falsified the Koran so as to suppress all mention of Ali's imamate and that of his descendants.

Also in keeping with their desire to move beyond the trauma caused by the *fitna*, the ulama sought to place the first four caliphs on an equal footing. All were "rightly guided" (*rashidun*) by God. They alone had been chosen by the community of believers and applied a "participative policy."[5] They alone ruled as modest sovereigns, rejecting pomp and devoting their lives to the public good. After them, dynastic governments profoundly altered the original meaning of the caliphal institution, going so far as to imitate non-Muslim monarchies like the Sasanians of Persia and the Byzantines. In short, the reign of the four rightly guided caliphs represented a true golden age during which the will of God was said to have been perfectly implemented on earth. This myth was above all constructed by the opponents of the Umayyads and Abbasids, who sought to underscore the difference between this ideal caliphate and the practical reality of the dynasties that succeeded it, which were often described as tyrannical.

This assertion of the ulama's power was rapidly followed by the decline of the caliphate as a political power, mainly as a result of centrifugal political forces. The last to wield absolute power was al-Ma'mun's successor, Caliph al-Mutawakkil (d. 861). Alongside the Alid and Kharijite revolts, all later caliphs were confronted by the growing power of the empire's provincial governors, particularly along its eastern fringes in Iran and Central Asia. These emirs or sultans (from the Arabic terms *amir* and *sultan*, both referring to the de facto holders of power) succeeded in forcing the Abbasid caliphs to allow them to autonomously govern their provinces and dispose of tax revenue as they saw fit. Among other things, this allowed the emirs to maintain armies of their own. Although they formally recognized the authority of the caliphs, in reality they governed alone, founding veritable dynastic states.

Gradually, the provinces closest to the political center in turn took their independence, generally under the political leadership of Turkish emir dynasties. Between 868 and 905 Egypt, Palestine, Syria, and a portion of Iraq were thus governed by a Turkish dynasty, the Tulunids. Between 945 and 1055 an Iranian Shi'a dynasty, the Buyids, seized power in Baghdad. Appointing their own ministers (*vizir*) and senior officials, these emirs reduced the caliphate to a symbolic power. Like the Tulunids, the Buyids at first consisted of a military junta that emerged thanks to the army's transformation into a force exclusively consisting of mercenaries, slaves, and volunteers. Launched under Caliph al-Mu'tasim (d. 842), this reform of the army favored the creation of a new, non-Arab military elite composed of Turks, Slavs, and Iranians.

Significantly, it was in the eleventh century—at a time when the caliphate had long since been reduced to a purely symbolic power—that ulama with ties to the caliph sought to systematically theorize the caliphate in a vain attempt to strengthen its legitimacy. Well-placed in the Abbasid court, Abu al-Hassan al-Mawardi (d. 1058) supplied (doubtless at the express request of Caliph al-Qa'im) an exhaustive list of the qualities a caliph must possess in a work entitled *The Ordinances of Government*, which remains a reference to this day. This work, which does not refer to any of the exceptional qualities attributed to the rightly guided caliphs, is striking for containing a number of attributes that were in fact never actually united in the person of a single caliph. Among other things, these included the need to belong to Muhammad's tribe, the Quraysh, and be well versed in religious studies. It was thus very much an effort to supply an ideal definition of the caliphate, as distinct from its actual practice.

While it today constitutes an authority on the matter, al-Mawardi's theorization of the caliphate was much criticized, often by ulama with ties to rivals of the sitting caliphs. Some argued that there was nothing necessary about membership in the Quraysh tribe. Others refused the—in truth, profoundly theocratic—idea that the caliph had to be well versed in religious studies. In their view, he should be satisfied with applying the law as they themselves had defined it. Such an idea obviously served to reinforce their own standing as the caliph's indispensable assistants. Over the course of debates between religious scholars and in a context marked by an endless series of often violent protest movements, the ulama were by default reduced to elaborating a minimal definition of the caliphate. On this definition, the necessity of the caliphate was grounded in the need to maintain social and political order, the condition sine qua non of implementing the religion. It was therefore necessary to obey the caliph even if he was unjust. Indeed, one must even avoid criticizing him for fear of destabilizing the entire social order. Only in a very few circumstances—among them, severe mental impairment—was it therefore justified to remove a caliph from power.[6]

In fact, the caliphate never recovered any of its efficacy in the years preceding the advent of Ottoman reign in the sixteenth century. Indeed, al-Mawardi himself directly witnessed the caliphs' impotence. Tasked on various occasions by the Abbasids with negotiating the scope of caliphal power vis-à-vis the Buyid emirs, he also served as a diplomatic emissary to the Seljuks, a Sunni Turkish dynasty that had established a state in Iran and who the caliph had expressly asked to rid him of the Buyid emirs.

This was done in 1055, when the armies of Tughril Beg took Baghdad. Though freed of the Shiʻa Buyids, the Abbasid caliphs had merely traded one guardian for another and never succeeded in restoring their power. In 1258 the final Abbasid caliph, al-Mustaʻsim, was killed during the Mongol conquest and sack of Baghdad. One of his cousins, al-Mustansir, succeeded in reaching Egypt, which had since 1250 been dominated by a dynasty of Turkish generals, the Mamluks. But though they acknowledged al-Mustansir's title as caliph, it once again conferred no more than symbolic power. By the thirteenth century, the title of caliph had lost so much of its meaning that many sovereigns often more or less officially appropriated it to signify that they governed in keeping with divine law. In this context, the largely trivialized term "caliph" had become merely an equivalent of "emir" and "sultan."[7]

The Crisis of the Imamate (819–874)

The crisis of the caliphate had its counterpart in a crisis of the imamate. As with the caliphate, this crisis accelerated the crystallization of Twelver orthodoxy in a context marked by the emergence of a class of Shiʻi ulama as architects and guardians of the dogma and the emergence of the state power of Twelver Shiʻa dynasties.

As we have seen, at the time of the sixth Imam, there emerged a corps of Shiʻi ulama. Trained in his teachings, they served as his agents (*wakil*) and were responsible for representing him among the faithful. The role of these agents significantly evolved beginning with the ninth-century crisis of the imamate, when several Imams died, leaving behind children incapable of ensuring the continuity of the imamate as a learned office.[8] The eighth and ninth Imams—respectively, Ali al-Ridha (d. 819) and Muhammad al-Jawad (d. 835)—both designated seven-year-old boys as their successors, provoking perplexity and debate among the faithful, particularly the scholars who had been trained by their fathers. In the absence of infallible scholarly religious authority, several of these ulama began to autonomously practice religious exegesis.

In doing so, they were also to play a central role in building consensus among the various factions of the faithful, perpetuating the teachings of the deceased Imams and administering the Imams' day-to-day affairs. In this particularly fluid context, they also played a central role in propagating Shi'a doctrine. In contrast to the Umayyad period, during which the Islamic faith was largely restricted to the Arab ruling elites, the reign of the Abbasids was characterized by the massive conversion of the empire's subjects of all ethnolinguistic origins. For the Shi'a, it was vital to profit from this to explain their point of view and win over new followers. In particular, this period witnessed the emergence of Persian Shi'i ulama at a time when Islam was rapidly spreading into the regions of the former Sasanian Empire.[9]

As with the caliphate, which had been emptied of its theocratic dimension by the ulama's self-assertion, the rising power of Shi'i ulama increasingly led them to challenge the Imams. The reign of the eleventh Imam, Hassan al-Askari (d. 874), focused all their criticism. It seems the young man lived a life of ease as a courtesan at the caliph's court, showing little interest in the austere tasks of elaborating and teaching doctrine. To remedy this situation, some ulama went so far as to write a book of religious law and attribute its authorship to him. This shows the degree to which the agents of the Imam had acquired considerable power even while they continued to believe it necessary to maintain the fiction of the imamate. Such circumstances encouraged them to reconceive the duties of their office. Thus, while some ulama continued to claim that the Imam was an extraordinary and infallible being inspired by God, others gradually came to see the imamate as purely a matter of scholarly mastery, claiming that, while the Imam was indeed a great religious scholar, he did not have access to the hidden secrets of the world and was in no way infallible.[10]

This crisis of the imamate allows us to better understand the deus ex machina of the twelfth Imam's occultation. The reality is that, after the death of the eighth Imam in 819, the ulama had acquired such power that they no longer needed the Imam. During the Minor Occultation and working closely with the Shi'a notability who had joined the Abbasid court, they continued to run the Imam's office, issuing religious law rulings and collecting taxes. In the tenth century, with believers gradually

losing hope in the Imam's imminent return, the ulama made his occultation a permanent feature of their organization: henceforth they would
officially be the community's ultimate reference and exercise some of the
Imam's powers in his absence. As we shall see, there were numerous
debates regarding the extent of this transfer of power, with significant
repercussions for the ideology of Shi'a Islamist movements in the contemporary period.

The rise to power of Shi'i dynasties after the occultation allowed the
ulama's role as central actors in Shi'a communal and religious life to be
consolidated. The most significant experience in this regard was that of
the Buyids (955–1045). They were perhaps initially Zaydis, and it seems
that their experience of state power led them to embrace a more moder-
ate Shi'a doctrine, allowing them to coexist with the caliphate as well as
see to the day-to-day administration of Sunni-majority populations.
Whatever the case, they pursued a policy of protecting Twelver Shi'i
ulama. The latter played a decisive role in marginalizing the Alid doctrines
that had resulted from the Imams' various quarrels of succession. To this
day, Twelver Shi'a describe the Ismailis, the Druze, and the Alawites as
"extremists" (*ghulat*), in particular because they attribute divine characteristics to human beings and recognize the existence of prophets after
Muhammad.

The ulama of the Buyid period ultimately emptied Shi'a doctrine of
its esoteric dimension, which today persists only in those movements that
originated in Ismailism. This process was part of the rapprochement with
the Mutazilites, the rationalist current whose ideas Abbasid Caliph al-
Ma'mum had vainly tried to impose on the Sunni ulama. This rapprochement had already begun before the Buyids came on the scene. Indeed,
Abu Sahl al-Nawbakhti, a Baghdad Shi'a leader born into one of the great
Shi'i families that had been part of the Abbasid court since the time of
Imam Ja'far al-Sadiq, had doubtless ordered a Mutazilite scholar to pro-
duce a work on the imamate.[11] Among other things, this notable sought
to empty the imamate of any revolutionary content. The Imam's Second
Coming was not imminent; in the meantime, it was not legitimate to revolt against the powers that be. Several Mutazilites subsequently

embraced Shi'ism and, in this way, the rationalism that had been marginalized in official Sunni Islam ultimately triumphed in Twelver Shi'a orthodoxy. It was also later incorporated into Zaydism.

An esoteric doctrine that at regular intervals generated millenarian protest movements, "Alidism" was thus transformed into a rationalist "Shi'ism" that distanced itself from the revolutionary spirit. This is explained by the gradual consolidation of power by Shi'i ulama and notables with ties to established governments, a process that started in the Abbasid period and continued under the Buyids. During the latter's reign, Shi'i ulama—now fully exposed to the light of day and driven to publicly debate their ideas—felt it necessary, not just to clarify their positions, but to also once and for all eradicate the radical esoteric ideas that so shocked the majority-Sunni population and that might otherwise pose a threat to Buyid rule.[12]

In particular, they went to great lengths to avoid mentioning many of the Imams' reported remarks regarding the metaphysical nature of the Imam. They also sought to quash the polemics concerning the falsification of the Koran. For it had until then been commonly accepted in Alid circles that the critical revision established by Uthman was a product of censorship. The unabridged version of the Koran, in their view, among other things contained the esoteric aspects of the divine message and had been passed down from one Imam to the next until the twelfth, who had taken it with him into occultation. As a consequence, the true Koran would be known to mankind only on the day of the Imam's return. Under the Buyids, the ulama began to claim the exact opposite: Uthman had indeed compiled the entire Koran, and the Imams' remarks referred only to the commentaries and interpretations of Imam Ali.[13]

As only the Imams could access the Koran's esoteric content and claim infallibility, in their absence the ulama could claim to be no more than the interpreters of scriptural sources. In reality, they developed a form of religious exegesis very similar to that already practiced by Sunni ulama, particularly those belonging to the Shafei school, from whom they extensively borrowed. It was during the Buyid period, moreover, that Shi'i scholars carried out a systematic critical revision of the hadiths of the Imams, which in Shi'a religious exegesis enjoy the same status as those of Muhammad. This effort, which had already been initiated by the Imam Ja'far al-Sadiq, involved a major process of selection: sources that did not suit a doctrine in transition that was in the process of detaching itself from esoterism were passed over in silence or simply suppressed.

Also like their Sunni counterparts, who had come to advocate obedience to the established government, even when unjust, the Shi'i ulama actively worked to deradicalize Shi'a political doctrine, producing political texts that allowed for coexistence and even collaboration with temporal powers other than that of the Imam. Protected by the Buyids, al-Shaykh al-Mufid (d. 1022)—a central player in the transition to rationalism—sought to distinguish between illegitimate non-Shi'a power (the Abbasids) and legitimate Shi'a power (in this instance, the Buyids). In theological terms, both of these types of power were unjust—only the government of the Imam was just—but it was permitted to collaborate with the latter. Al-Mufid's disciple, al-Sharif al-Murtadha (d. 1044), went even further, claiming that such collaboration was obligatory if it allowed one to preserve or extend Shi'a rights.[14]

The fall of the Buyids—brought down by the Seljuk Turks, who professed Sunnism—followed in 1268 by that of the Abbasids after their conquest by the pagan Mongols did not prevent Shi'i ulama from continuing to display a high degree of political pragmatism. Far from it: some of these ulama went so far as to claim that a non-Muslim sovereign, if he behaved justly, was preferable to an unjust Muslim sovereign,[15] and a number of Shi'i ulama and notables even assiduously frequented the Mongol court before any of the latter had embraced Islam. In this, the Shi'i ulama showed no less political realism than their Sunni counterparts. The revolutionary spirit that many authors and commentators have since the Iranian Revolution of 1979 characterized as an intrinsic characteristic of Shi'ism thus in fact corresponds to a very contemporary reinvention of tradition.

In concluding, two essential points must be underscored in regard to the similarities and differences between Sunnism and Shi'ism. First, in Twelver Shi'ism, the doctrine of the Imam's occultation did not just render the clergy's existence necessary and legitimate but also gave it great latitude in the practice of exegesis. In Sunnism, by contrast, while a clergy does in fact exist, the direct relationship that it postulates between God and believer has the effect of undermining its legitimacy, regularly impeding its efforts to claim a monopoly on religious knowledge. As we shall see, this fundamental difference in the status of the clergy in these two forms of Islam was to have a decisive impact on the development of the Sunni and Shi'a varieties of Islamism as well as the stances they respectively adopted vis-à-vis the clerical institution. The second point to be underscored concerns the matter of exegesis. Freed of the direct supervision of the Imams, Twelver exegesis developed in a context of great freedom. By contrast, the consolidation of the four canonical schools of Sunni jurisprudence imposed a narrower framework on exegesis. While the emergence of these schools did not end the practice of exegesis, Sunni ulama were henceforth required to belong to a school of jurisprudence and above all refer to the dogma laid down by their predecessors.

Sufism and Shi'ism: Mysticism and Popular Worship

As we have seen, the rationalist and exoteric turn taken by the Twelver Shi'i ulama following the occultation of the last Imam allowed for a sort of rapprochement between Sunni and Shi'a orthodoxies. If one considers the popular devotional practices associated with the mystical currents of Sunnism, one also finds many commonalities.

The mystical currents of Sunnism are intellectually and historically linked with Shi'ism. For in their lifetimes, the spiritual and esoteric teachings of the Imams, in particular those of Ali bin Abi Talib (d. 661), Ja'far al-Sadiq (d. 765), and Ali al-Ridha (d. 819), attracted many disciples. Though the Imams did not necessarily share the political stance of the Alids, the latter sought divine contact with God and access to the hidden aspects of divine truth.[16] Criticizing the Umayyad drift toward a monarchy of pomp and lucre, they practiced asceticism, often withdrawing from society to better pursue a life of meditation and study. It seems that a number of them were in the habit of wearing wool clothing to indicate their renunciation of luxury, with the result that they came to be known as "Sufis," from the Arabic word *suf*, or "wool."

Sufism was gradually developed on the basis of these mystics' teachings and lifestyle. The first written texts date mainly from the tenth and eleventh centuries. Starting in the twelfth and thirteenth centuries, Sufism organized itself into brotherhoods that exist to this day. These brotherhoods rapidly expanded in the aftermath of the Mongol invasions. Originating in Central Asia, the Mongols conquered vast swaths of land throughout Asia after unifying under the leadership of Genghis Khan (d. 1227), their incursions extending into the Middle East and reaching the gates of Western Europe. Initially shamanists, the Mongols subsequently adopted several religious traditions after coming into contact with the populations they had conquered, including Buddhism, Christianity, and Islam. The latter religion was ultimately adopted by several sovereigns of the Ilkhanate dynasty, who between 1256 and 1335 reigned over what is today Iran and Iraq. The representatives of an open and pluralistic religious culture, the Ilkhanate Mongols ushered in a period of religious tolerance.

At the same time, their largely syncretic beliefs gave rise to an Islamic revival movement largely driven by the Sufi brotherhoods. The latter spread in a context also marked by the resonance of millenarian beliefs blurring the boundaries between Sunnism and Shi'ism, something that explains why many brotherhoods mixed mystical Sunnism with worship of the figure of Imam Ali. Whereas the largely uncentralized state exercised little control over society, the brotherhoods sometimes transformed themselves into small, virtually autonomous local chieftainships centered on a shrine and often possessing an army. Though initially confined to an elite that generally held itself aloof from government, the practice of Sufism in this way became a popular movement capable of controlling sometimes large numbers of people and was therefore an influential social and political force.[17]

To this day, Sufi communities bear the names of eponymous founders, with most of them referring to Shi'i Imams. They claim that their practices derive from the esoteric teachings of the Imams as transmitted by a chain of disciples (*silsila*). In this way, the Sufi orders contributed to making Ali "one of the central figures of Muslim spirituality in general,"[18] the division between Sunnis and Shi'a notwithstanding. They also made it possible for esoteric doctrines to win a place of their own in Sunni Islam. For some major Sunni theologians were Sufis. In South Asia, Sufism very early on emerged as the dominant form of Sunni Islam, and the Sufi brotherhoods there were closely associated with the state. They today remain at the heart of Muslim religiosity in a context that is otherwise characterized by a high degree of religious syncretism.

There are many commonalities and exchanges between Sufism and Shi'ism. There is thus genuine proximity at the level of their ideas and ritual practices. Such is the case of the notion of *wilaya*, which is sometimes translated by "saintliness" in English and refers to intimacy with God. As we have seen, this is a pillar of Shi'a doctrine but is also found in Sufism, whose mystics also claim to have direct access to God. In contrast to the Imams, however, among whom intimacy with God is given at birth and not a life choice, the Sufis possess *wilaya* through their initiation into the esoteric teachings and strict, ascetic discipline of the body. In both Sufism and Shi'ism, *wilaya* confers extraordinary powers: Imams and Sufi mystics can perform miracles (*karama*) and transmit God's blessing (*baraka*), even after their death.

This is why pilgrimage to the tombs of these holy men, for whom splendid mausoleums have been built, features as a central aspect in both Sufism and Shi'ism. They include Muhammad, Fatima, the Imams, and their relatives (sons, daughters, sisters, brothers, uncles, etc.), as well as—for the Sufis—a large number of mystical teachers. During these pilgrimages, the faithful fervently touch the inner wall of the tomb while reciting religious incantations in order to enjoy the blessing of the departed. Owing to these practices, Shi'a and Sufis have regularly been criticized by fundamentalist Sunni movements, particularly the Salafist movements that emerged over the course of the twentieth century, for whom the belief in *wilaya* is a form of polytheism.

The Safavid Episode

As we have seen, interaction with the government generally played a decisive role in the definition of Islamic doctrine, whether it be Sunnism or Shiʻism. The Safavid dynasty's establishment of Shiʻism as the state religion of Iran was a decisive episode in this regard.

The Safavid Empire first originated in one of the Sufi brotherhoods that proliferated after the Mongol conquests. Founded in the region of Ardabil in present-day northern Iran by a Kurdish or Turcoman Sufi master named Safi al-din Ardabili (d. 1334), the brotherhood rapidly extended its influence elsewhere, particularly in Mesopotamia and Anatolia. Over the course of the fifteenth century, its conversion to Shiʻism accompanied the brotherhood's transformation into a radical armed movement whose leader, Shah Ismaʻil (d. 1524), was crowned king in 1501 after his army vanquished local rivals. As soon as he was crowned, he announced that Twelver Shiʻism would be the official religion of the state he had just founded.

The establishment of Twelver Shiʻism as state religion in Iran had wide-ranging repercussions. On the one hand, it put an end to the religious indeterminacy that had characterized the preceding period. For populations that mainly practiced Sufi Islam, the distinction between Sunnism and Shiʻism was anything but obvious. Though Sunnism was dominant in this context, there was widespread popular worship of Ali and the family of the Prophet. While it facilitated the shift to Shiʻism, this indeterminacy did not allow for the establishment of an official religion, which had to be based on dogma that was at once clear and unambiguously distinct from that defended by rival Sunni and neighboring powers, first and foremost the Ottomans.

Because their territory was majority Sunni, the Safavids did not have any Shiʻi ulama who might serve as organic intellectuals. They thus decided to invite to their court Arab ulama from the great Shiʻi population centers of the day: the southern part of what is today Iraq, present-day Bahrain, al-Hasa (the Eastern Province of contemporary Saudi Arabia), and the Jabal Amil region in what is today southern Lebanon. Among these immigrant ulama, the largest number consisted of South Lebanese "Amilites," who often reached very high office in the first decades of Safavid rule. Because they had been persecuted by the Sunni Ottoman sultans and had the habit of participating in polemical debates with Sunni ulama, they were particularly well equipped to advance the

Safavids' project, which was in reality to transform Shi'ism into an official Islam capable of responding point-by-point to its official Sunni counterpart.[19]

The interaction of these ulama with the government once again had the effect of rapidly transforming doctrine in several respects. On the one hand, the ulama brought the Safavids into the fold of Twelver orthodoxy. For they at first had little familiarity with the ulama's Shi'ism and were in truth closer to the radical *ghulat* doctrines (Ismailism, Druzism, Alawism) that deified Imam Ali and recognized other prophets after Muhammad. The first Safavid sovereign, Shah Ismail, thus presented himself as both the hidden Imam and the reincarnation of Ali. On the other hand, the ulama for the first time had to conceive of Shi'ism as a state religion rather than just a communal doctrine. Their collaboration with the Buyids had demanded nothing of the sort since the latter never tried to transform Shi'ism into an official religion. However, conceiving of Shi'ism as the state religion required them to define the conditions under which a Shi'a state not led by the Imam might be legitimate as well as those governing the practical exercise of Shi'a religious law.

Before the Safavids, most Shi'i ulama held that the Imam's occultation had suspended certain collective aspects of religious life: Friday prayer and the sermon accompanying it; the implementation of legal punishments prescribed by the Koran; the collection of certain taxes.[20] The ulama who supported the Safavid government—and, in particular, the Amilites—claimed that things had changed with the advent of a Shi'a state. Henceforth these practices could be restored, not just because the political leaders were Shi'a but also because the ulama, as the Imam's delegates in his absence, could legitimately exercise most of the latter's prerogatives. Moreover, the Safavid sovereign Shah Tahmasp (d. 1576) bestowed the official title of "representative of the Imam" (*na'ib al-imam*) on Ali al-Karaki (d. 1534), an Amilite scholar. It can thus be said that the ulama had truly been substituted for the Imams in order to transform Shi'ism into a ruling doctrine.[21]

This substitution did not take place without debate among religious scholars. Some thought things had gone too far and also looked disapprovingly on the temporal power accumulated by certain of their colleagues. They formed what is known as the *akhbari* current (from the Arabic *akhbar*, a synonym of "hadith"). Hostile to Safavid institutional innovations, they also believed that the Imams' infallibility meant they had already answered all questions that might arise for the faithful. One thus had to stick to the letter of scriptural sources and abandon exegesis, a superfluous and even dangerous practice that led one to stray from the spirit of the Imams. Their opponents, the state ulama, formed what is known as the *usuli* school (from the Arabic *usul al-fiqh*, which refers to the science of developing religious law). They believed that many problems inevitably arose from social and historical change and that, as representatives of the Imam in his absence, scholars could deduce his will—and thus that of God—by the use of reason (*aql*). Despite the *akhbari*'s attacks, in the late eighteenth century the *usuli* ultimately triumphed, with the result that their views today represent the mainstream of Twelver Shi'ism.

By reestablishing these suspended religious practices, the Safavids made it possible for the ulama to occupy various official positions. Apart from overseeing prayer in the mosques, the ulama served as judges. New positions were created, among them those of *sheikh al-islam* and *sadr*. The *sheikh al-islam* (literally, "leader of Islam") was responsible for decreeing and disseminating official religious doctrine. The *sadr* (literally, "leader") was the religion's chief administrator and was, among other things, responsible for administering mortmain goods, distributing their dividends to those who were entitled to receive them, overseeing worship, and supervising courts. What's more, the state granted the ulama a portion of property taxes, thereby ensuring that they were on a solid economic footing. This close interaction with the Safavid state had the effect of transforming the ulama into a full-fledged clergy.

The Ottoman-Safavid Rivalry

The construction of Twelver Shi'ism as a state ideology under the Safavids also profoundly altered the regional geopolitical configuration over the long term by creating the conditions for recurrent conflict between the Shi'a Persian Empire and its Sunni neighbors, particularly the Ottoman Empire. When the Safavids founded their state, the Ottoman Empire was indisputably the greatest Muslim power. Ruled over by a Turkish dynasty, the empire first spread to the borders of Europe in the fourteenth century and continuously expanded its territory after that, conquering Constantinople in 1453 (thereby putting an end to the Byzantine Empire) and pursuing its eastward expansion, particularly in Anatolia and the Arab regions. The Ottomans immediately saw the emergence of the Safavids as a threat, not just because it put a brake on their territorial expansion but also because the latter commanded the loyalty of a portion of the Turkoman population in the Ottoman territory of Anatolia, where the Safavids' elite military corps, the Qizilbash, originated.

Within just a few years of the Safavid state's foundation, the Ottomans had conquered most Arab regions, including Iraq, Syria, Egypt, and the holy towns of Mecca and Medina on the Arabian Peninsula. The annexation of these regions officially put an end to the Abbasid caliphate, allowing the Ottoman sovereigns to present themselves as caliphs and the guardians of the holy places of Islam. In other words, they were now the main representatives of Sunni orthodoxy; for them, the threat posed by the Safavids was at once territorial and ideological in nature. In fact, they pursued what was a sometimes very severe policy of repression against Shi'ism on their territory. The rivalry between the Ottomans and Safavids was reflected in a series of wars in the southern Caucasus and Iraq. The cradle of Shi'ism, Iraq passed under Ottoman sovereignty shortly after the Safavids came to power. In the seventeenth century, however, the Safavids succeeded in occupying the better part of what is today Iraq, controlling Baghdad for several years as well as the holy cities of Najaf (where the tomb of Iman Ali can still be found today) and Karbala (where the mausoleum of Imam Hussein stands). It was only in 1639 that the Ottomans definitively reestablished their sovereignty over these regions. The Safavids officially recognized this in the framework of the Treaty of Qasr-e Shirin, which ended the war between the two empires.

Southern Iraq and particularly the region of Najaf and Karbala nevertheless remained a frontier zone where Ottoman sovereignty held sway only in fits and starts and where the Safavids and their successors retained considerable influence, financing Shi'i religious institutions and restoring the Imams' mosques and mausoleums at great cost in what was a typically Iranian architectural style. Following the fall of the Safavids in 1722 under the onslaught of Sunni Afghan tribes, southern Iraq naturally became a refuge zone for many Iranian ulama. The latter sought to escape the chaos of war, anti-Shi'a persecution, and the religious policy conducted by the new sovereign, Nader Shah (d. 1747). Having expelled the Afghans and reestablished the empire's unity, Nader Shah founded a new dynasty, the Afsharids, and stripped Shi'ism of its status as state religion. For Nader Shah believed that such close association with Shi'ism had been a mistake that, among other things, created tension with neighboring states. He promoted an ecumenical religious policy and attempted— unsuccessfully—to convince the Ottomans to recognize Twelver Shi'ism as merely a fifth school of Islamic jurisprudence.

The exodus of many Iranian ulama to southern Iraq had important long-term consequences. One of these was to establish the Shi'i clergy in the holy cities of what is today southern Iraq as a religious, social, and political force relatively independent of the Ottoman and Iranian states alike. As representatives of the Imam in his absence, they directly collected religious taxes and thus possessed their own economic resources. And that is without counting the subsidies and various donations of some Shi'i states. Starting in the late eighteenth century, Iran's Qajar dynasty (1794–1925) reestablished the organic link between the state and Shi'ism and supported Shi'i religious institutions in Iran and elsewhere. At the same time, the small but very rich Shi'a state of Awadh in northern India played a preeminent role in the growth of the holy cities of southern Iraq, in particular financing the construction of a canal to bring the waters of the Euphrates to Najaf.[22] In this context, the religious seminaries of southern Iraq, supplied with a constant flow of students from Iran and other Shi'i population zones, acquired a central position in the Shi'a teaching and religious authority system.

Over the course of the second half of the nineteenth century, the town of Najaf established itself as the main center for training ulama and the seat of religious authority. It was here that the *marja'iyya* (*al-taqlid*) was born. Literally the "source of imitation," the *marja'iyya* is an institution of religious authority in which any Shi'a who has not received a high level of training in the religious sciences allowing him to autonomously practice exegesis has to follow the opinions of a particularly erudite scholar, or *marja'* (*al-taqlid*), an expression that may be translated by "reference" or "source of imitation." To this day, the *marja'* exercise religious and social leadership. For, in addition to exegesis, they are solely authorized to collect religious taxes, and the most prominent of them are at the head of globalized networks of religious, educational, and charitable institutions. As we shall see, they also wield great political influence.

In the contemporary world, finally, the Safavid heritage persists in the existence of an official Shi'a Islam. While it cannot be reduced to it, this Shi'a orthodoxy is nevertheless an essential attribute of the Iranian state. No matter the political regime that dominates it, this state seeks to retain its status as the tutelary power of Shi'i the world over, using Shi'ism as a springboard with which to more or less aggressively wield influence from one period to the next. Most Sunnis thus subscribe to a representation that depicts Shi'ism as intrinsically Iranian: in their eyes, to be Shi'a is to be Iranian or, at least, a vector for the influence and interests of Iran. As we shall see, this raises many problems for the coexistence of Sunnis and Shi'a in several Middle Eastern countries, undermining processes of national integration.

South Asian Syncretism in the Mughal Empire (1526–1858)

As the Ottomans and Safavids fought one another for the status of leader of the Muslim world, contemporaneous political and cultural developments on the Indian subcontinent show that doctrinal differences between Sunnism and Shi'ism do not prevent the formation of political alliances or the production of syncretic cultures. Shortly after the Safavids came to power, Babur (d. 1530) laid the foundations of the Mughal Empire, which dominated India from 1526 to 1858. The Mughal sovereigns originated in one of the Mongol tribes that migrated westward from Central Asia in the wake of the great conquests of Genghis Khan and, later, Timur (d. 1405), from whom Babur directly descended.

From the outset, the Safavids supported the Mughal sovereigns, helping them consolidate their power and even recuperate lost territory. Jalaludin Muhammad Akbar (d. 1605), the third and doubtless most important Mughal emperor, made Persian the official language of the empire and developed a policy to actively attract Persian literati to his court. This was in part a matter of local context: Persian was the language of administration and court life in several Central and South Asian states, a fact that had given rise to a class of Persian bureaucrats and literati with close ties to established governments.

For all that and with few exceptions, the Mughal sovereigns never converted to Shi'ism, and that strand of Islam never enjoyed majority status among Indian Muslims, who generally remained a minority vis-à-vis the Hindu population. Like their predecessors, the Mughals practiced a form of Sunni Islam highly imbued with Sufi mysticism. Such was their religious and cultural openness that their court became a refuge for many religious dissidents. There were thus both Sunnis and Shi'a among the influential Persians of the Mughal administration. The Shi'a may have been attracted by the prospect of a career in high public office or even been sent by the Safavids to assist their allies. The Sunnis were sometimes dissidents who had refused to convert to Shi'ism. In periods during which these mystical orders were persecuted, some Shi'a Sufi brotherhoods also found refuge in Mughal territory.[23]

As the Mughal Empire waned in the eighteenth century, Shi'i kingdoms formally attached to the empire (but in truth largely autonomous of it) emerged, particularly in northern India. The largest of these was Awadh. Founded in 1722 by a high-ranking Persian official in the Mughal court at the time of the fall of the Safavids, the kingdom adopted a religious policy similar to that of the latter. Having established Shi'ism as state religion, the sovereigns of Awadh welcomed many Safavid notables, among them ulama, to whom they granted privileges. They lavishly financed Shi'i religious institutions, some of them, as we have seen, in

Mesopotamia. Faithful to the prevailing religious syncretism, however, they did not follow the Safavids in their anti-Sunni and anti-Sufi policy. Since a majority of the population was Sunni, so too were government officials and some high-ranking court dignitaries, including those responsible for administering the *imambara* (the South Asian equivalent of the Arab and Iranian *husseiniyya*, structures where Shi'a commemorated the martyrdom of Imam Hussein) and mortmain goods. Moreover, the kingdom's great religious studies institute, the Firangi Mahal, was run by a Sunni family but, since it offered instruction in rationalist philosophy, logic, and mathematics, received both Sunni and Shi'i students.[24] Shi'a who intended to become clerics subsequently left for Iraq and Iran to complete their training. As in Iran before the Safavids, popular worship of the Prophet's family was commonplace in India. There, Sunnis and Shi'a jointly participated in the rituals of Ashura, which commemorates the martyrdom of Imam Hussein at Karbala in 680. So strong was this religious syncretism that Hindus also took part in processions, with the result that, in some regions, the most famous storytellers of the Karbala tragedy, who traditionally officiate during these ceremonies, were Hindus. For this reason, the rituals of Ashura played a central role in maintaining good relations between the various religious communities.

Political and Religious Rapprochement (Nineteenth and Twentieth Centuries)?

Starting in the late eighteenth century, the Muslim world found itself confronted with accelerating European expansion: Britain's subjugation of India (1757), Napoleon Bonaparte's expedition to Egypt (1798), the establishment of a British protectorate over the Arab emirates of the Persian Gulf (from 1820), the French conquest of Algeria (1830), British subjugation of Egypt (1882), the fall of the Ottoman Empire (1918) following its defeat alongside the Axis powers with which it had allied itself during the First World War, British and French mandates over the Arab territories of the Ottoman Empire in the Near East (1920),[25] and the abolition of the Ottoman caliphate by Mustafa Kemal Atatürk and its replacement by a secular Turkish republic (1924). These are just a few examples of the European powers' growing political and economic encroachment at this time.

This situation pushed Muslim intellectual and political elites to ponder the causes of this unfavorable balance of power. What were the sources of European power? Why had Muslims—the recipients of the ultimate divine message—been incapable of achieving the same degree of technological and economic advancement?

Their various responses to these questions laid the foundations for what came to be known as the Nahda, or Renaissance, Movement. While some secular politicians and intellectuals thought that it was necessary in some areas to follow the Europeans' example—in the development of national identity, for example, or state centralization and the practice of modern scientific disciplines—religious scholars and intellectuals added that it was also and above all necessary to rediscover the true meaning of Islam by returning to the religion of the Prophet and the first four rightly guided caliphs. Also known as "Islamic reformism," this religious perspective on the Europeanization of the Muslim world was principally organized around three great figures who closely collaborated with one another: Jamal al-Din al-Afghani (d. 1787), a Shi'a ulama from Iran, and his disciples Muhammad Abduh (d. 1905), an Egyptian professor at al-Azhar University, and Rashid Rida (d. 1935), a Syrian ulama with ties to the nationalist movement. The thinking of these three men converged around a number of themes. First of all, they wished to revive religious exegesis so as to rid Islam of the errors that had accumulated over time. It was no longer appropriate to merely imitate the ancient ulama who had founded the canonical schools of jurisprudence. To the contrary, exegesis had to be reinvented, an enterprise requiring the confident use of reason. Breaking with the dominant Sunni tradition but consistent with Shi'a practice, the reformists were thus true rationalists. Even as they insisted on a return to authentic Islam, they did much to import into the Muslim world institutions and concepts that originated with the European Enlightenment. For they were deeply persuaded that what they perceived as the decline of Islam as a civilization required that some ideas and practices be borrowed from Europe. In addition to reforming the educational system by including some modern disciplines to which they had extensively contributed, the reformists called for new political institutions based on popular sovereignty and the separation of powers to be established to help fight despotism.

Among the Muslim reformers, the trajectory of Jamal al-Din al-Afghani is instructive, particularly as regards the question of relations between Sunnis and Shi'a at this time. Born in Iran and educated in Najaf, al-Afghani was, like all Shi'i ulama, strongly imbued with rationalism and believed that "Islam was the religion of free will."[26] It was on this basis that he called for Islam to be liberated from the idea—widespread among traditional Sunni clergy—of predestination, which in his view lent to a type of resignation vis-à-vis European imperialism. An itinerant activist preacher, he traveled across the Muslim world, becoming a political adviser to some rulers, particularly in Afghanistan, and generally exercised significant influence over the political and intellectual debates of his time. His travels also took him to Europe, first to London and then to Paris, where, among other things, he engaged in an intellectual debate with Ernest Renan regarding Islam's ability to integrate modern science.

Like all reformists, Jamal al-Din al-Afghani had been a tireless promoter of Islamic unity across ethnonational frontiers and doctrinal divisions. In this respect, the reformists were agents of Sunni and Shi'a rapprochement. Though al-Afghani was an Iranian Shi'a, his ideas had their greatest impact in Egypt, a profoundly Sunni Muslim society where al-Azhar University was in the process of establishing itself as the Sunni world's leading religious studies center. One of his main disciples there was Muhammad Abduh. Far from being a marginal figure in the religious institution, Abduh occupied central institutional positions: he was a student and then professor at al-Azhar and subsequently held the office of judge and, later, grand *mufti*, the supreme religious authority at the national level. Al-Afghani and Abduh were forced to flee Egypt owing to their anti-Ottoman positions, and it was from Paris that the two men jointly edited an intellectual and political revue that published several of the foundational texts of reformism. Their work was subsequently carried on by the Syrian Rashid Rida, a Sunni, who, among other things, began a dialogue with Lebanese Shi'i reformist ulama.

The collaboration among these three ulama from different denominations and intellectual traditions testifies to the capacity of reformism
to overcome intra-Muslim divisions. It must be underscored, however,
that this rapprochement was political, not religious, in nature. In the context of European expansion, in other words, priority was given to the
political unity of Muslims, even if this meant neglecting the doctrinal and
theological questions central to divisions between Sunnis and Shi'a. No
intellectual synthesis was advanced to overcome these differences, which
were instead swept under the carpet. Indeed, to maximize the reach of
his message, all his life al-Afghani deliberately cultivated mystery as to
his religious identity. Even as it indicated the possibility of overcoming
the issue of denomination, this stance was thus also indicative of the scale
of difficulties in this area. It was precisely by passing himself off as a Sunni
that al-Afghani was able to become the leading voice of reformism, sug-
gesting that, for Shi'a, rapprochement with the Sunnis required them to
abandon their specificities.[27]

The other forms of Sunni-Shi'a rapprochement also mainly took place
in the political domain. While al-Azhar University attempted to organize
private meetings and dialogue between its professors and their Shi'i—
and, in particular, Lebanese[28]—counterparts starting in the early twentieth century, these exchanges were institutionalized following the fall
of the Ottoman Empire in the framework of large international conferences intended to mobilize all Muslims on behalf of major political causes.
The first such conference took place in Jerusalem in 1931 on the initiative
of Muhammad Amin al-Husseini, leader of the Arab opposition to the
establishment of a Jewish state in Palestine, *mufti* of Jerusalem, and the
highest-ranking Islamic religious authority in Palestine, which had since
1920 been occupied by the British.[29] On this occasion, the Sunni *mufti*
invited the great Iraqi Shi'a ulama Muhammad Hussein al-Kashif al-Ghita
(d. 1953) to lead the prayer in Jerusalem's al-Aqsa mosque.

Subsequently, various attempts were made in the framework of associative and intellectual circles, most of them with ties to al-Azhar, to
pursue this dialogue between the various currents of Islam. This was the
case of the Association for the Rapprochement of the Islamic Legal

Schools, which was created in 1947. Founded in Cairo on the initiative of a young Iranian ulama, Muhammad Taqi Qummi, it was supported by both the great ulama of al-Azhar and religious intellectuals and included Iranian, Iraqi, and Lebanese Shi'i ulama. Rather than being ignored, in this framework disagreements were recognized and accepted by ulama who were far from occupying marginal positions in the religious landscapes of their countries, leading some Sunnis among them to recognize Shi'ism as a school of Islamic jurisprudence in its own right alongside the four Sunni schools. When he became rector of al-Azhar in 1958, one of the founding members of the association, Mahmud Shaltut (d. 1963), thus decided to place the study of Zaydi and Twelver Shi'a religious law on the university's program. In a famous fatwa of 1959, he recognized Twelver Shi'ism as a fifth school of Islamic jurisprudence and no less legitimate than the four Sunni schools. Significantly, these attempts at doctrinal rapprochement between Sunnis and Shi'a rapidly ran out of steam starting in the late 1950s, particularly once they no longer benefited from the active support of the Egyptian regime. In 1952 Gamal Abdel Nasser (d. 1970) took power with a group of young officers. For a time he saw the Sunni-Shi'a dialogue as contributing to a hoped-for unification of the Arab world, but he ultimately came to distrust it following Iran's rapprochement with Israel and the subsequent failure of the United Arab Republic in 1961, a brief experiment to unify Egypt and Syria that notably neglected to include Iraq. As we shall see, though initially a cause of ecumenical enthusiasm, the Iranian Revolution of 1979 ultimately deepened the sectarian divide. In any case, it was very much the regional political context that was each time responsible for reducing or deepening this divide.

Chapter 3

ISLAM AS IDEOLOGY

SUNNI AND SHIʿA ISLAMISM

In contrast to reformism, which was above all an intellectual movement, the Islamists introduced militancy and turned Islam into a modern political ideology. This transformation did nothing to dispel the Sunni-Shiʿa division since the two groups each produced their own version of Islamism. These, in turn, come in a variety of forms, depending on the national, cultural, and historical context. Yet a major characteristic of what can today be described as Islamism's "historic wing"—that is, the version that more or less hews to the teachings of the founding fathers (1920–1970)—is its deep attachment to Muslim unity over and beyond doctrinal and theological differences.

At the Junction of Tradition and Modernity

At the outset, Islamism was an anticolonialist movement championed by intellectuals situated halfway between traditional religious knowledge—that of the ulama and religious seminaries—and modern knowledge based on disciplines formed in Europe. This twofold influence allowed the classical tradition to be reinvented: by selecting certain elements and excluding others, a sort of synthesis was produced and acknowledged as such. Consider, for example, the careers of the two founding fathers of Islamism, Hassan al-Banna (d. 1949), who in 1928 founded the Muslim Brotherhood in Egypt, and Abul Ala Maududi (d. 1979), who in 1941 founded the Jamaat-e-Islami (the Islamic Society), which is today one of the largest Islamist movements in the South Asian countries that emerged from the breakup of the British Raj on the Indian subcontinent (Pakistan, Bangladesh, Sri Lanka, and India).

Hassan al-Banna grew up at a time when Egypt, formally independent since 1922 and governed by a constitutional monarchy, continued to be directly influenced by the former British colonial power, which among other things kept troops in the region of the Suez Canal. He was not a religious scholar but rather a schoolteacher. He had grown up in a deeply religious family of small landowners, and, more important, his father had been educated at al-Azhar University. The latter was the author of various types of treatises and textual commentaries exhibiting a diverse and inclusive religious background: integrated into Sufi brotherhood circles, he was as interested in mystical thinkers as he was in reformist ideas and orthodox ulama like Ibn Hanbal.[1]

Immersed in this atmosphere, the adolescent al-Banna began to frequent several of the religious societies and youth associations that proliferated in Egypt in the 1920s. Often inspired by Christian missionary associations, they were particularly frequented by the educated middle classes and sought to reinforce the Islamic ethic and lifestyle among young people. Strongly influenced by reformist ideas, Hassan al-Banna was also heavily imbued with Sufi mysticism and very early began to frequent the circles of the Hasafiyya brotherhood, where he made friends for life in some cases. With a presence throughout much of Egypt, the brotherhood's networks facilitated his frequent changes of residence, including moves to Cairo and then Ismailia on the banks of the Suez Canal, where he began his career as a teacher and created the Society of the Muslim Brothers.

By the start of the Second World War, the Muslim Brotherhood had become one of the most important political organizations in Egypt in terms of both its influence and the size of its membership. Part political party, part Sufi brotherhood, it was organized into sections spread throughout the country. The Muslim Brotherhood's strategy consisted of infiltrating existing organizations—sporting clubs, intellectual associations, labor unions—and participating in elections. On the model of the master/disciple relationship of the Sufi brotherhoods, its members owed their "guide" (*murshid*) absolute personal fealty. An immediate strong suit of the Muslim Brotherhood was its ability to recruit members across a broad array of social environments, from civil servants and students to peasants and workers.[2]

Islamism's other major intellectual reference, Abul Ala Maududi was born in the state of Hyderabad, a central Indian principality long ruled by a Muslim dynasty autonomous of the Mughal emperors. Like Hassan al-Banna, Maududi received an education that combined traditional religious instruction—his father intended him for a career as an ulama—with modern subjects. Raised in an educated middle-class family, he nevertheless had prestigious religious forebears. On his father's side, he descended from a lineage of Sufi saints from Delhi belonging to the most powerful Sufi brotherhood of the Indian subcontinent, the Chishtiyya, which had served at the court of the Mughal sovereigns. On his mother's side, he descended from a lineage of great Mughal army generals and Hyderabad princes. Maududi's father, a lawyer, was a fervent Sufi and ascetic. Abul Ala Maududi initially embarked on a career in journalism, and, while he is sometimes described as an ulama, he made no secret of his mixed intellectual training, which combined traditional religious studies and modern Western knowledge.[3]

Like Hassan al-Banna, Abul Ala Maududi was directly confronted with the problem of colonization. For India had fallen under British control starting in the mid-eighteenth century, with particular consequences for its Muslim population, which constituted a demographic minority vis-à-vis the country's Hindus but had long been politically dominant. In particular, Islam had been the state religion of the Greater Mughal Empire, into which India had been incorporated in the sixteenth century. The British deposed the last Mughal emperor in 1857 following the Indian Rebellion, a revolt by native British East India soldiers against British rule. Although their mutiny jointly mobilized Hindus and Muslims against the colonial power, the British, convinced that the Muslims had spearheaded the revolt, set about breaking the Muslim elites. In general, British colonization broadly favored the rise of the Hindu middle classes.

During Abul Ala Maududi's youth, the Muslims of India thus strongly felt themselves to be a people in decline and were nostalgic for their

glorious past. Maududi's family was particularly imbued with this senti-
ment, his father determined to raise his children in a way that preserved
them from Western influences. While still very young, Maududi became
involved in various protest movements, including the Caliphate Movement, which in the wake of the First World War mobilized to preserve
the Ottoman caliphate at a time when the war's victors were busily dis-
mantling the last great Muslim empire. More generally, he was involved
in various intellectual movements and currents that sought to unite Muslims and thereby restore the glory of Muslim India or, failing that, develop solutions that would allow Muslims to recover a form of political
sovereignty in a country increasingly ravaged by communal tensions between Muslims and Hindus. He thus began to militate against the Shud-
dhi (or "purification") Movement, a Hindu group that sought to convert
the country's Christians and Muslims to Hinduism.[4]

In 1941, Abul Ala Maududi founded the political organization Jamaat-
e-Islami. Like Hassan al-Banna with the Muslim Brotherhood, he modeled it on the Sufi brotherhoods. For Maududi, the latter were "the best
institution of Islam" since they allowed for the organization of a community of pious believers entirely devoted to their leader and were imper-
meable to the negative influences of society.[5] In contrast to the Muslim
Brotherhood in Egypt, however, Jamaat-e-Islami never became a mass
political movement. To the contrary, the organization saw itself as constituting an avant-garde. Rather than pursue large-scale recruitment, it
sought to create an elite characterized by moral rectitude, discipline, and
total commitment to the cause. It was fiercely criticized by the ulama, who
had organized themselves into other movements to fight colonialism. In
their view, Maududi, who did not belong to their world, was in no position to legitimately speak on behalf of Islam. Maududi, for his part, believed the ulama fundamentally incapable of confronting the problems
of the modern world.[6]

While Shi'a Islamism developed in symbiosis with the clerical institution, as we shall see, it also contained important secular intellectual
figures with profiles similar to those of al-Banna and Maududi. The foremost of these was Ali Shariati (d. 1977). Raised in a family of Iranian
clerics, in the early 1960s he studied literature in France, where he

frequented the intellectual world as well as anti-colonialist circles and, in particular, supporters of Algerian independence. His writing reflects this synthesis between Islam and modern intellectual disciplines. In a way similar to the reformists and Sunni Islamists, he called for a return to an original Shi'ism purged of the clerics' exegetical errors. He thus contrasted "Alid" Shi'ism, that of Imam Ali, with "Safavid" Shi'ism, the institutional and clerical version of Shi'ism that had in his view confined the Shi'a in an eschatological waiting game. Widely appreciated among educated young people, Ali Shariati provoked distrust among the clerics, including the most militant, who did not look kindly on his anticlericalism. He was close to the Freedom Movement of Iran, though never a member. Created in 1961, this organization sought to restore Islam to the center of Iranian identity. It mainly consisted of lay intellectuals, some of whom subsequently occupied important positions in the provisional governments established following the 1979 revolution. One such was Mehdi Bazargan (d. 1995), who for a few months served as prime minister.

Shia Islamism and the Clergy in Iraq

While one must not disregard the influence of figures like Ali Shariati, Shi'a Islamism nonetheless fundamentally remains a clerical ideology—that is, one in which the thinkers and leaders are clerics. This is why it is impossible to separate the history of Shi'a Islamism from that of the Shi'i clergy in the two great centers of Shi'a doctrinal development: Iran and Iraq.

The historical matrix of Shi'a Islamism is to be found in 1950s and 1960s Iraq. As we have seen, the territory of present-day Iraq has been central to Shi'a history since the Middle Ages. It was there, among other things, that the central institution of Shi'a religious authority, the *marja'iyya* (*al-taqlid*), first developed, with a handful of particularly erudite scholars, the *marja'* (*al-taqlid*; see chapter 2), providing spiritual guidance to the Shi'a faithful. To this day, the southern Iraqi city of Najaf remains central to the *marja'iyya*. It is there that the Shi'a world's most important *marja'* live and teach. The historic importance of this region to Shi'ism explains why the Shi'a represented a majority of the population at the time the British created Iraq in 1921.[7] Yet Iraq was constructed "against its society,"[8] with the state deliberately centered on the old Sunni Ottoman elites (see chapter 6).

As in Egypt a few years earlier, the 1950s saw Iraq transition from a monarchical regime supported by the former British colonial power to a republican regime originating in a military coup (1958), with General Abd al-Karim Qasim (d. 1963) at its head. The latter was supported by the Communist Party, which was the largest political organization in Iraq at the time and had a solid base among Shi'a, who in general tended to support protest parties en bloc.

The fall of the monarchy presented three challenges for the Shi'i clergy of Iraq. In addition to the difficulties presented by communist ideology, the clergy had to confront the socioeconomic consequences of the Qasim regime's reforms. These included an agrarian reform that weakened the class of large landowners who were among the main contributors to institutions overseen by the clergy and an education reform that deprived the ulama of their central role in the educational system.[9] Finally, while the Shi'a population's interest in the Communist Party may be explained by reference to Shi'a marginalization under the monarchy, it also reflected a process of secularization that over time threatened the very survival of the clerical institution, which then, as now, largely depended on voluntary payment of religious taxes by the faithful.

This particular context explains why communism was initially Shi'a Islamism's main ideological and political target in Iraq. Najaf took a leading role in the Islamist counterattack. In concert with young activists drawn from the town's small shopkeeping families, whose businesses were heavily dependent on the religious institution's continued prosperity, young ulama set about bringing the faithful back into the fold of Islam. They were drawn from prestigious scholarly families, the great dynasties of transnational, multicultural, and multilingual clerics characteristic of Shi'ism.

Though they themselves were full members of the clerical institution, these young ulama were critical of their elders, whom they saw as prisoners of conservatism and thus incapable of coming to grips with the challenges posed by secularization. They thus sought to modernize the religious institution in order to bring it into line with a society in transition. One of them, Muhammed Baqir al-Sadr (d. 1980), was heavily influenced by the Muslim Brotherhood in the manner in which he conceived and organized the ulama's counterattack. The Muslim Brotherhood had been active in Iraq since 1948 and was similarly worried about the success enjoyed by the Communist Party. For several years, Muslim Brothers had been in contact with the ulama of Najaf and even hoped to attract Shi'i to their movement. It was Muhsin al-Hakim (d. 1970), the most important *marja'* of the era, who is said to have rejected Shi'a involvement in the Iraqi Islamic Party, which had been the Muslim Brotherhood's official organization since the 1960s.[10] This stance reveals what is yet another enduring characteristic of Shi'a Islamism: even as it presents itself as the standard-bearer of a unified and universal Islam, it is also a communal ideology that has always been reluctant to dilute its Shi'a specificity within a generic Islam. For this reason, the young ulama of Najaf chose to rely on their own political organization and in 1958 founded al-Da'wa al-Islamiyya (the Islamic Call) Party, with Muhammed Baqir al-Sadr at its head.

Its clerical sociology played an important role in the emergence of rival poles within Shi'a Islamism. For while it postulated the ideal of a central religious authority as the source of consensus, the institution of *marja'iyya* was always traversed by conflict of varying intensity among several major religious scholars, all of whom laid claim to the status of *marja'*. The emergence of a Shi'a version of Islamism put a new spin on these rivalries. Before, the competition for religious authority was informed by a host of economic, familial, ethnic, regional, and national factors. The most powerful *marja'* were those who could mobilize support networks in several segments of society—within the religious institution itself and among the well-to-do as well as in several ethnic groups, in several regions, and outside the national borders. The ideologization of Islam, however, made politics central to the competition for the *marja'iyya*, giving rise to a militant type of *marja'* historically exemplified by Muhammad Baqir al-Sadr. In this context, the *marja'* were increasingly called on to take a stance on major political issues and, in particular, define their position vis-à-vis the question of the state and government—issues that most of their predecessors had gone out of their way to avoid.

A first great quarrel over these issues took place in 1960s Iraq, with the emergence of another Shi'a group, the Message Movement, with ties to a pole of religious authority that rivaled that of the Narjaf *marja'iyya*. Renamed the Islamic Action Organization in 1979, this movement was closely linked to the family, ethnic, and local networks of Muhammad al-Shirazi (d. 2001). Initially, he was no different from the other young ulama of prestigious scholarly families who desired to fight communism and secular ideologies. In the new context of the 1960s, however, the adversary was above all Arab nationalism, which soon came to be incarnated by the Ba'ath, an openly secular and socialist party that took power for the first time in 1963. For Muhammad al-Shirazi, the threat represented by the Ba'ath was all the greater to the extent that he was among the thousands of Shi'a who, though born in Iraq, had remained Iranian citizens.

While he largely agreed with Muhammad Baqir al-Sadr and his followers that the clergy needed to directly address the popular classes and rely on a political organization, Muhammad al-Shirazi was not part of the clerical networks of Najaf and wished to establish himself as an autonomous pole of religious authority and political action. To do so, he mobilized his family networks, the particular identity of the town of Karbala, and a violent critique of the clerical establishment of Najaf. For, in contrast to the other major ulama, he had studied, not in Najaf, but in Karbala. Although it was the site of Imam Hussein's tomb and thus an important place of pilgrimage, it was not a major center of religious studies. In the late 1960s it was one of al-Shirazi's nephews, Muhammad Taqi al-Modarresi, who created the Message Movement, the second Iraqi Shi'a Islamist movement destined to play an important role on the scene of regional Shi'a Islamism.

The Iranian Experience

The trajectory of Iranian Shia Islamism is also intimately linked to that of the clergy, which, as in Iraq, mobilized to fight the progress of secular ideologies and the modernizing authoritarian political regimes that threatened to undermine its social and economic foundations. In Iran, the main enemy was not communism but rather the regime of the Pahlavi sovereigns (1925–1979), led by Reza Shah Pahlavi (who ruled from 1925 to 1941) and his son, Mohammad Reza Pahlavi (1941–1979), who would be overthrown by the revolution in 1979. Starting in the 1930s, this regime sought to modernize Iran on the model of the secular republic that Ataturk built in Turkey following the First World War and the collapse of the Ottoman Empire. To that end, it undertook many reforms. Those of the education and justice system sought to liberate these two sectors from clerical control; the reform of the bureaucracy aimed to create a modern and efficient state apparatus as well as a base of support for the new regime; that of the army established military conscription. And that is without mentioning a tax reform intended to boost state revenue and a vestimentary reform that sought to impose European customs on Iranians and that, among other things, prohibited women from wearing the veil. Finally, Reza Shah, who wished to rediscover Iran's "authentic" national origins, devoted himself to symbolically reviving the pre-Islamic period, in particular by purifying the Persian language of the Arabic influences that, as he saw it, had gradually distorted it.

Logically enough, the Iranian Shiʿi clergy soon took sides with those who opposed this rapid modernization, occasionally entering into alliance with other opposition movements, including nationalists and communists. As in Iraq, it was a many-faceted mobilization. At the end of the Second World War, the Devotees of Islam, a radical movement founded by a young, Najaf-educated cleric, was the first religiously inspired political organization to theorize the need for overthrowing the Pahlavi regime, which engaged in the assassination of intellectuals and political leaders. At the same time, high-ranking clerics mobilized against the regime's reforms, and some were major supporters of Mohammed Mosaddegh's (d. 1967) nationalist government. While prime minister, in 1951 Mosaddegh decided to nationalize the Anglo-Iranian Oil Company, the British company that operated the Iranian oilfields, a move that led to his ouster in a 1953 coup d'état jointly fomented by Britain and the United States.

It must be noted that the Devotees of Islam Movement was short lived and never supported by high-ranking clergy. This stands in stark contrast with Iraqi Shi'a Islamism: whereas Iraqi Shi'a Islamism produced lasting political organizations with close links to the clerical institution, Iranian Shi'a Islamism mainly centered on the figures of individual clerics and subsequently existed in symbiosis with the theocratic regime of the Islamic Republic. The best known of these clerical figures was of course Ruhollah Khomeini. Like Muhammed Baqir al-Sadr in Iraq, Khomeini came from a family of clerics and had close ties with the *marja'iyya* in the town of Qom, home to Iran's foremost religious seminaries.

His frontal confrontation with the regime of Mohammed Reza Pahlavi began with the onset of the White Revolution in 1963. This reform movement featured, among other things, an agrarian reform and a modernization of electoral law giving women the right to vote, something that Khomeini publicly opposed. He also voiced his opposition to strengthening ties between Iran and the United States and the alliance with Israel. As a result, Khomeini was on several occasions arrested between 1963 and 1964 and subsequently sent into exile. Following a brief stay in Turkey, he spent the better part of his exile in Najaf before traveling to France a few months before the fall of the shah in February 1979.

Little is known about Khomeini's life in Najaf. His relations with Iraqi Shi'a Islamist activists and, in particular, al-Da'wa leader Muhammad Baqir al-Sadr seem to have been complicated. For al-Da'wa enjoyed the political—and doubtless also financial—support of the Iranian regime. Indeed, the latter had an interest in supporting the opposition to the Iraqi regime with which it was at odds over many issues: in addition to territorial disputes, Iraq accused Iran of manipulating Iraqi Shi'a in order to undermine the nation's stability. In response, Iraq sought to fan Arab nationalist feelings among the Iranian Arabs of the Khuzestan region— known to the Arabs as Arabistan (that is, the "land of the Arabs")—which is located in Iran along its border with Iraq. The Shah moreover calculated that supporting the Iraqi Shi'i clergy in the transnational competition for religious authority was a good way of weakening the Iranian clergy. While they generally held to the same ideological line as Khomeini, the clergy of Najaf and al-Da'wa could not openly support him in these circumstances. Only Muhammad al-Shirazi, who had publicly supported Khomeini at the time of his arrest in 1963, clearly appears to have been in contact with him during his time in Najaf.

The Question of the Islamic State

Whether in its Sunni or its Shi'a variety, Islamism is above all an ideology centered on action and winning power. At first, it gave little attention to doctrinal problems, particularly when they involved sensitive issues. As with the Muslim reformists, the essential thing for the Islamists was to unite Muslims over and beyond their cultural, sectarian, intellectual, and theological differences. Unity was not to be had by gradually winning everyone over to what had been declared the only valid doctrine. Hassan al-Banna was even occasionally involved in efforts to bring about rapprochement between Sunnis and Shi'a under the aegis of al-Azhar University. One of his favorite maxims, borrowed from Rashid Rida, was "Cooperate with each other on agreed upon matters and forgive each other when it comes to disputed questions."[11] This ecumenical approach was shared by Sunni and Shi'i ideologues alike, who moreover extensively borrowed from one another. The Shi'a were thus great readers of Maududi, several of whose books had been translated into Persian by Ruhollah Khomeini. As we have seen, Muhammad Baqir al-Sadr had links with the Iraqi Muslim Brotherhood and drew on it for inspiration in creating al-Da'wa. Later, after the Iranian Revolution of 1979 brought Khomeini to power, many Sunni Islamists saw this first successful takeover as a model to follow.

At first, the Islamists' objectives were very general in nature: to defend Islam against the spread of secular ideologies such as nationalism and communism, fight colonialism, and redefine Islam as a total system offering practical solutions to the problems of humankind in all domains. To this end, the Islamists affirmed their desire to establish an "Islamic state" on the basis of Sharia. The notion of the Islamic state had first been formulated by the reformist Rashid Rida. It was from Rida that Hassan al-Banna drew his inspiration in setting forth this concept, which marshaled two sources of legitimacy: that of the caliphate, with the Islamic state seen as its modern incarnation, and that of the European state. In a way once again typical of reformism, this amounted to merging the Muslim legal norm with what was in the process of establishing itself as the universal political norm.[12]

Hassan al-Banna did little to develop the Islamic state concept, and it was to Abul Ala Maududi that the task would fall of specifying what distinguished it from a simple Muslim state. Maududi was induced to clarify this concept by the debates in which he participated regarding the creation of a state for Muslims in India. For as we have seen, Indian Muslims were concerned about their loss of status at a time marked by the rise of the Hindu middle classes. Mobilizing to maintain their position, they first attempted to negotiate a specific status for themselves in the context of a Hindu-majority India and subsequently devoted their efforts to creating a separate state entity.

In contrast to the partisans of the Muslim League, who demanded that India be divided into two states—one with a Hindu majority and the other with a Muslim one—Abul Ala Maududi refused to take a simple communal approach to the issue of Islam's place in India. For him, the question was not simply a matter of achieving political sovereignty but also of the kind of state that was to be created. In his view, the secular Muslim nationalism advocated by the Muslim League was too directly inspired by the West. In founding Jamaat-e-Islami, Maududi explicitly sought to create a "counter-League" devoted to establishing an Islamic state.[13] In this state, not only would Muslims constitute the majority and hold the reins of power; they would also live under laws based on Sharia. Against democracy, which he saw as subject to the vagaries of popular will and potentially far removed from the will of God, Maududi posited the concept of "theodemocracy"—yet another modern version of the caliphate in which sovereignty belonged to God alone, the source of all laws. In 1947 the British Raj was finally divided on a religious basis between a Hindu-majority state (India) and a Muslim-majority one (Pakistan). The partition was accompanied by major population transfers, with millions of Hindus and Muslims crossing the border to join their respective communities, though neither state ever achieved total religious homogeneity. In this new context, Jamaat-e-Islami's objective became to Islamize the Pakistani state and society. Its ideas, as we shall see, greatly influenced General Muhammad Zia ul-Haq (d. 1988), who in the late 1970s launched a policy of Islamization that undermined the coexistence between Sunnis and Shi'a (see chapter 8).

One encounters the same focus on the question of the Islamic state in Shi'a Islamism, albeit at a different scale: due to its clerical sociology, Shi'a Islamism is obsessed with the question of institutionalizing the ulama's role in government, a question totally absent from Sunni Islamism. Muhammad Baqir al-Sadr was the first to have "Shi'ized" the question of the Islamic state. In the tradition of the great Shi'i political thinkers of the early twentieth century who had supported Iran's experiment with constitutional monarchy, he attempted to reconcile the idea of clerical oversight of the state with the principle of popular sovereignty: in his Islamic state, a council of great ulama holds a supervisory role— that of censorship, in fact—in regard to any laws adopted by Parliament that might contravene Islam.

Within Shi'a Islamist circles, however, it was above all the doctrine of *wilayat al-faqih*, or "Guardianship of the Islamic Jurist," that most influenced the manner in which the Shi'a version of the Islamic state was conceived. Developed by Ruhollah Khomeini during his years of exile in Iraq, it identified the specifically Islamic nature of the Islamic state as consisting not so much in the conformity of its laws with Islam as in the fact that the state was directly controlled by a *marja'* vested with all of the powers of the Prophet and the Imams. This doctrine represented a significant break with the manner in which Shi'i ulama had traditionally approached matters of government and state. From the time of Ja'far al-Sadiq and the subsequent occultation of the twelfth Imam, it is to be recalled, the dominant Shi'a doctrine began to close the gap with Sunnism by seeking to determine the necessary conditions for coexistence with the powers that be. In this spirit, Shi'i theologians could just as well support an absolute monarchy as a constitutional one or, today, a classic democratic system.

The Iranian Revolution for the first time allowed Shi'i Islamists to pass from theory to practice. An effort was thus made to abolish the frontier between political and religious authority, an effort embodied by the establishment of the supreme leader of the revolution. This institution placed supreme political authority in the hands of an ulama, making the new regime a full-fledged theocracy. For, according to the Iranian Constitution of 1979, the supreme leader had to be a *marja'* who, in addition to his religious competencies, demonstrated such leadership qualities as courage and effectiveness in administering the state. Yet the institution of the supreme leader coexists with institutions elected on the basis of universal male and female suffrage, including the Parliament and the president of the republic. The supreme leader is himself elected for life by the Assembly of Experts, a learned body consisting of eighty-six ulama elected by the people.

The practice of the Islamic state significantly evolved following the death of Khomeini in 1989 and the profound crisis of religious legitimacy that it ushered in for the Islamic Republic.[14] Since none of the *marja'* of Qom supported the doctrine of *wilayat al-faqih*, a few weeks before his death Khomeini had the constitution modified to allow for the possibility of separating political and religious authority. Henceforth the supreme leader of the revolution no longer necessarily had to be a *marja'* but could instead be a simple *mujtahid*—that is, an ulama who, though well versed in religious studies, had not been recognized by his peers as the most knowledgeable among them. In reality, Khomeini's practice of power had led him to conclude that the preservation of the Islamic state could require that concessions be made in the religious domain: the essential thing was not that the state be led by a *marja'* but that it be in the hands of a man familiar with religious law and possessing political skill. In his view, this was the case of Ali Khamenei, since 1989 supreme leader of the Islamic Republic. Although not a religious studies virtuoso, the latter unreservedly subscribed to *wilayat al-faqih* and had furthermore held important political offices, including that of president of the republic. With Khamenei, the Islamic state would be led by a man who was ideologically faultless but also undeniably had what it took to serve as a head of state. For all that, Khamenei's appointment to the post of supreme leader of the Islamic Republic marked a lasting retreat from the utopia of the Islamic state.

While Ali Khamenei did not lay claim to the status of *marja'* for several years, contenting himself with promoting the *marja'iyya* of uncharismatic, not especially influential clerics in order to prevent himself from being overshadowed by any great Iranian ulama, he was always uncomfortable with this separation of political and religious authority. Starting in 1994 he thus sought to position himself as *marja'* by putting pressure on the religious institutions of Qom. They resisted with all their strength, and even the militant ulama who had participated in the Islamic Revolution refused to recognize his *marja'iyya*. Hussein-Ali Montazeri (d. 2009), in particular, became one of Khamenei's main clerical opponents. Until 1987 Montazeri, first in line to succeed Khomeini, subsequently found himself sidelined for his criticism of the regime's "betrayals."

Faced with this resistance, Khamenei ultimately declared that his *marja'iyya* did not apply in Iran but only abroad. It was not to prove a success. In reaction to Khamenei's initiative, Mohammad Hussein Fadlallah (d. 2010) officially declared his *marja'iyya*, provoking an open crisis with the supreme leader of the Islamic Republic, who responded by embarking on a systematic effort to discredit this new rival. A Lebanese ulama, Fadlallah had been a prominent figure in al-Da'wa in Iraq. After returning to Lebanon in the 1960s, he became associated with the pro-Iranian Shi'a movement Hezbollah, eventually coming to be seen by many observers as its "spiritual father," although it is doubtful that he ever held such a status. His refusal to submit to the authority of Khamenei was only one of many manifestations of the latter's rejection by non-Iranian *marja'*. Though he continued his struggle to achieve the status of great transnational *marja'*, Khamenei was in these conditions ultimately obliged to recognize the intrinsically plural nature of the *marja'iyya*, an institution that showed remarkable resilience vis-à-vis the Islamic Republic's efforts to place it under its control.

Radicalizations: Sayyid Qutb and His Legacy

At the end of the Second World War, the Muslim Brotherhood in Egypt was at once feared and courted by the other political organizations. Fearing that they would attempt a coup d'état, in 1948 Prime Minister

Mahmoud El Nokrashy, who was aligned with the nationalist movement, decided to ban them. Immediately after doing so, he was assassinated by a radical young Muslim brother. Though Hassan al-Banna firmly condemned this act, the founder of the Muslim Brotherhood would himself be assassinated a few weeks later in 1949 by the regime's police. Not surprisingly, the Muslim Brotherhood subsequently supported the monarchy's opponents, in particular the Free Officers Movement that took power in 1952. Several officers of this military junta were members of the Muslim Brotherhood. Gamal Abdel Nasser, the coup's mastermind, himself had close ties to the organization, which further provided the popular base necessary for the putsch's success.

Yet relations between the new regime and the Muslim Brotherhood soon deteriorated. Accused of being behind an attempted assassination of Nasser, the latter were severely repressed. This was to be a turning point in the movement's history, a period marked by mass arrests, torture, and public trials. The best-known figure of this black period was Sayyid Qutb, a teacher and man of letters who had been made responsible for Muslim Brotherhood propaganda in the early 1950s. Arrested in 1954, he subsequently spent the better part of his life in penal servitude before being executed by hanging in 1966. It was while imprisoned that he wrote a series of texts advocating armed revolutionary action by an avant-garde. His writings were to particularly influence a rising generation of Muslim Brothers who had come of age in this difficult political context, leading them to revisit some of the ideological and political principles laid down by Hassan al-Banna. These included his project for a mass Islamism that was reformist in its approach to politics and favorable to participation in existing political institutions.

In contrast to Hassan al-Banna, who had been able to organize a mass movement but wrote little and thus left behind no detailed ideological system, Sayyid Qutb was above all an ideologue. A great reader of Abul Ala Maududi, he likewise held to a revolutionary interpretation of Islam, theorizing the need for an Islamic avant-garde to take power by force. For him, the Islamization of the masses would follow from the Islamization of the state, an approach that greatly differed from that of Hassan al-Banna, for whom educating the masses was the priority. At the conceptual level, Qutb developed several notions that would prove central to radical Sunni Islamism. In addition to reviving the notion of *jihad*—the war against disbelievers in the name of God—he took up the paired concepts of *ubudiyya* (worship) and *hakimiyya* (sovereignty) already posited by Maududi: in the Islamic state, only God—and not the people, single party, king, or autocratic leader—exercised sovereignty. For the law flowed directly from God. In that state, God was also the only object of worship, in contrast to the cult of personality that, then as now, was paid to the leaders of many Arab political regimes.

The theorist of a radical break with the established social and political order, Qutb also adopted Maududi's view that contemporary Muslim societies had returned to a state of *jahiliyya*, or the ignorance prevailing before Muhammad's revelation of God's message. Consequently, the Islamic avant-garde had first to withdraw after the example of the Prophet, who had migrated (*hijra*) from Mecca to Medina in order to better prepare the forthcoming *jihad* against the idolaters. Another key concept of radical Islamism logically followed from this rejection of the surrounding society in *jahiliyya*: *takfir*, a term that is most often translated as "excommunication" or "anathema" and which more specifically refers to the fact of declaring someone a *kafir*, or unbeliever. In the eyes of the radical Islamists, all those who do not conceive and practice Islam as they themselves understand it are unbelievers against whom it is legitimate to fight and kill. This is why contemporary jihadist movements are often described as *takfirist* or "excommunicators."

This last point was singled out for particular refutation by Hassan al-Hudaybi (d. 1973), who succeeded Hassan al-Banna as guide of the Muslim Brotherhood. He did not hesitate to describe the partisans of *takfir* as "Kharijites" and warned the followers of Sayyid Qutb against "the utopia of the Islamic state," which in his eyes should not be substituted for the slow but deep re-Islamization of society on a day-by-day basis.[15] In reality, the line advocated by al-Banna and al-Hudaybi, which may to this day be described as reformist, is entirely in keeping with the traditional Sunni vision of the relations between religion and politics. It is based on the idea of the necessity of compromising with the powers that be should they wander from the straight and narrow path of Islam. By contrast,

Qutb and his followers belong to a similarly well-established tradition of rebellion against governments that do not respect authentic Islam.[16]

In the 1970s and 1980s Sayyid Qutb's ideas served as the inspiration for a whole series of radical movements dedicated to revolutionary action, particularly in Egypt. Gamal Abdel Nasser's death in 1970 inaugurated a new historical period in that country. The new president, Anwar al-Sadat, gave signs of good will to Islamist protest, tolerating Islamist movements and accepting a limited Islamization of law. While the reformist Islamists were satisfied with this rapprochement, the most radical continued to reject the government and society as a whole, withdrawing into themselves in keeping with a sectarian dynamic. Mainly consisting of small groups, these movements were made up of young people principally drawn from the modern educational system, often with a background in scientific disciplines.

Known as *Al-takfir wa al-hijra* (excommunication and migration), the Society of Muslims is representative of these movements. Under the leadership of Shukri Mustafa, a young agricultural engineer who read Qutb and Maududi in prison in the 1960s, its members formed a countersociety that held itself aloof from the society of *jahiliyya*. In 1977 they kidnapped and assassinated an eminent al-Azhar University ulama and former minister before being arrested and subsequently sentenced to death. A few years later, in 1981, the small *Al-jihad* (the *jihad*) group, led by a young lieutenant and an electrical engineer, who served as their mastermind, assassinated President Sadat. Having received the Nobel Peace Prize a few years earlier alongside Israeli prime minister Menachem Begin, Sadat had signed a peace treaty between Egypt and the Jewish state in 1978—in the eyes of many Egyptian opposition movements, an unpardonable sin.[17]

Chapter 4

AN ISLAMIST INTERNATIONAL?

Most Islamist movements are organized as transnational networks. The factors explaining this are similar for Sunnis and Shi'a alike. Thus when the various forms of Islamism first emerged, Cairo (for the Sunni world) and Najaf (for its Shi'a counterpart) generated centripetal intellectual and religious dynamics owing to their position as centers of religious knowledge. When the Egyptian, Iraqi, and Syrian movements were severely hit by repression, a portion of their activists were forced into exile, simultaneously accelerating these movements' transnational diffusion and encouraging multiple hybridizations and reorganizations.

Palestine as Pan-Islamic Cause

The Muslim Brotherhood's involvement in the Palestinian cause powered its spread beyond Egypt. Starting in 1935 Hassan al-Banna's brother, Abdel Rahman, traveled to Jerusalem to enter into contact with the great *mufti* Muhammad Amin al-Husseini.[1] Born into a powerful family of Jerusalem notables, this ulama had been appointed by the British to lead the Supreme Muslim Council, an institution responsible for overseeing the religious affairs of the Muslims of Palestine. He quickly became a key figure in the opposition to the project of creating a Jewish national homeland. Above all, he sought to mobilize Muslims the world over on behalf of what he hoped would become a great pan-Islamic cause. He played a central role in the Arab Revolt of 1936, in which Palestinian society mobilized against British colonial rule and Jewish immigration.

Al-Husseini actively supported the Muslim Brotherhood as it created cells in most Palestinian towns. The Egyptian Muslim Brotherhood moreover participated in the 1936 revolt through a paramilitary organization, the Phalange for Palestine, which carried out armed attacks on Palestinian territory and was subsequently involved alongside Arab armies in the first Arab-Israeli War (1947–1949). The Muslim Brotherhood's Palestinian involvement constituted a decisive step in the history of the movement in Egypt, increasing the importance of the aforementioned Secret Organization, a military branch of the movement that, in addition to training volunteers for the Phalange for Palestine, also supplied military training to thousands of militants under the leadership of active and former Egyptian Army officers.

The collapse of the Arab armies, the resulting mass exodus of Palestinians, and the creation of the state of Israel in 1948 led the territorial and political organization of the Palestinian branch of the Muslim Brotherhood to be revamped. For, in the immediate aftermath of the war, it was mainly present in territory placed under the sovereignty of the new state of Jordan. This country, created from the union of the West Bank (formerly an integral part of Palestine) and Transjordan, received the better part of the Palestinian refugees of 1948. As a result, the Muslim Brotherhood became an organization mainly composed of Palestinians but operating in a Jordanian framework. With the West Bank occupied by Israel following the Six-Day War of 1967, the Muslim Brotherhood of the West Bank found itself under Israeli administration and was subject to specific dynamics while at the same time retaining close ties with the Jordanian activists.

In both Jordan and the occupied West Bank, the Muslim Brotherhood was authorized to exist in the form of religious and charitable organizations. In this framework, it opted for a new approach based on peaceful coexistence with the powers that be. It was only with the outbreak of the First Intifada in 1987 that the political dynamics of the two branches began to evolve in markedly different directions. In the West Bank and the Gaza Strip, the Muslim Brotherhood was transformed into a new organization, Hamas (the acronym of the Islamic Resistance Movement), which opted for armed struggle against Israel. The Jordanian Muslim Brotherhood, for its part, continued along the path of legalism.

The Cairo Connection

Alongside their Palestinian involvement, the Egyptian Muslim Brotherhood sought to establish ties with influential political and religious figures in the Arab world by sending delegations to various countries. Contacts established with foreign students in Cairo often served to lay the groundwork for these trips and, more broadly, to create branches in several countries.

Starting in the 1930s, the Muslim Brotherhood established a presence in Yemen under the leadership of Yemeni students from al-Azhar and the Dar al-Ulum, the teacher-training institute where Hassan al-Banna had studied. Moreover, since Yemen possessed few qualified personnel who might help it develop its educational system, many Egyptians taught there, including Brotherhood activists. In a general way, there were strong ties between the Egyptian Muslim Brotherhood and certain movements opposing the Zaydi monarchy of Imam Yahya Hamid al-Din (d. 1948), in particular the Free Yemeni Movement. One of its founders, the Islamic judge Mohammed Mahmud al-Zubairi, had resided in Cairo in the 1940s, where he mixed with Muslim Brotherhood activists,[2] their vision of Islam profoundly influencing his movement.[3] The Muslim Brotherhood also played a central role in the complex series of events that resulted in the assassination of Imam Yahya in 1948 and the establishment of a short-lived constitutional monarchy. Until the 1990s the Yemeni Muslim Brotherhood did not possess a structured organization as this was prohibited by law. However, in the Arab Republic of Yemen, which had been created in the country's North in 1962 after the final collapse of the Zaydi imamate,[4] they exercised significant institutional influence, particularly in the educational system. In 1990 the unification of North and South Yemen and the creation of a democratic regime allowed the Muslim Brotherhood to join with other Islamist currents as well as various figures from the tribal and business worlds in creating the al-Islah (Reform) Party. The movement adopted a legalist approach, participating in elections and joining various governmental coalitions.[5]

The centripetal attraction of Cairo also explains the Muslim Brotherhood's presence in Sudan beginning in the 1940s via the intermediary of Sudanese students in Cairo and also Egyptians working in Sudan, particularly as professors. In this country, the Muslim Brotherhood initially militated in favor of the unification of Egypt and Sudan, something that limited their appeal among the educated, who tended to favor the creation of an independent Sudanese state. It was only in the mid-1950s, at a time when the Egyptian Muslim Brotherhood was subject to all-out repression on the part of Nasser's regime, that the Sudanese activists became autonomous, making common cause with the supporters of independence.[6] Yet they only really expanded following the creation of the Islamic Charter Front in 1964 by Hassan al-Tourabi (d. 2016), allying themselves with the country's powerful Sufi brotherhoods and gradually succeeding in infiltrating the army. In 1989 the military putsch of General Omar al-Bashir allowed the Sudanese Muslim Brothers to closely associate themselves with the government.

Syria provides another example of the central role played by Arab students from al-Azhar in the transnational diffusion of the Muslim Brotherhood. Most of the students who founded the Syrian branch were members of ulama families of middling economic and social status whose income was mainly dependent on small trade.[7] They created a network of youth associations that, from the mid-1930s, had a presence in most large Syrian towns. As in Egypt, some had close ties with Sufi brotherhoods. Such was the case of Mustafa al-Siba'i (d. 1964), who at the end of the Second World War united the various associations to form an organization also named the Muslim Brotherhood Society, which sought to resemble its Egyptian mother organization in all respects. When the Nasserian crackdown began in 1954, Mustafa al-Siba'i assumed general command of the Muslim Brotherhood in both countries. In contrast to the cases discussed above, where the Muslim Brotherhood found a modus vivendi with the powers that be and, in some cases, became closely associated with them, the Syrian branch was subject to particularly severe repression. Its leaders were forced into exile, a process that accelerated after the Ba'ath—a socialist and Arab nationalist party whose members were mainly recruited from the country's religious minorities—came to power.

One encounters a similar history in Iraq where, starting in 1963, a rival branch of the Syrian Ba'ath Party won power. The creation of the Iraqi branch was the work of Muhammad Mahmud al-Sawwaf (d. 1992). In 1948 he established a pro-Palestinian organization, the Society for the Salvation of Palestine, which contributed a handful of combatants to the 1947–1949 war. An ulama originally from Mosul, al-Sawwaf had studied and taught at al-Azhar in the 1940s. During his time in Cairo, he became very close with Hassan al-Banna, who personally appointed him "general guide" of the Muslim Brotherhood in Iraq. In 1951 he founded the Islamic Brotherhood Association, the official name of the Muslim Brotherhood in Iraq, which became the Iraqi Islamic Party in the 1960s. Forced into exile under Saddam Hussein, who fiercely repressed political organizations, the party resumed its activity in Iraq following the American intervention of 2003, which put an end to the power of the Ba'ath Party. In this way it became one of the main actors in the Sunni politico-religious field. In contrast to other Sunni political forces, the Iraqi Islamic Party always advocated participation in the political process launched under the aegis of the United States.[8]

The "Najaf Connection"

For Shi'a, Iraq and the religious seminaries of Najaf, in particular, were central to the diffusion of Shi'a Islamism in the Arab world. Like al-Azhar in Cairo, the religious seminaries of Najaf attracted many foreign students who resided in the town for periods of varying length. From the outset, the al-Da'wa Party thus included non-Iraqis, in particular Lebanese who, upon returning to Lebanon in the 1960s and 1970s, created cells of the movement. One of the main actors in this process of expansion was Mohammad Hussein Fadlallah. From a family of clerics from the mainly Shi'a Jabal Amel region of southern Lebanon, Fadlallah was born in Najaf, where his father taught religious studies. Among other things, Fadlallah played an important role as a member of the editorial committee of the journal *Islamic Enlightenments*, the mouthpiece of an association of reformist ulama linked to al-Da'wa and whose editor-in-chief was Muhammad Baqir al-Sadr. Upon returning to Lebanon in the mid-1960s, Muhammad Hussein Fadlallah gradually became a central figure on the Lebanese religious and political scene.

It was also via Najaf seminary students that al-Da'wa took root in Bahrain in the late 1960s. Though ruled by a Sunni dynasty, the Al Khalifa, the majority of the Bahraini population practiced Shi'ism, and there had long been a strong Shi'a clerical tradition there. The clergy was well integrated into the networks of the *marja'iyya*, which attracted many religious studies students. It was some of these students who founded Bahrain's al-Da'wa cell. One of them was Isa Qasim. Born into the lower classes rather than a great clerical family—his father was a fisherman—he returned to Najaf in 1972 to participate in his country's first parliamentary elections. Elected by a very large majority to represent his district, he was a key figure of parliamentary Shi'a Islamism at this time and starting in the 2000s established himself as the most influential Shi'a ulama in local political debates.

A somewhat different dynamic was at play in Kuwait. This country contains a large Shi'a minority—today, probably around 25 percent of the population. Unlike Bahrain, however, a strong Shi'a clerical tradition never emerged there. This is why, in establishing itself in the emirate over the course of the 1960s, the al-Da'wa Party relied on emissaries sent by the Najafi *marja'iyya* at the request of the representatives of local merchant notables, who wanted them to preside as imams in mosques and oversee Shi'i religious education networks. A Lebanese citizen, resident of Najaf, and al-Da'wa activist, Ali al-Korani had brought together in the emirate a group of young Kuwaitis from the new middle classes who were eager to breathe new life into Shi'a political representation in Parliament. For they believed that they were demographically underrepresented there and saw the Shi'i MPs as old men incapable of understanding the issues of a rapidly transforming society. It was these young people who formed the nucleus of al-Da'wa in Kuwait. In its various manifestations, the latter would long be the emirate's principal Shi'a Islamist movement.

The Gulf: Land of Exile and Migration

While the first contacts appear to have taken place in the 1940s, it was above all in the mid-1950s that hundreds of Muslim Brothers flocked to the monarchies of the Persian Gulf. This was the result of the conjunction of several factors. The persecution of the Muslim Brotherhood in Egypt and Syria encouraged the activists to seek places of exile. At the same time, the Gulf countries were desperately short of skilled workers. Drawn from the educated middle classes, the Muslim Brothers were thus welcomed with open arms, particularly in the educational system, the religious bureaucracy, and the cultural field. Finally, thanks to its petrol revenue, the Gulf experienced accelerated economic development in the aftermath of the Second World War. Further strengthened by the oil booms of the 1970s, the labor needs of the Gulf countries grew considerably, making it a region of mass migration. For many Muslim Brothers, political exile went hand in hand with economic migration, the Gulf offering many career opportunities in these circumstances.

These socioeconomic factors were joined by an ideological one. In the context of the Cold War, the Gulf countries remained aligned with the Western bloc while the Arab republics—Algeria, Egypt, Syria, and Iraq—switched to the Soviet camp. Starting in the late 1950s, the Egypt of Gamal Abdel Nasser embarked on an intense propaganda campaign denouncing the Western-aligned Arab regimes, calling on Arabs to unite under its banner. Explicitly founded as a state devoted to spreading and defending Islam, Saudi Arabia was behind a major ideological counterattack in the context of this "Arab Cold War."[9] Whereas Nasser talked of unifying the Arabs, the Saudis called for Muslim unity.

Given their commitment to what is known as the "Wahhabi" current of Sunni Islam, however, the Saudi ulama were little inclined to throw their support behind a project of this type. Wahhabi doctrine is based on the teachings of Muhammad ibn Abd al-Wahhab (d. 1792), an ulama who was the organic intellectual of the first Saudi state (1744–1818). To this day his descendants constitute a dynasty of religious scholars with ties to government and control important offices in the religious bureaucracy. Educated in the Hanbali school of religious law, Muhammad ibn

Abd al-Wahhab had focused on the issue of doctrinal purity. Throughout his life, he fiercely combatted the religious practices of his compatriots, which he saw as deviant, particularly those running counter to the principle of the uniqueness of God. In his eyes, all practices that consisted in joining the worship of human beings to the worship of God amounted to polytheism and should be strictly prohibited. For this reason, his favorite targets were the Sufis and Shi'a, who revere holy men, as we have seen.

Because the Wahhabi ulama mainly focused on doctrinal questions that were more likely to exacerbate divisions between Muslims than lead them to close ranks, the exiled Muslim Brothers were central to the counterattack organized by the Saudi Kingdom. They particularly became involved in institutions created in the 1960s to propagate Islam throughout the world and make Saudi Arabia the religion's new center of gravity. They thus actively contributed to the development of the Islamic University of Medina, which was created in 1961 to train foreign ulama and compete with al-Azhar, now firmly under state control, its prestige badly damaged. Alongside other Islamist ideologues and activists, including Abul Ala Maududi, they also played an important role in the World Islamic League created in 1962.[10]

The Muslim Brothers who passed through Saudi Arabia in this context included many of the movement's leading figures. In this connection, one might mention Sayyid Qutb's brother, Muhammad Qutb (d. 2014), the Syrian Sa'id Hawwa (d. 1989), and the Palestinian Abdullah Azzam (d. 1989). Indeed, such was the concentration of leading Muslim Brotherhood officials in Saudi Arabia that the kingdom was the site of preparations for the establishment of an International Organization of the Muslim Brotherhood, which was officially created in 1982.[11] Their presence also had a decisive impact on the Saudi politico-religious sphere, giving rise starting in the 1960s to a vast social movement known as Al-Sahwa al-Islamiyya (the Islamic Awakening). It was pioneered by young ulama trained by foreign Muslim Brothers, particularly Muhammad Qutb, who merged his brother's ideas with Wahhabism. Having constantly extended its reach, in the 1990s the Sahwa Movement occupied a central place in protests against the Saudi regime.

Other Gulf monarchies were affected by the Muslim Brothers' pere-grinations, particularly Kuwait and Qatar. In Kuwait, the first Muslim Brothers arrived in the 1940s and mainly occupied posts in the educational system and religious bureaucracy. In 1952 a Kuwaiti branch of the organization was created thanks to contacts between the emirate's merchant notability and the Iraqi and Egyptian Muslim Brothers.[12] Until Kuwait's invasion by Iraq in 1990, the better part of its members were foreigners. The influence of these foreign militants, who had been trained as activists in their countries of origin, reflected both their competence and the large number of expatriates residing in Kuwait, where they have constituted a majority since the 1970s. Well represented in the intellectual professions, Egyptians and Palestinians were particularly influential within the various Muslim Brotherhood organizations that succeeded one another, which they sought to make into an assistance network for the foreign activists residing in the country as well as a hub in the Muslim Brotherhood's transnational network.[13]

It was the trauma of the Iraqi invasion that undid Kuwait's ties with this transnational network. Since the Palestinian Liberation Organization (PLO) had supported Saddam Hussein, the thousands of Palestinians residing in Kuwait were deported following its liberation. More generally, Arab expatriates, seen as having been disloyal toward their host country during the invasion, were the object of generalized suspicion. In the eyes of Kuwaiti activists, moreover, the transnational leadership of the Muslim Brotherhood had not been sufficiently active in its support for the liberation of Kuwait. In fact, it was above all the young Kuwaitis who had organized resistance networks during the occupation that took charge of the Muslim Brotherhood's organizations in the emirate following the liberation. It was they who created the Islamic Constitutional Movement in order to participate more actively in political life with the reestablishment of an elected Parliament.

In Qatar, a Muslim Brotherhood network was established in the 1950s following the arrival of Abd al-Badi Saqr, an Egyptian with close ties to Hassan al-Banna. Saqr was appointed to head the national education system and then the National Library, opening the path for an influx of Muslim Brothers into the country, where they played a central role in modernizing the educational system.[14] It was Saqr who arranged for Yusuf al-Qaradawi, whom he had got to know during a stint in prison, to come to Qatar in 1961. Once there, this graduate of al-Azhar founded the College of Sharia, the country's leading institute of religious studies. In the 1990s al-Qaradawi became a star of the al-Jazeera cable television channel by virtue of his weekly program, *Sharia and Life*. He is today one of the world's most popular Muslim preachers.

Shi'i Exiles in the Gulf

In the 1970s the repression became particularly intense in Iraq, indiscriminately targeting Shi'a Islamist militants, religious studies students and professors, and all Shi'a suspected of subversive activities—a category that included in particular anything that could be seen as helping to spread Iranian influence. In this context, some Gulf countries became places of exile for many Shi'a Islamist activists fleeing Iraq.

Since it possessed only an embryonic Shi'a clerical class and still had the most open political regime of any Gulf state, Kuwait was the principal destination for Shi'a Islamist exiles prior to the 1979 revolution, when all the Iraqi exiles took up residence in Iran. They included major figures from al-Da'wa and the Message Movement: in the case of al-Da'wa, Muhammad Mahdi al-Asefi (d. 2015) and Izz al-Din Salim (d. 2004); in that of the Message Movement, Muhammad al-Shirazi and most members of his family, including his nephews Muhammad Taqi and Hadi al-Modarresi. Many of these exiles were easily integrated into existing Shi'i community institutions (mosques and religious schools), thereby compensating for the lack of personnel with training in religious studies. They moreover created new religious institutions, one of the Message Movement's priorities. The result was to make Kuwait the main center of its activities in the 1970s. This reflected Muhammad al-Shirazi's skill at establishing relations of trust with both the local Shi'a population and members of the ruling dynasty. This allowed him to create a number of institutions, including a religious teaching seminary, a mosque, a *husseiniyya*, and a library, all of which continue to exist to this day. In the 1970s the seminary attracted many Shi'i students from the Gulf and played a key role in spreading the Message Movement to Saudi Arabia. Central actors of state power, the Wahhabi ulama of that country had always exhibited a visceral hostility toward Shi'ism. Yet Saudi Arabia contained a Shi'a minority mainly concentrated in the kingdom's Eastern Province, around the towns of Qatif and Hofuf. As in Bahrain, with which the Saudi Eastern Province was closely linked, Saudi Shi'a society had long possessed a strong clerical tradition. It exists to this today and explains the significant involvement of Saudi Shi'a in transnational Shi'i clerical networks. Given these circumstances, Saudi Arabia could not be a land of exile for Iraqi Shi'i Islamists. Most officials of the Saudi branch of the Message Movement were thus trained in Kuwait in the seminary that Muhammad al-Shirazi had created. Foremost among them was the branch's founder, Hassan al-Saffar, who remains to this day a leading figure of Saudi Shi'a Islamism.

From Kuwait, the Message Movement also spread to Bahrain, where its leader, Hadi al-Modarresi, had moved in 1973 after having spent some time in the Emirate of Sharjah, part of the United Arab Emirates. Like his uncle in Kuwait, he succeeded in forming ties with local notabilities, allowing him to obtain Bahraini nationality. In a context in which the regime saw Shi'i religious movements as a way to thwart the Marxist and Arab nationalist organizations that constituted its principal opposition, these contacts facilitated his activities.

Exporting the Revolution

The advent of the Islamic Republic of Iran in 1979 changed the transnational dynamic of Shi'a Islamism. Formerly tied to the Shi'i religious institutions of Iraq, it now came to center on the activities of the Iranian state. Starting in 1979 the latter made exporting the Islamic revolution a major part of its foreign policy. The objective was to encourage the establishment of other Islamic republics or, at the very least, of regimes favorable to Iran. Failing that, it sought to strengthen the power of Shi'i communities in the domestic political equation. These efforts to export the revolution first and foremost targeted countries with large Shi'i minorities (generally incorporated into nation-states in a position of statutory, political, and socioeconomic inferiority) and in which Shi'a Islamist movements had already been active, particularly those originating in Iraqi transnational networks.

It was around these networks that the policy of exporting the revolution initially centered. In reality, this policy was as much a matter of import as it was of export:[15] while the Islamic Republic hoped to expand the revolutionary dynamic, it was in fact often primarily responding to the appeals of preexisting Shi'a Islamist movements that counted on its support to consolidate their positions. At first it was the Shirazis—that is, the militants of Muhammad al-Shirazi's Message Movement—who were the most active in this respect. They profited from the contacts they had made well before the revolution with Khomeini's entourage to organize from Iran various subversive activities targeting Iraq, Bahrain, and Saudi Arabia.

Believing that war would decide the fate of Saddam Hussein's regime, the Shirazis were particularly active in the Persian Gulf. For in 1980 Hussein had invaded Iranian territory, launching a war that continued until 1988 and which the Iraqi Shi'i Islamists expected would bring about the fall of the Ba'ath regime. In November 1979 the Shirazis played a leading role in sparking a series of protests and riots in Saudi Arabia's Eastern Province. In the course of this unrest, protesters waved portraits of Khomeini while chanting slogans hostile to the Al Sauds and their American allies, demanding that the latter leave the kingdom or face the consequences. When these demonstrations were put down, many cadres of the Saudi Message Movement left the country for Iran, where the group was renamed the Organization for the Islamic Revolution in the Arabian Peninsula—a name that perfectly captured its objective. Bahrain was another favorite target of the Shirazis. In 1981 it had been the scene of an attempted coup d'état orchestrated on the part of the Islamic Liberation Front of Bahrain, an Iranian-backed movement led by Muhammad al-Shirazi's nephew, Hadi al-Modarresi. Among the countries where the Shirazis had established a solid foothold, only Kuwait was not subject to a campaign of destabilization. There the Shirazis had excellent contacts with the proregime merchant notability, a group that was naturally little inclined to embrace revolutionary ideals. And, in general, they considered the Shi'a situation to be rather good there.

The decision by the al-Da'wa networks to embrace the project of exporting the revolution was above all triggered by the assassination of Muhammad Baqir al-Sadr in 1980 and the massive exodus of their cadres to Iran that followed. Like the Shirazis, their action took various forms depending on the local context. Better established than the Shirazis thanks to their participation in the networks of the Najaf *marja'iyya*, they often favored an approach to exporting the revolution that focused on spreading ideas rather than direct revolutionary action, particularly in the Gulf countries. In Bahrain they thus clearly dissociated themselves from the attempted coup d'état of 1981, favoring a pressure-group strategy instead. Outside of Iraq, where they pursued a revolutionary strategy as far as their circumstances permitted, al-Da'wa networks were only occasionally involved in political violence. In the 1980s they orchestrated a series of armed attacks against various targets in Kuwait. In addition to the French and American Embassies, these included the emir himself, who narrowly escaped an attack in 1986. These attacks aimed, not to overthrow the regime, but rather to dissuade the emirate from continuing to finance the Iraqi war effort against Iran. It seems that few Kuwaitis were involved in these attacks, which were carried out by Iraqis and Lebanese. In their aftermath, in any case, none of al-Da'wa's leading figures were troubled by the police.

With the war with Iraq having taken a more favorable turn for Iran following its expulsion of Iraqi troops from its territory, in 1982 the Islamic Republic sought to get a better grip over the activities of the various movements involved in one way or another in exporting the revolution. It imposed the creation of an Iraqi opposition front, the Supreme Assembly for the Islamic Revolution in Iraq, in which each movement was represented in proportion to its supposed political power. It was in this period that Hezbollah first emerged in Lebanon after various preexisting militant networks, including those of al-Da'wa, requested help from Tehran in fighting Israeli troops. The latter had invaded southern Lebanon in order to create a buffer zone intended to protect Israeli territory

from attacks carried out by Palestinian organizations from Lebanese
territory. Led by a few hundred Pasdaran, the Islamic Republic's principal paramilitary organization, Hezbollah rapidly became a powerful
military and political organization proclaiming its submission to the religious and political authority of the supreme leader of the revolution
in Iran. After the Lebanese Civil War ended in 1990, Hezbollah established itself as the Shi'a community's main political representative and
one of the most active sworn enemies of Israel (see chapter 11).

The Primacy of National Dynamics

Among Sunnis and Shi'a alike, the organization of Islamist movements
into transnational networks is predicated on a vision of the pan-Islamic
world as an alternative to the nation-state order. In this respect like others,
Islamism reflects the historical conditions in which it was born, a time
marked by European imperial expansion. In the eyes of the Islamists, the
nation was from the outset a foreign reality that divided Muslims. Islamism was in this way in step with the protest ideologies that dominated the Middle East at this time, all of which were characterized by a
desire to establish endogenous state models, whether "Arab" or "Islamic."
For all that, the transnational expansion of the Egyptian Muslim Brotherhood and Iraqi Shi'i movements did not lead to the establishment of
integrated transnational political organizations with centralized command structures.

As we have seen, with the creation of the International Organization
in the 1980s, the Muslim Brotherhood attempted to formalize international coordination among the various movements that historically derived from its Egyptian core or that identified with the ideas of Hassan
al-Banna. Though the organization is at pains to operate in secrecy, it is
reputed to be more of an empty shell than an effective body of coordination. In the view of many non-Egyptian activists, the International
Organization is excessively dominated by Egyptians and is for this
reason incapable of closely assessing various national contexts or determining which position is most appropriate in a given context. Some
movements sometimes call on it to settle internal conflicts. When the

Jordanian Muslim Brotherhood was given the opportunity to join the government in 1989, it thus called on the International Organization to arbitrate disagreements among its members. In vain: the organization's response, when it finally came, was belated and ambiguous.[16]

Among the Shi'a, three rival centralizing bodies now exist: that of the Iraqi movements, that of the *marja'iyya*, and that of the Iranian state. Like the Egyptian Muslim Brotherhood, the Iraqi Shi'i movements sought to portray themselves as the model to be followed for the movements with which they were historically associated but without attempting to create an international organization. As a result, while there are ties linking the activists of various movements, these remain informal. They are reflected in regular meetings and mutual support, but there is no coordination, much less a common public agenda.

In Iraq, Ali al-Sistani is today the most widely followed *marja'* at the global level and is sometimes called on by individual activists and political movements for advice or arbitration. His opinions have never been a matter of general consensus. In 2005, for example, the main Bahraini Shi'a Islamist movement, al-Wefaq (Accord), found itself divided over the question of whether it should participate in the 2006 parliamentary elections. Ali Sistani's entourage was thus called on by the movement's leadership, with the *marja'* of Najaf apparently recommending their participation. Yet Sistani's advice failed to sway those who favored boycotting the elections, with the result that al-Wefaq split into two organizations.

A similar observation may be made regarding Iran's role. Starting in 1982 Iran attempted to tighten its control over transnational Shi'a Islamist movements. Far from unifying Shi'a Islamism under the banner of the Islamic Republic, this policy had the effect of splitting it into two major tendencies. The first, which Shi'i Islamist activists generally refer to as "Hezbollah" or the "Line of the Imam" (the Imam in question is Ruhollah Khomeini, seen as a political and religious leader), identifies with the Iranian political model and declares its submission to the religious and political authority of the supreme leader of the revolution. Organizations belonging to the Line of the Imam include Lebanese Hezbollah, the Supreme Council for the Islamic Revolution in Iraq (which in 2007 became

the Islamic Supreme Council of Iraq), and Hezbollah al-Hejaz, a radical
Saudi organization.

The second tendency brings together movements that either are
openly critical of the Islamic Republic or wish to remain independent.
Several factors explain their estrangement from Iran. Some of these movements have voiced reservations regarding Iran's foreign policy choices,
particularly in relation to Iraq. Observing that the rank-and-file soldiers
of the Iraqi Army, most of whom were Shi'a, did not defect in large numbers to take up the cause of the Islamic Revolution during the Iran-Iraq
War and that, in a general way, Iran continued to be seen as a foreign ag-
gressor, Iraqi al-Da'wa thus thought it better to distance itself from Iran
so as to portray itself as an Iraqi national party. In the late 1980s, moreover, Iranian foreign policy sharply changed direction with the rise of a
pragmatic wing personified by Ali-Akbar Hashemi-Rafsanjani (d. 2016).
Elected to the presidency in 1989, Rafsanjani sought to reintegrate Iran
into the international community and thus halted all efforts to aggressively export the revolution in preference to a more classic policy of influence. This shift disappointed some, particularly among the Shirazis,
who in the 1990s were sacrificed on the altar of improved relations with
the Gulf monarchies.

As hopes for the revolutionary utopia faded, in the 1990s the Iranian
regime also found itself confronted with a crisis of religious legitimacy,
with a number of Shi'i Islamist movements definitively refusing to submit themselves to the authority of the new supreme leader of the revolution, Ali Khamenei. Some of these movements (Iraqi al-Da'wa, for example, where a lay faction had taken the upper hand in the late 1980s)
ultimately rejected what had been a central tenet of Shi'a Islamist
ideology—namely, that all forms of political authority should be subordinate to the supreme religious authority embodied by the *marja'iyya*.

As for the pro-Iranian movements, their declarations of allegiance
to the Supreme Leader of the Islamic Republic did not lead to centralized oversight by Tehran or even a unified political project. Lebanese
Hezbollah is a perfect illustration of this. In the 1990s the movement
abandoned its project of exporting the Islamic Revolution—that is, of
establishing an Islamic Republic in Lebanon—on the grounds that the

country's multidenominational sociology made it both impossible and undesirable to transplant the Iranian experience there. At the same time, the role actually played by Ali Khamenei in the party's internal life was diminishingly small: he intervened only if directly asked to do so, and his opinions were far from clear cut. In 1998, hesitating over whether it should join the government, Hezbollah thus sought his advice. In response, he seems to have advised them to make a decision in keeping with the movement's interests. Other movements, it should be stressed, followed the example of Lebanese Hezbollah. In Iraq, the Supreme Council for the Islamic Revolution in Iraq thus changed its name in 2007 to the Islamic Supreme Council of Iraq in order to indicate that it had abandoned its plan of establishing an Islamic Republic in that country, once again on the grounds that such a project was unworkable there.

As we have seen, when Sunni or Shi'a movements appeal to the transnational level, it is above all to request arbitration or advice regarding their participation in national political institutions. In both cases, transnational bodies have either shown themselves incapable of taking decisions or have preferred to let the movements decide for themselves. What's more, the idea has gradually taken root among Shi'i Islamists that, in what concerns issues that are not matters of general ideology but rather contextual political choices, decisions are best taken at the national level: the most detailed understanding of national political contexts is to be found among leaders at the national level, and it is they who know best how to respond to them. At the level of their general ideology, the question of whether they should participate in a classical electoral system was long ago settled by Shi'i movements as well as those originating in the Muslim Brotherhood: wherever possible, they are clearly encouraged to do so.

In reality, while they have made a place for themselves in transnational activist networks, these various organizations have mainly defined their political agenda in keeping with what political scientists who are specialists of social movements call the "structure of political opportunities"— that is, the possibilities for political action within a given context. This context, however, is everywhere defined by national political institutions. When these institutions make it possible for them to exist as more or less official political organizations, as in Jordan and Kuwait, the movements never fail to seize the opportunity. Elsewhere—the United Arab Emirates, for example—they opt for social action by way of formal or informal associative frameworks and/or "open clandestinity."[17] Granted semilegal status by Nasser's successors starting in the 1970s, the Egyptian Muslim Brotherhood is an example of the latter approach.

To conclude, it should be noted that, on the ideological level, while the pan-Islamic ideal continues to be seen as a desirable goal, the project of establishing a unified Islamic state across national borders is no longer on the agenda, having been swept aside in order to focus on the national framework.[18] A number of ideologues, Sunni and Shi'a alike, have theorized the legitimate existence of ethnonational identities among Muslims as well as the legitimacy of citizenship-based belonging in the national framework.

Chapter 5

FROM PAN-ISLAMISM
TO SECTARIANISM

Beginning with the Iranian Revolution of 1979, a series of critical episodes shattered the pan-Islamic approach to relations between Sunnis and Shi'a that had since the 1920s characterized Sunni and Shi'a Islamism. In a context in which some no longer saw the struggle against Western imperialism as a priority, all Muslim countries had achieved independence, and Iran presented itself as a power determined to revise all aspects of the status quo, and defining the "true Islam" became a matter of paramount political importance. Muslims and non-Muslims alike are today preoccupied with this question. All seek to establish, each in their own way, one way or another of being Muslim as an absolute model, thereby discrediting other ways of living one's faith.

Iran in the "Shi'a Ghetto"

As we have seen, the ideology and institutional architecture of the Islamic Republic of Iran are profoundly Shi'a. The Iranian Constitution specifies that the state religion is not Islam but rather Twelver Shi'a Islam, and this despite the fact that Iran contains a number of religious minorities, including Sunnis. Similarly, the Guide of the Revolution, the embodiment of supreme religious and political authority, must be of Shi'a denomination. At the same time, however, Iran has in several respects sought to erase its Shi'a identity, presenting itself as the champion of Islamic unity. As early as 1979 the regime thus forbade openly anti-Sunni public statements and made participation in collective prayer with Sunnis obligatory during the pilgrimage to Mecca.[1] In his writings and speeches, moreover, Ruhollah Khomeini on several occasions underscored his view that the first two caliphs, Abu Bakr and Umar, had been good Muslim leaders. This allowed him to demonstrate that truly Islamic government had existed apart from the four years of Ali's reign and thereby to take a step toward the Sunnis.[2]

In foreign policy, the Islamic Republic extensively mobilized pan-Islamic themes, calling on Muslims to unite against Western imperialism and unjust regimes. In this spirit, the regime sought to revive the rapprochement activities between Sunnis and Shi'a that had, as we have seen, collapsed in Egypt in the early 1960s. To this day, "Unity Weeks" and international conferences devoted to Sunni-Shi'a dialogue are a regular occurrence in Iran. Since 1990 they are officially overseen by an association created by the Guide of the Revolution, Ali Khamenei. Significantly, the Iranians took the same name as the Egyptian association founded in 1947—the Association for Rapprochement between Islamic Legal Schools—and constantly refer to the legacy of Mahmud Shaltut, the al-Azhar rector who recognized Twelver Shi'ism as Islam's fifth school of law. The association's activities concern Sunnis, Twelver Shi'a, Zaydis, and Ibadis but exclude the Ismailis, the Druze, and the Alawites on the grounds that they do not subscribe to the *khatimiyya*, the dogma according to which Muhammad was the last prophet sent by God.[3]

A pillar of the foreign policy of the Islamic Republic, exporting the revolution was also conceived as a vector for unifying the Muslim world behind Iran. In fact, the revolutionaries' victory was at first welcomed by many Sunni Islamist militants, chief among them various branches of the Muslim Brotherhood. Faithful to their pan-Islamic credo, the latter sent emissaries to Tehran as early as 1979 to congratulate Khomeini, whose objectives seemed perfectly in sync with their own efforts to unify Muslims in order to fight the West. What's more, Khomeini was objectively the first to establish that "Islamic state" whose necessity the Muslim Brotherhood had theorized. Like most Shi'a Islamist ideologues, he was a great reader of Sunni Islamist thinkers, from Sayyid Qutb to Abul Ala Maududi.

In Sunni Islamist circles, it was the Palestinians whose enthusiasm for the Iranian Revolution proved most lasting. Support for the Palestinian cause had been a constant of the foreign policy of the Islamic Republic, which saw it as a radical refusal to extend any recognition to Israel and thus as a fight for the total eradication of the Jewish state. Although relations with Yasser Arafat's (d. 2004) Palestinian Liberation Organization rapidly deteriorated, Islamic Iran was at first a strong supporter, in 1979 giving it the premises of the Israeli Embassy in Tehran in what was one of its first major foreign policy actions.

It was in these conditions that, with the Palestinian Muslim Brotherhood continuing to pursue its policy of nonconfrontation with the Israeli occupier, Fathi Shiqaqi (d. 1995) in 1981 founded Islamic Jihad, a radical revolutionary movement seeking to create an Islamic state encompassing all Palestinian territory—that is, Israel and the occupied Palestinian territories. A fervent admirer of Khomeini, Shiqaqi was also the author of a laudatory work on the Iranian Revolution. Unequivocally titled *Khomeini: The Islamic Solution and the Alternative*, it referred to the writings of Mahmud Shaltut in order to play down the importance of the doctrine of the return of the Hidden Imam in Shi'ism, a major point of disagreement between Sunnis and Shi'a.[4]

Iran subsequently drew closer to Hamas. This movement originated in the Palestinian Muslim Brotherhood's transformation into an armed organization fighting Israel in the context of the First Intifada (1987–1993).[5] This rapprochement may largely be explained by the isolation of Hamas, which was not invited to attend the negotiations in Oslo between the PLO and the Israeli government and subsequently refused to recognize the validity of the agreements signed in 1993.[6] While most Arab countries had either already made peace with Israel or were prepared to do so in exchange for the Jewish state's return of Arab land occupied following the 1967 war, Iran persisted in its desire to present itself as the leader of the "front of refusal" of any normalization with Israel. It is in this context that Iran became an ally of Hamas. The alliance was further strengthened in 2006 when the international community refused to recognize the victory of the Islamist movement in Palestinian legislative elections, preferring to nullify the elections rather than live with a Palestinian Authority under the leadership of Hamas, which the European Union had placed on its list of terrorist organizations in 2001.

For all that, Iran's relations with the Palestinian Islamists—all Sunnis owing to an absence of Shi'a in Palestine—remain the only example of strong and relatively stable ties between the Islamic Republic and Sunni movements. Elsewhere, such relations were short-lived. There are various reasons for this. The first of them is Iran's often ultrarealist foreign policy choices, which sometimes ran deeply counter to its pan-Islamic ideology. One of the most striking examples in this regard is the rapid deterioration of relations with the Syrian Muslim Brotherhood.

Like so many others, the latter sent a delegation to meet with Khomeini in Tehran in 1979. More specifically, they hoped that he would support their struggle against the Ba'ath Party regime. Having come to power in 1963 following a coup d'état, this socialist and Arab nationalist party sought to fast track the secularization and modernization of Syria, an approach ultimately in line with the policy formerly promoted by Iran's Pahlavi monarchy. Among other things, this took the form of pressure to unveil women and the promotion of Syria's pre-Islamic past. The Ba'ath enjoyed particularly strong support among middle class and disadvantaged members of many religious minorities. For, though Syria had always had a majority-Sunni population, it contained large Christian and Alid Muslim minorities—specifically, the Druze, Alawites, and Ismailis.

The Alawites—whose very affiliation with Islam was a matter of debate, as we have seen, with the Twelver Shi'a condemning their doctrines as a form of *ghulat*, the extremist doctrines that deified Ali—rapidly succeeded in dominating the leadership of the Ba'ath Party. Particularly after Hafez al-Assad (d. 2000), an Alawite air force officer, came to power in 1970, Alawites with ties to the president's family quickly took over positions of power. More broadly, al-Assad sought to mobilize his community of origin, helping to draw the Alawites out of the marginal position they had historically occupied. Then as today, the latter represented only around 10 percent of the Syrian population.

In this context, the Muslim Brotherhood, which particularly recruited from the Sunni shopkeeping petite bourgeoisie, rapidly transformed itself into an opposition organization, a part of which turned to armed struggle alongside other Islamist organizations. One of the main themes around which they mobilized consisted precisely in denouncing a system of religious minority domination in a majority-Sunni country. As a result, Islamist protest in Syria rapidly distanced itself from the historical ecumenism of the Muslim Brotherhood, with the Syrian branch going out of its way to systematically denounce the Alawite heresy, even when this meant dusting off the polemical texts of medieval ulama who stigmatized the Alawites as "more infidel than the Jews and Christians, even more infidel than the idolaters."[7]

A reflection of the specificity of the Syrian social and political situation, the anti-Alawite discourse of the Syrian Muslim Brotherhood was also fueled by the Islamic Republic of Iran's refusal to support their cause. Like so many other Muslim Brothers, Sa'id Hawwa had already made several trips to Saudi Arabia. Filled with enthusiasm at the prospect of exporting the Islamic Revolution to Damascus, in 1979 he hastened to Tehran. In vain. Even before the revolution, the Syria of Hafez al-Assad had actively supported Iraqi and Iranian Shi'i Islamists, in particular welcoming the exiled militants of the Message Movement and inviting Khomeini to take up residence in Syria after his expulsion from Najaf in 1978. This should in no way be seen as an expression of religious solidarity. On the one hand, most Shi'i clerics held the Alawites in contempt, as we have seen. On the other, Ba'ath was a socialist and Arab nationalist party and thus at a huge ideological remove from the intellectual universe of Shi'a Islamism. Ba'athist Syria was much more interested in weakening its adversaries: Iraq was governed by a rival Ba'ath Party, and Pahlavi Iran was Israel's main ally in the Middle East.[8]

The Islamic Republic of Iran, for its part, saw several advantages in an alliance with Syria. In addition to keeping faith with a supporter of Shi'a Islamist movements from the very beginning, this alliance served the objective of occupying an influential place in the front against normalization with Israel, in which Syria was a major player. In particular, the alliance with Syria gave Iran access to Lebanese territory: by openly supporting Hezbollah in its struggle against Israel—support that included military training—the Islamic Republic could claim to play a leading role on the front lines of the war between Islam and the "Zionist entity." Finally, with the outbreak of the Iran-Iraq War in September 1980, Syria and Iran came to share another direct enemy. In exchange for Syria's support during this war, Iran supplied Syria, which possessed little in the way of oil resources, with cut-rate petroleum.

The desire to reconcile fidelity to Shi'a identity and pan-Islamism was not the least of the Iranian contradictions. Only minor doctrinal compromises were made in the effort to move closer to Sunnism. Moreover, the choice to support the Syrian Ba'athist regime rather than its Islamist opponents—an example of Iran's many realist decisions—shows that the Islamic Republic has always privileged a narrowly defined vision of the Iranian national interest over Islamic solidarity.

The Saudi Counteroffensive

The Islamic Republic's confinement to the "Shi'a ghetto"[9] was also a result of the policies of its adversaries, first and foremost Saudi Arabia. As we have seen, well before the Iranian Revolution, the kingdom had positioned itself as a pan-Islamic power in order to counter pan-Arab Nasserian propaganda. Like the Iranian revolutionaries, the Saudi kings did not stop at religious boundaries and were unhesitating in their support for non-Sunni Muslim religious movements in conflict with authoritarian Arab nationalist governments. When republican forces defeated the Zaydi imamate in North Yemen in 1962, plunging the country into civil war, King Faisal bin Abdulaziz Al Saud thus chose to give political and military support to the forces loyal to the imamate while Nasser's Egypt supported the republicans. Similarly, when the Iraqi Shi'a religious institution was subjected to a particularly intense wave of repression in the early 1970s, emptying its religious seminaries of foreign students, the same King Faisal publicly supported the Shi'i religious authorities against the Ba'athists.

The Iranian Revolution naturally undermined Saudi pan-Islamism. Henceforth the kingdom found itself confronted with another state power claiming leadership of the Muslim world. The Islamic Republic, what is more, immediately put Saudi Arabia into the category of unjust regimes to be destroyed. High on the list of grievances directed against the Al Saud was their unshakeable alliance with the American "Great Satan" and their adherence to a deviant current of Islam. Among other misdeeds, the latter was responsible for the massacre of thousands of

Shi'a, sought to limit Shi'a access to the holy places of Arabia, and had destroyed the tombs of Fatima and four Imams (Hassan al-Mujtaba, Ali Zayn al-Abidin, Muhammad al-Baqir, and Ja'far al-Sadiq) in Medina's al-Baqi' cemetery. All that without mentioning the discrimination to which the Saudi Shi'a minority was subjected. It was in this spirit, moreover, that the Islamic Republic's ecumenical policy had always in principle excluded dialogue with the Wahhabi ulama: the statutes of the Association for the Rapprochement between Islamic Legal Schools clearly list fighting Wahhabism as one of its objectives.[10]

Saudi Arabia soon felt the consequences of this new competition. In November 1979 two major events rang out like a warning shot. The Great Mosque of Mecca was for several days occupied by a Salafist-millenarian Sunni group. A few days later the Saudi government, which had had to call on the French GIGN (Groupe d'intervention de la Gendarmerie nationale) to liberate the sanctuary of Mecca, was confronted with a popular Shi'a uprising in the Eastern Province that had been planned to coincide with the celebrations of Ashura (the commemoration of Imam Hussein's martyrdom) on the initiative of the Saudi branch of the Message Movement. While it is now known that these two events were in no way connected, they were at the time both seen as resulting from the enthusiasm generated by the Iranian Revolution.

Alongside the campaign of repression, Saudi Arabia reacted by revisiting its status as leader of the Muslim world. Initially developed for the purpose of fighting pan-Arabism, it now had to serve the purpose of confining Iranian revolutionary Islam to the "Shi'a ghetto." In this framework, a pan-Islamism blind to doctrinal and sectarian differences was no longer appropriate: to the contrary, in order to discredit the Islamic Republic's pretensions, it was now necessary to define the contours of true Islam and distinguish between good and bad Muslims. To that end, the Wahhabi ulama, whose dogmatism had prevented them from playing a leading role in enacting pan-Islamic solidarity over the preceding period, were now fully empowered to act as propagandists.

They were even particularly well equipped for this. As we have seen, Wahhabism is fundamentally an Islam of rupture that had emerged in opposition to Sufism and Shi'ism. Its ulama are virtuosos of doctrinal polemic. Moreover, the great figures of Hanbalism are among the major references of Wahhabism, including some figures who are well-known for their anti-Shi'a texts. These include Taqi al-Din ibn Taymiyya, whose writings, as we have seen, were mobilized by the Syrian Muslim Brotherhood to denounce Alawite sectarian domination.

It was under the leadership of the Wahhabi ulama that, in the early 1980s, Saudi Arabia published a number of new and old anti-Shi'a works and more generally encouraged the denunciation of Shi'ism as a deviant form of Islam. In addition to the works of Ibn Taymiyya and other medieval polemicists, this effort drew on various contemporary ulama and ideologues from the traditional Wahhabi clerical and militant spheres. Among others, one might here mention the Syrian Muhammad Surur Zayn al-Abidin (d. 2016), who in the early 1980s authored an anti-Shi'a book, *The Era of the Mages Has Come*,[11] that was widely circulated by Saudi institutional networks.[12] A former member of the Syrian Muslim Brotherhood, he moved to Saudi Arabia in the 1960s and ultimately came to reject the brotherhood's ideology, in particular holding that it was not sufficiently attentive to the issue of doctrinal purification. In Saudi Arabia, he was behind one of the two great factions within the Sahwa Movement, which, it is to be recalled, originated within the Muslim Brotherhood.

There was nothing very novel about the polemical literature sponsored by Saudi Arabia. In it, the Shi'a are called *rafidha* (or *rawafidh*), a pejorative term literally referring to "those who refuse" the legitimacy of the first three caliphs. A large portion of it is devoted to refuting the doctrine of the imamate by way of more or less sophisticated arguments. In addition to likening Shi'ism to a type of idolatry of human beings, this literature often claims that Shi'ism directly derives from Judaism: the Wahhabi ulama extensively repeat an apocryphal tradition according to which the theory of the imamate was forged by a certain Abdallah ibn Saba, a Yemeni Jewish convert to Islam who is said to have encouraged the Alids to elevate Ali to the rank of divinity and thereby directly caused *fitna*, or discord.[13] The Shi'a, for their part, have always denied the existence of this figure.

In addition to the doctrine of the imamate itself, Saudi polemicists wrote extensively about Shi'a ritual practices and, in particular, the processions of Ashura, the pilgrimages to the tombs of the Imams, and the ritual insult directed at the companions of Muhammad. This ritual was first established in the Safavid period as a propaganda tool: the believers employ specific expressions to publicly inveigh against the companions. It is to be noted that, for the Wahhabis, the issue of the companions is particularly sensitive as they are eager to base religious law on scriptural sources, in keeping with Hanbali tradition. To accuse the companions of having falsified the Koran is to fundamentally challenge the ulama's status as transmitters of the Prophet's hadith and thus the validity of all Sunni exegesis.

Other practices are held to be appalling and contrary to Islam. Dissimulation (*taqiyya*), which authorizes Shi'a to hide their sectarian identity when necessary, is presented as evidence of their intrinsic treachery. One might also here mention temporary marriage (*mut'a*), a specifically Shi'a practice that allows a legal union of predetermined duration, something the Wahhabi ulama claim was condemned by the Prophet himself.[14]

In the framework of this counteroffensive against the Iranian Revolution, the clerics of the Committee of Grand Ulama, the official body responsible for setting the religious norm in Saudi Arabia, also directly criticized the Iranian state and its leaders. In a short text entitled "Advice for Combatting the Ideas of the *Rawafidh*," the charismatic president of the committee between 1993 and 1999, Abd al-Aziz ibn Baz (d. 1999), thus called on Muslims to not be fooled by the messages of the Islamic Republic, noting in particular that, owing to the practice of *taqiyya*, its leaders were, like all Shi'a, hypocrites who hid their true beliefs and intentions.[15] The Saudi ulama also transmitted more general considerations regarding Iran and its visceral hatred of Arabs as well as the discrimination to which Sunni Iranians were subjected.

A New Ideology: Salafism

As might be expected, the Iranian Revolution, far from unifying the Muslim world, ushered in a period that continues to this day and is marked by intense struggles over the definition of "true Islam." One effect of these struggles has been the global spread of Salafism, a current of contemporary Sunnism that defines itself in opposition to what are seen as deviant currents of Islam such as Shi'ism and Sufism as well as against the Islamism associated with the Muslim Brotherhood.

The word "Salafism" is polysemic and covers various historical, social, and political realities. A common denominator of the various currents, movements, and individuals who today claim to be adherents of Salafism or can be associated with this term is their adoption of a radically antirationalist theology[16] and identification with an original, pure Islam, that of the "pious ancestors," or *salaf salih* (the source from which the Arabic term *salafiyya* is derived as well as the English-language term "Salafism")—that is, Muhammad and his companions. For the Salafists, all has been said in the eternal Koran. Given the limits of human reason, one cannot claim to understand that text's full meaning without the help of the Prophet's hadith as they were transmitted by his companions.

In this very broad sense, the Hanbalis were the first Salafists par excellence.[17] The Hanbalis were the fiercest critics of all forms of philosophical speculation, which they accused of leading Muslims astray from true Islam. In comparison to other schools of law, Hanbalism takes the greatest pains to base the law on scriptural sources and in particular places great importance on the study of the hadith, an activity in which its ulama often excelled. The founder of the Hanbali school of law, Ahmad ibn Hanbal, particularly fought the Mutazilites. The latter, it is to be recalled, taught that the Koran had been created at a specific historical moment and, as a consequence, did not supply a detailed response to all practical legal problems that arose for Muslims as a result of social and political change. As we have seen, though Mutazilism no longer exists, many of its ideas made their way into Twelver Shi'ism and certain currents of Zaydism. This is one of the main sources of conflict between Salafism and Shi'ism.

While today's Salafists copiously refer to the Hanbali ulama of the Middle Ages, especially ibn Taymiyya and his disciples, the term "Salafism" was rarely used in the latter's time. It was in the early twentieth century that it was popularized and made synonymous with modernist reform by certain reformist intellectuals and ulama, including some

Muslim Brothers. Yet these intellectuals supported a rationalist approach that was a priori totally at odds with the manner in which Hanbali ulama traditionally employed references to "the school of the pious ancestors." At the same time, however, Saudi Wahhabis also laid claim to the epithet "Salafist." Indeed, owing to the positive connotation that the reformists' activities had conferred on the term, King Abdulaziz Al Saud, founder of the Kingdom of Saudi Arabia in 1932, preferred to refer to his state's official ideology as "Salafism" rather than "Wahhabism."[18]

In the context of that time, the differences between modernist reformism and Wahhabism as to the status of reason and its use were obliterated by the shared desire to return to original Islam and, above all, to promote Islam vis-à-vis European imperialism. Indeed, many reformists saw a reason for hope in the epic story of the Saudi state's construction over the course of the first three decades of the twentieth century. For contrary to most Muslim states, Saudi Arabia was never colonized and was constructed, among other things, by ridding the Hejaz of the Hashemites, who had notoriously allied themselves with the British during the First World War. In fact, some reformists—Rashid Rida in particular—actively collaborated with Saudi ulama and politicians.[19]

Today those who claim to be followers of Salafism do not refer to the modernist reformists and often criticize the liberties they took with scriptural sources. Their principal references are associated with two intellectual traditions: Hanbali-Wahhabism and La Madhhabiyya.[20] As we have seen at length, Hanbali-Wahhabism is the prevailing religious tradition in Saudi Arabia and is based on the teachings of the Hanbali ulama of the Middle Ages as well as those of Muhammad ibn Abd al-Wahhab, who was educated in the Hanbali tradition and claimed to be a follower of this school of law. Its main representatives in the contemporary period are Saudi Arabia's official ulama, among whom Abd al-Aziz ibn Baz and Muhammad ibn al-Uthaymeen (d. 2001) are the best known and have exerted the greatest influence over Salafism.

La Madhhabiyya, which can be translated as "abandoning the law schools" (*madhhab*), is an intellectual movement that originated in the ideas of Muhammad al-Shawkani (d. 1834), a Yemeni ulama who criticized the systematic imitation of the ulama associated with the canonical law schools and encouraged educated Muslims to revisit the hadith on their own in order to recover the original meaning of Islam. His ideas spread widely in colonial India, giving rise to the Ahl-i Hadith (People of Hadith) Movement, an important influence on Abul Ala Maududi's Jamaat-e-Islami, and from there traveled to Syria and Iraq, where its followers merged it with Hanbalism. Today this current influences Salafism by way of Muhammad Nasir al-Din al-Albani (d. 1999). A specialist of the hadith, this Syrian ulama taught in Saudi Arabia in the 1950s and 1960s. His writings had a decisive influence on some politico-religious movements, particularly of Sahwa's rival groups, the Saudi Muslim Brotherhood. The most famous of these movements was the Salafist Group for Preaching and Combat, which was responsible for seizing the Great Mosque of Mecca in 1979.[21]

In the 1920s, then, the term "Salafism" gradually began to spread as a way of referring, not to modernist reformism, but rather to a form of religious purism focusing on the search for original Islam. Under the influence of intellectuals and ulama working in the religious and educational institutions of Saudi Arabia, however, Salafism assumed an increasingly ideological form starting in the 1970s, a process that accelerated following the Iranian Revolution.[22] These figures were the source of a wide range of publications regarding the very definition of the term "Salafism," which they tended to present in an all-encompassing manner, similar to that in which the Islamists conceived Islam itself—that is, as a comprehensive ideological system covering every aspect of life. Nasir al-Din al-Albani was one of the principal actors in these developments. While these authors sometimes argued among themselves over the true nature of Salafism, they contributed to its emergence as a new Islamic ideology. With the backing of Saudi financial power, it soon became widespread.

As an ideology, contemporary Salafism is also a social project for monitoring the masses (already a significant aspect of Hanbalism in its early days) that seeks to translate religious law into the form of clear and simple commandments for the benefit of laymen. In doing so, it aims to ensure that religion is correctly practiced in the public sphere. It is this project that explains the success enjoyed by Salafism among the uneducated lower classes. Salafism does not ask these social categories to have mastered religious exegesis but rather explains that emulating the Prophet in all areas of life is the best way to practice original Islam in all its purity. This accounts for the particular manner in which the Salafists present themselves. Men must dress themselves in the same way that Muhammad (supposedly) did. They must wear long beards with their mustaches shaved above their lips. Whether wearing pants or djellaba, they must never allow their clothes to fall below their ankles. Often the djellaba ends at mid-calf. Depending on the country, their heads, which are often shaved, are covered with a white cap or—in the Gulf countries, for example—the white veil traditionally worn by men (the *ghutra* or *shmag*) without the string of black fabric (the *agal*) that normally holds it. Women, for their part, hide their face and body under long pieces of black fabric. It should be noted here that there is sometimes disagreement among Salafist religious authorities in this regard: Nasir al-Din al-Albani thus held that women are not obliged to fully conceal their faces, provoking the ire of many Saudi grand ulama.

The Salafists are moreover distinguished by the extreme codification of their everyday lives. Thus they punctuate their sentences with religious expressions and also accompany many everyday acts (meals, hygiene, sleep, etc.) with religious rituals and expressions. They subject themselves to many prohibitions. Everything that compromises their health, such as smoking or using drugs, is prohibited on the grounds that it harms the body God created. Listening to music is also forbidden. They of course abstain from all the Sufi-inspired popular religious practices widespread in many Sunni Muslim societies, whether it be music and dance, appeals for the blessing of holy men, or pilgrimages to the tombs of Sufi masters. This desire to distinguish themselves by strictly imitating the Prophet and fastidiously observing a large number of prohibitions can lead to sectarian self-segregation, particularly in societies where Muslims are a minority, with the Salafists endeavoring to limit contact with "impious" societies.

At the political level, adherence to Salafism continues to this day to give rise to radically opposed attitudes. These may generally be categorized as consisting of three types. The majority currently practices withdrawal from political life. In this, it is perfectly in line with the Hanbali and Wahhabi traditions, both of which are characterized by legalism: while ulama and Muslims in general are duty bound to observe and enforce Islam, it is forbidden to overthrow—or, for that matter, publicly criticize—a Muslim government that fails to strictly conform to these same principles. For the Hanbali and their Wahhabi emulators, nothing must be done that might undermine the stability of government to the degree that social and political order are the necessary conditions of the religious order. Should the sovereign stray from Islam, he must be tirelessly lavished with advice, though this must be done discreetly so as not to undermine his legitimacy.[23] These "quietist" Salafists—"academic" ('*ilmiyya*) is the preferred term in Salafist circles because they toe the line laid down by the great ulama of Salafism—advocate withdrawal from political life in order to prioritize the purification of doctrine and education. They do not organize themselves as a party, do not vote, and do not seek to challenge the existing political order, though their fringe lifestyle may nevertheless profoundly affect the social order in the places where they reside. For these Salafists, the question of the nature of the state is not relevant for it is possible to be a true Muslim under nearly every type of political regime. In cases where it is not, it is possible to emigrate to a more favorable social and political context. As can be seen, this type of Salafism is very far removed from the Islamism that originated in the Muslim Brotherhood tradition, which centers on the question of the Islamic state and is organized into activist groups. This also explains why, in addition to the fact that it corresponds to the dominant ethos of the Saudi ulama, the Saudi government saw it as a perfect Islamic counter-model to revolutionary Shi'a Islam.

The second major category of contemporary Salafism is politically structured and activist. It believes it is possible to implement the project of supervising the masses in order to promote pure Islam by taking over the government or, at the very least, influencing it via existing social and political institutions—for example, by creating parties and participating in local and parliamentary elections. Initially, this politicized current was above all to be found in some Gulf countries with elected assemblies, particularly Kuwait and Bahrain. In these two countries, the Salafists began participating in parliamentary elections in the 1990s and 2000s, respectively. In Egypt and Tunisia, the overthrow of authoritarian regimes in the context of the 2011 Arab Spring mobilizations and the new political opportunities it presented allowed Salafist parties to emerge.

In countries where they choose to participate in institutional politics, the Salafists are rivals to the currents and movements that originated in or have affinities with the Muslim Brotherhood. Depending on the political context in which they are active, the Salafists often develop a violent critique of the Muslim Brotherhood and have sometimes even been supported by the ruling government as a way to weaken the latter. In Egypt, the Salafists have shown themselves to be more ideologically radical and socially conservative than the Muslim Brotherhood, whose ideology has significantly evolved, particularly in what concerns the place of sharia in legislation and women's participation in politics. Salafists argue, for example, that sharia should be the sole source of legislation and oppose extending the suffrage to women.[24] In 2013 Mohamed Morsi, the Muslim Brotherhood president who was democratically elected following the fall of Hosni Mubarak's regime, was overthrown by a military coup d'état that brought General Abdel Fattah al-Sissi to power. Whereas the Muslim Brotherhood was subjected to massive repression, the Salafists, mainly regrouped in the al-Nour Party (the Light), positioned themselves as steadfast supporters of the new authoritarian government.

Finally, the third major Salafist political attitude consists of jihadist Salafism, particularly as it is embodied by the al-Qaida organization (the Base) and, more recently, the Islamic State of Iraq and the Levant, better known in many areas under its Arab acronym, Daesh. The emergence of this movement is due to two factors: on the one hand, the intellectual encounter between the activism of the Muslim Brotherhood and Salafism; on the other, the involvement of Arab Islamists supported by Saudi Arabia and the United States in the struggle against the Soviet occupation of Afghanistan between 1979 and 1989. Initially conducted by myriad Afghan groups, the struggle against the Soviets quickly drew the attention of a number of Arab Islamists, most of them from or associated with the Muslim Brotherhood. The central figure here was Abdallah Azzam. Associated with the Palestinian and Jordanian Muslim Brotherhood, this Palestinian had also studied religion in Syria and at al-Azhar in Egypt. Following a trip to Saudi Arabia, he became involved in the Afghan cause in the aim of ending the factional quarrels among Afghan combatants and encouraging the Muslim world to throw its full support behind the jihad against Soviet communism.

Breaking with the ulama's rhetoric, in 1984 Abdallah Azzam wrote a seminal work in which he explained that jihad in Afghanistan was an individual duty for all Muslims. To contravene it was to fail to apply true Islam. This interpretation resulted in his expulsion from the Jordanian Muslim Brotherhood, which refused to send anything other than humanitarian aid to Afghanistan.[25] Following his break with the organization and assisted by the young Saudi multimillionaire Osama bin Laden (d. 2011), Azzam became involved in creating an autonomous jihadist military organization in Afghanistan made up of Arab jihadists. After linking up with a radical Egyptian organization headed by Ayman al-Zawahiri, an Egyptian with close ties to radical Islamism, bin Laden became its leader. In Afghanistan, Zawahiri sought to re-create the Islamic Jihad organization, which had been decimated in Egypt following the assassination of Anwar al-Sadat in 1981, and while he was at it channel the better part of Osama bin Laden's money toward the Egyptian fighters. It was from this collaboration that al-Qaida was born in the late 1980s.[26]

Iran-Saudi Arabia: A New Cold War

In the aftermath of the 1991 Gulf War, during which an international coalition led by the United States liberated Kuwait from occupation by its Iraqi neighbor, relations between Iran and Saudi Arabia warmed. This is explained by several factors. On the one hand, the pragmatic turn taken by Iranian foreign policy in the late 1980s cleared the way for a less ideological approach to relations with the Gulf monarchies. On the other, the war had the effect of reshuffling the deck of regional geopolitics. Iraq lost its status as an ally of Western powers and the Gulf monarchies. Though it was officially neutral in the conflict, Iran did not fail to seize this opportunity to weaken Iraq and supported the international coalition, in particular by opening its air space to Coalition forces and offering asylum to some members of the Kuwaiti royal family. The Gulf monarchies, for their part, were weakened by the war: the need to call on an international coalition to protect them from the expansionist machinations of Saddam Hussein had exposed their dependence on the American security umbrella. And it was a particularly critical period in Saudi Arabia: the Sahwa Movement had organized the first major campaign of popular protest against the regime, criticizing the presence of American troops in the kingdom and demanding democratic reform as well as true respect for the principles of Islam.

It was in this context that a general rapprochement took place between the Gulf monarchies and Iran, in 1994 resulting in the resumption of diplomatic relations between Saudi Arabia and the Islamic Republic. These had been broken off in 1987 after Iranian pilgrims had provoked riots during their pilgrimage to Mecca, causing the death of more than four hundred people among the pilgrims and Saudi security forces.

Starting in 2003, however, a new regional-political disruption once again strained relations between Iran and its Gulf neighbors, with significant consequences for relations between the region's Sunnis and Shi'a: the toppling of Saddam Hussein's regime by a new international coalition led by the United States. To understand all its causes and consequences, this decision must be put into context.

After al-Qaida's attack against New York's World Trade Center on September 11, 2001, the administration of George W. Bush embarked on a grand project to reconfigure the Middle East along democratic lines. Having attacked the Taliban's Sunni Islamist regime in Afghanistan, it turned its attention to Iraq, which was (falsely) accused of hiding arms of mass destruction and, more broadly, of being one of the main obstacles to democracy in the region. By choosing to overthrow Saddam Hussein, the United States swept aside some of the issues that had led it to leave the dictator in place following the 1991 Gulf War. In the absence of a satisfactory scenario for Iraqi political transition, the Coalition had at the time chosen not to follow through on its military victory. It was generally acknowledged that, despite his flaws, Saddam Hussein (whose regime relied on the support of the country's Sunni Arab minority) had until then perfectly fulfilled his role as a rampart against the exportation of the Iranian Revolution to the Middle East. Should he be removed, there was a risk that Iraq, where the population was majority-Shi'a and Shi'a Islamism was well developed, would fall into the hands of a Shi'a Islamist regime allied with Tehran.

When the United States attacked Iraq in 2003, it had not really prepared a transition plan to avert this danger. The predictions of 1991 rapidly came true. Having attempted in vain to install a government composed of ideologically secular Shi'a exiled in the United States, the Americans had to accept that they had no choice but to deal with the Shi'a Islamist opposition and that, what's more, Iran would inevitably play an important role in the Iraqi transition. Under pressure from Ayatollah al-Sistani—Iraq's (and the world's) leading Shi'a religious authority—elections were rapidly held in 2005. The winners were a coalition of Shi'a Islamist movements driven, like a large share of the Shi'a population, by a powerful and irrepressible desire for vengeance against the former regime as well as the feeling that it was finally their turn to dominate Iraq. In this context, successive Iraqi governments all ultimately approved the marginalization of Iraq's Sunni Arabs, transforming the democratic project into an endless round of ethnoreligious score-settling characterized by guerilla warfare, terrorist attacks, and religious-cleansing campaigns as well as the generalized breakdown of the Iraqi state.

It is in this context that the religious question acquired new relevance at the regional level. The leaders of Iraq's Arab neighbors—all Sunni—grew deeply concerned about the growing power of the Shi'a in Iraq, which in their eyes left the door wide open to the extension of Iranian influence networks throughout the Middle East. King Abdallah of Jordan was the first to publicly express this worry. During a now-famous press conference in December 2004, just a few weeks before Iraq's first legislative elections, he warned against the creation of a "Shi'a crescent" stretching from Lebanon to the Persian Gulf. In his mind, this expression, which will go down in history, referred to a vast Shi'a alliance led by Iran aiming to challenge the political status quo in the region.

More generally, Arab leaders became alarmed at the prospect of a global alliance between the Americans and Shi'a in which the latter would become the tool by means of which the former would seek to rebuild the Middle East on new foundations. It was said that the Americans, having discovered that Saudi Arabia had helped spread the radical religious ideology that inspired the September 11 attacks, no longer saw any profit in their alliance with the kingdom and were tempted to make Iran their main ally in the region. Rumors cleverly stoked by the Bush administration spoke of projects to divide Saudi Arabia by ceding to Bahrain its Eastern Province, which is populated by Shi'a and holds the entirety of its petroleum resources. Doing so would have had the effect of creating a new, majority-Shi'a, oil-rich state in the Gulf.

To guard against the negative effects of this "Shi'a crescent" and the grand Shi'a-American alliance supposedly on the horizon, Arab leaders took steps to bolster the loyalty of their Shi'i citizens. Some Gulf countries thus gave in to long-standing demands regarding the collective status of Shi'a as a religious community and their ability to fully observe their faith. After hosting a large conference of national dialogue among the representatives of the various currents of Islam present in the kingdom, Saudi Arabia thus agreed to lift restrictions on the construction of Shi'i mosques and other religious buildings. A major reform of Shi'i religious courts, which issue rulings on family matters on the basis of Shi'a law, was also implemented. This in particular allowed the number of Shi'i courts to be increased. Kuwait, for its part, created an autonomous Shi'a institution to manage mortmain goods, and, for the first time in its history, Qatar appointed a Shi'a religious judge to oversee Shi'i family affairs.

While changes in Iraq thus had several immediately positive effects for some Shi'i communities, they also increased tensions in other countries and radicalized the Salafist movement—and particularly jihadist Salafists—in regard to the sectarian issue. An example of this is provided by the evolution of al-Qaida. Before the change of regime in Iraq, Osama bin Laden and the organization's other figures were not concerned with the Shi'a question, which was totally absent from their writings.[27] Confronted with Sunni marginalization in Iraq and the expansion of Iranian influence, an al-Qaida branch was established in Iraq under the leadership of Abu Musab al-Zarqawi (d. 2006). A former small-time criminal, this Jordanian had also spent time in the anti-Soviet jihad in Afghanistan, where he struck up a close relationship with one of the main ideologues of jihadist Salafism, the Palestinian Abu Muhammad al-Maqdisi, known among other things for his many anti-Shi'a writings. Following the fall of the Taliban regime in Afghanistan in 2001, Zarqawi found refuge in Iraqi Kurdistan and was involved in the activities of several armed Salafist groups, among other things planning several attacks in Jordan.[28]

Following the fall of Saddam Hussein's regime, resistance to the American occupation in Iraq was mainly led by Sunni groups of various ideological stripes, former supporters of Saddam Hussein, tribes, and Islamists. Abu Musab al-Zarqawi led the local branch of al-Qaida there, its leadership largely consisting of foreign fighters while Iraqis supplied its rank-and-file troops. In addition to the Americans, they targeted the Shi'a. Shi'i religious processions, mosques, religious and political figures, and neighborhoods, as well as markets frequented by the Shi'a population, were among his favorite targets—so much so that he acquired the reputation of being among those mainly responsible for anti-Shi'a violence in Iraq and for fanning the flames of sectarian division in the Middle East. Zarqawi targeted Shi'a both as allies of the Americans and as followers of a deviant religion. Drawing on ibn Taymiyya, who was among those who denounced the alliance between the Shi'a and the Mongols, he liked to observe that the Shi'a had regularly served as the accomplices to impious foreign powers. At a more mundane level, provoking a generalized civil war between Sunnis and Shi'a in Iraq was for Zarqawi a way of maintaining a chaotic situation that favored the long-term establishment of jihadist groups in the country.[29]

In many respects, the emergence of Daesh in 2014 took place in response to a similar dynamic. For, in addition to the fact that it partly absorbed the networks of al-Qaida and other jihadist Salafist groups, the organization owed its success to its ability to capitalize on Sunni feelings of marginalization, which became more pronounced in the final years of the government (2006–2014) of Prime Minister Nuri al-Maliki, a Shi'a and member of the al-Da'wa movement. The Daesh phenomenon thus cannot be reduced to its purely ideological, jihadist-Salafist dimension since only a small minority of Muslims subscribe to that doctrine, a fact that naturally limits its reach. Like al-Qaida but in much broader fashion, Daesh succeeded in creating a broad coalition of Sunnis dissatisfied with the policies that Shi'i governments had adopted toward them.

Following the change of regime in Iraq, the mobilizations of the Arab Spring deepened the polarization between Sunnis and Shi'a at the regional and local levels. Starting in Tunisia and subsequently spreading to Egypt, in 2011 these protests reached Arab countries where the issue of Sunni-Shi'a relations was in one way or another an important element of the political equation: Yemen, Bahrain, Saudi Arabia, and Syria. Calls to overthrow or reform the regime in these four countries took place in a context in which sectarian identities were already highly politicized and in which Saudi Arabia and Iran possessed influence networks and/or were suspected of playing a role in political dynamics. It was under the influence of these two factors—internal and external—that the conflicts took a sectarian turn, ultimately coming to be seen as zero-sum contests between Sunnis and Shi'a, Saudi Arabia and Iran. It must be emphasized that this process developed under the impact of objective factors, including the respective sociologies of regimes and opposition movements, as well as a result of what the sociology of mobilizations calls the conflict's "cognitive framework"—that is, the manner in which its various actors perceive it and their ability to spread that perception in public opinion, particularly via the media.

In Yemen, the protests took place in a context marked by a war that had been under way since 2004 between the army and the Houthi rebel movement. Among other things, the war had served to justify the increasingly authoritarian practices of President Ali Abdallah Saleh (d. 2017), in office since 1990. The Houthis are a Zaydi revivalist movement that gradually emerged in the 1980s, its leaders drawn from the former aristocracy of the Zaydi imamate that dominated the northern part of the country until 1962. Having lost status under the republican regimes that succeeded the imamate, this group sought to once again play a role in political life. In the 1990s the movement was politicized, winning representatives in Parliament. It then split, giving rise to the Young Believers movement under the leadership of al-Houthi, a large family of Zaydi ulama. At first, one of its main goals was to fight the growing influence of Salafism among Zaydis. After the Young Believers violently criticized the Yemeni government's alliance with the United States in 2004, a vicious circle of repression and retaliation soon degenerated into war. In

2014 the conflict underwent a radical reversal when President Saleh, who had been forced from power in 2012 following the mobilizations of the Arab Spring, allied himself with the Houthis, giving the rebel movement a second wind. Immediately thereafter, the movement conquered the capital Sanaʿa and forced the government to resign.

Starting in 2004, the Yemeni government sought to discredit the Houthis by portraying them as Iranian agents seeking to reestablish the Zaydi imamate, a portrayal soon seconded by the Saudis, who in 2009 launched their first anti-Houthi military intervention. This move was interpreted by Arab and international public opinion as mainly intended to counter the expansion of Iranian influence networks in Yemen. And Iran was indeed among the Houthis' supporters, even if it is difficult to evaluate the nature and extent of this support. Whatever the case, the conflict in Yemen rapidly came to be seen as a proxy war between Saudi Arabia and Iran, with most media outlets relegating its extremely complex local issues to the background or simply ignoring them.

A similar dynamic was at work in the civil war in Syria, which resulted from the repression of the mobilizations of 2011. In this country, where the regime is above all supported by sectarian minorities and has a particularly strong foothold in the Alawite community, the sectarian geography of protests shows that they mainly concerned regions with a Sunni Arab majority.[30] Sunni religious actors, moreover, immediately played a key role in them.[31] This is hardly surprising given the sectarian sociology of opposition to the Baʿathist regime since the 1970s, though it must be noted that, questions of sectarian identity aside, the actors of the 2011 mobilization differed from their predecessors: while Muslim Brotherhood protests above all drew on the urban petite bourgeoisie, participants in the 2011 mobilization mostly came from rural and periurban zones, areas inhabited by lower-class people left behind by the economic liberalization that got under way in the 1990s. Nor did the Muslim Brotherhood dominate the mobilizations or the armed opposition to the regime that followed. For repression had reduced the latter to a movement of out-of-touch exiles, their place contested by a constellation of religious actors: ulama, pietist movements, and local Islamists without historic or organizational ties to the Muslim Brotherhood. To this local context must be added the regional configuration. As we have seen, since the 1980s Syria had been one of the Islamic Republic of Iran's most reliable allies. In Lebanon, its support alongside Iran decisively contributed to the rise of the Shi'a Hezbollah movement. Moreover, Syria had vigorously confronted Saudi Arabia in the aftermath of the assassination of Lebanon's prime minister, Rafiq al-Hariri, in 2005. It was thanks to support from the Saudi kingdom, where he had made his fortune, that this Sunni billionaire had emerged in the 1990s as the strongman of the Lebanese Sunni community. He had also long been on excellent terms with Syria, which in 1976 profited from the civil war (1975–1990) to establish troops in Lebanon, where it came to represent the supreme political authority. No important political decisions could be taken without its approval. Furious at Syria's decision to support one of his main political rivals, however, in 2004 Rafiq al-Hariri made an about-face, throwing his support behind France and the United States in support of UN Resolution 1559, which demanded that Syria withdraw its troops from Lebanon and that the militias—that is, Hezbollah—surrender their weapons. While Syria was indeed forced to withdraw from Lebanon in 2005, al-Hariri paid for it with his life, assassinated a few weeks later in an attack that few could doubt had been ordered by Syria and carried out by Hezbollah. From this moment on, Saudi Arabia, on the one side, and Syria and Iran, on the other, were led to support political camps in open conflict in a political space polarized between pro- and anti-Syrians.

In this context, Saudi Arabia and most of the Gulf monarchies immediately saw the 2011 mobilizations as an opportunity to weaken both Syria and Iran. They thus supported the Syrian opposition, particularly relying on long-established networks with Sunni religious actors. Their main objective was not ideological. They sought neither to encourage a democratic transition nor to establish a Sunni Islamic regime but rather to weaken Iran by depriving it of an important ally and, while they were at it, make the future leaders of Damascus beholden to them. As in Yemen, the involvement of the Gulf monarchies and particularly Saudi Arabia in the Syrian conflict encouraged it to be read in sectarian terms: what was at stake was the preservation of a Shi'a regime allied with Iran against a Sunni opposition supported by the Gulf monarchies. As in the Yemeni conflict, Arab public opinion regarding the Syrian conflict is deeply po-larized along sectarian lines. In Yemen's civil war, Sunnis tend to support the government while Shiʻa tend to back the Houthi rebels. In Syria, Sun-nis often hope for the opposition's victory while Shiʻa want the regime to be preserved.

Finally, it must be underscored that the stance taken by the Gulf mon-archies in regard to the Yemeni and Syrian conflicts is also explained by the turn taken by the Arab Spring in Bahrain and Saudi Arabia. For the mobilizations also rapidly took a sectarian turn in these countries. Start-ing in February 2011 the main opposition currents in Bahrain came to-gether in mass demonstrations imitating the modus operandi of the Egyptian mobilizations. As we have seen, the Bahraini regime is in the hands of a Sunni dynasty, but Shiʻa form the majority of the population. In this context, opposition to the regime has since the 1980s been domi-nated by Shiʻa Islamist currents. This fact quickly lent a Shiʻa hue to a mobilization that initially sought to use slogans concerning the democ-ratization of institutions and Sunni-Shiʻa national unity to insulate itself from the sectarian question. After negotiations had begun between the main opposition movement, al-Wifaq, and the regime's reformist wing, the conservatives of the ruling dynasty once again took control, calling for help from their Saudi neighbor and protector. In response, the latter sent Bahrain a contingent of the Peninsula Shield, a joint armed force of the Gulf Cooperation Council, a regional cooperation organization that since 1981 has brought together the six monarchies of the Persian Gulf (Saudi Arabia, Kuwait, Bahrain, Qatar, United Arab Emirates, and Oman).

The fact that the mobilizations quickly spread to some Shiʻi areas around the Eastern Province town of Qatif, where sporadic rioting broke out in 2011 and 2012, only increased Saudi alarm vis-à-vis the events in Bahrain. Though it never reached the scale of the mobilization in Bah-rain, the disorder strengthened the Saudis in their belief that the momen-tum of Shiʻa protest had to be broken. In their view, not only would success on the part of the Bahraini opposition have galvanized their own Shiʻa population, but it would also have represented a new victory for Iran—an absolutely unacceptable prospect. To counter the wave of pro-tests, the Bahraini and Saudi regimes thus sought to place restrictions on public opinion. They discredited the opposition and protesters by denouncing them as agents of Iran and presenting the mobilizations as a product of foreign manipulation. They also sought to sow concern among the Sunnis as to the protesters' true motivations, describing them as driven by a project of sectarian domination that would, after the fashion of Iraq, reduce the Sunnis to the status of a marginalized community.

Of course, these regimes also resorted to direct repression, hunting down protesters, hundreds of whom were arrested, imprisoned, and sentenced, sometimes to death. In 2016 the execution of the Saudi Shi'a ulama Nimr al-Nimr, a figurehead of the mobilizations in Saudi Arabia, provoked a wave of protest among the region's Shi'i populations, especially in Iran, where the Saudi Arabian Embassy was ransacked, leading to the two countries severing diplomatic relations.

PART TWO

MANAGING SECTARIAN DIFFERENCE

Chapter 6

IRAQ

ON THE FRONTIER OF SUNNISM
AND SHIʻISM

Though it had been the heart of the Muslim Empire under the Abbasids, the region corresponding to present-day Iraq assumed a peripheral status once it fell under Ottoman sovereignty in the sixteenth century. As we have seen, this frontier zone was fiercely fought over by the Ottoman and Safavid Empires, with each side claiming to embody and defend Sunni and Shiʻa Islam, respectively. As a consequence, contemporary Iraq finds itself on an old fault line that simultaneously divides Sunnis and Shiʻa and brings them into contact. This line does not just juxtapose Sunnis and Shiʻa as religious groups but also Sunnism and Shiʻism as identities and state ideologies. It is a divide that the Iraqi state has to this day never been able to properly manage.

A Border Zone

Iraq was officially established in 1921 under British rule from the union of three Ottoman provinces: Mosul, Baghdad, and Basra. At the time they contained around three million inhabitants. A little more than half were Shiʻa,[1] a very large majority of them Arab. The Kurds, who represented around a quarter of the population, were mainly Sunni but included a Shiʻa minority, the Feylis. While Iraq was the historic cradle of the partisans of Ali, Shiʻism was long a largely urban phenomenon there that concerned only a minority of the population. What is more, a large portion of this urban Shiʻa population was of Iranian origin, in part because the towns of the South had become a refuge for many Iranian Shiʻi ulama following the fall of the Safavids in 1722 (see chapter 2). There, the latter came to fully dominate religious education, their hegemony continuing to this day. Thus even though they had spent the better part of their lives in Iraq, the last two great *marja'* of Najaf, Abul Qasim Khu'i (d. 1992) and Ali Sistani, were Iranian citizens.

Outside of the towns, in the countryside and desert zones, most inhabitants of the Ottoman provinces that were to become Iraq had long practiced Sunnism. It was only starting in the nineteenth century that the tribal Arab populations of the South overwhelmingly embraced Shi'ism. Several factors explain this. One of these was Wahhabi pressure, which led many tribes of the Arabian Peninsula to flee to Iraq to escape forced conversion to "pure Islam." These populations offered a fertile breeding ground for proselytization by Shi'i ulama, who for their part wished to create a tribal army to defend them against Wahhabi incursions and ensure their autonomy vis-à-vis the Ottoman government, which they wanted to keep at arm's length. Thanks to the construction of canals to bring the waters of the Euphrates into town, moreover, Najaf and Karbala experienced accelerated economic development and became important commercial crossroads that attracted the surrounding populations, a fact that also exposed them to the influence of Shi'i preachers.

Finally, the conversion of Arab tribes to Shi'ism was also an involuntary consequence of the Ottoman policy of sedentarization. This was intended to increase the volume of cultivated land and thus taxable activities. Via a policy of land distribution, it transformed many tribal chiefs into great landowners and thousands of nomads into landless peasants, the former being tasked, among other things, with putting the latter to work and collecting taxes. This profound disruption to the tribal order created new divisions between the reforms' winners and losers. Often the former remained Sunni while, for the latter, adopting Shi'ism was a way of protesting against those dominating them. In this context, being Shi'a was clearly a matter of protest and resistance.[2]

With the exception of Baghdad, a religiously mixed city, the Sunnis above all lived in the country's North. As was also the case among the Shi'a, they were strongly divided between town-dwellers and country/tribal people. Another formative division was that between Arabs and

Kurds, who each represented around half of the Sunni population. In the Ottoman period, the Kurds of the mountainous regions had enjoyed broad autonomy under the rule of tribal emirates. There, the Sufi brotherhoods, which were on the decline among Sunni Arabs, were very powerful and remain so to this day. In contrast to the Shi'a, whose relations with the Ottoman government oscillated between open hostility and peaceful coexistence and who, thanks to an autonomous economic foundation based on Shi'i religious activities, lived at a remove from the Ottoman central government, the Sunni elites, Arab and Kurd alike, were well integrated into the machinery of the Ottoman administration.

The Unequal Integration of Shi'a

The construction of the Iraqi state largely took place by excluding the Shi'a. This can largely be explained by the attitude of Shi'i ulama, who spearheaded the largest uprising against British occupation. In 1920 they raised a great tribal army headed by the leading *marja'* of the time, Muhammad Taqi Shirazi (d. 1920). In the pan-Islamic spirit so widespread at the time, Shirazi sought to pass himself off as a leader of the resistance to European imperialism, calling on Muslims of all denominations to present a common front. Defeated, the ulama continued to oppose British policy, boycotting the elections to the Constituent Assembly in 1922 and to Parliament in 1923. Mahdi al-Khalissi (d. 1925), one of the great ulama of Najaf, forbade participation. Once again in pan-Islamic spirit, he also argued that the Ottoman government, even if unjust, was preferable to this phantom government at the beck and call of the non-Muslim British.[3] After some vain attempts to co-opt him, he was deported shortly thereafter with several other great Shi'i ulama and died in exile in Iran.

The Shi'a resistance therefore explains why the British decided to turn toward the former Ottoman elites, who were mainly drawn from the Sunni Arab population, to form the backbone of the Iraqi state. During the First World War many local Ottoman Army officers defected to join the army of the sharif of Mecca. As the head of a dynasty of guardians of the holy places descended from the Prophet, the latter allied with the British against the Ottomans and raised a tribal army on the Arabian

Peninsula. In exchange, the sharif hoped to be awarded leadership of a large Arab state after the war and further be acknowledged as the new caliph. Having broken their promises in this regard, in compensation the British offered the throne of the monarchy of Iraq to one of the sharif's sons, Faysal. The latter naturally filled the key positions of the new state with his own men, which thus came under the control of a coalition consisting of the old Sunni Ottoman notables and officers from the sharifian army, themselves also Sunnis. The confessional homogeneity of the state elite was only disrupted by a few Jews, who had been recruited for their high level of technocratic skill and familiarity with European languages.[4] With the British, the new state's ruling elites shared a profound suspicion toward the Shi'a, who were looked on as "aliens, Persians, who owed neither loyalty nor commitment to Iraq."[5] Above all, they portrayed the ulama as theocratic despots who, if they were allowed to have their way, would keep Iraq in a state of backwardness. This suspicion was also fueled by the presence of thousands of Iranians who, by virtue of agreements passed at the time of the Ottoman Empire, possessed a number of privileges: they were not subject to Ottoman taxes or military conscription and also benefited from an extraterritorial status—that is, they fell under the legal authority of Iranian consulates and were consequently exempt from Ottoman law.[6] In these conditions, many Shi'a residing in the Ottoman provinces that were to become Iraq had for the sake of convenience opted for Iranian citizenship. Not surprisingly, then, doing away with the Iranians' special status became an obsession for the rulers of Iraq.

Moreover, Faysal and his entourage had developed a distinctive conception of the new state. Fueled by the Arab nationalist ideology that had been spreading for several years among the Arab populations of the Levant, they wanted Iraq to be an "Arab state"—a notion hardly compatible with the ethnocultural reality of the population. They also embraced a typically Arab and Sunni vision of the history of Islam and the Arab world, seeing themselves as its heirs.[7] On this basis, Iraq's new rulers established a profoundly inegalitarian form of citizenship intended to identify "authentic" Iraqis. It was based on a dichotomy between citizenship and nationality. The first code of nationality thus created two categories of Iraqi citizen. Category A included Iraqi citizens of Ottoman nationality (*taba'iyya*), those who had been Ottoman citizens or whose parents or grandparents had been. Category B grouped together Iraqi citizens of Iranian nationality. Only the former category enjoyed the full array of social and political rights associated with citizenship. Because most of them had either Iranian citizenship or no citizenship at all, the Shi'a were overwhelmingly included in category B, a fact that prevented them, among other things, from presenting themselves as candidates for jobs in the state administration.[8]

In these circumstances, it is little surprise that large numbers of Shi'a, particularly those drawn from the new educated middle classes, should have supported the opposition parties—the Iraqi Communist Party and Ba'ath, in particular—that ultimately overthrew the monarchy. As we shall see, Shi'a as well as Kurds were overrepresented in the Arab world's communist organizations, to which they were attracted by an ideology that spoke of establishing justice for all citizens without consideration of ethnic or sectarian hierarchies. Their support for Ba'ath moreover showed that, contrary to the prejudices held by the monarchy's elites, the Shi'a could subscribe to Arab nationalism. In fact, though members of the Shi'a clerical elite were often of Iranian origin, the great majority of the Iraqi Shi'a population came from Arab tribes.

In these conditions, the fall of the monarchy and the rise to power of republican regimes starting in the late 1950s should have allowed the unbalanced sectarian sociology of ruling elites to be corrected. But it was not to be. In 1963 the Ba'athist coup d'état against the regime of General Abd al-Karim Qasim ended in a ruthless hunt for the communists who, as mentioned previously, supported it, provoking the ire of Shi'i clergy. Although Ba'ath included many Shi'a, some of the Sunni putschist militants hunting communists in the streets of Baghdad galvanized themselves by chanting anti-Shi'a slogans, playing on the consonance between the Arab terms *shi'i* (Shi'a) and *shuyu'i* (communist) to assert their rejection of communist and Shi'a domination alike.[9]

In fact, the Ba'ath rise to power coincided with the rise of the party's military faction. Because it was very difficult for Shi'a to reach the higher ranks of the army, which were dominated by the old Ottoman and

Sharifian elites, the vast majority of the party's Shi'a were civilians while its soldiers were mainly Sunnis. Professional solidarities thus overlapped with religious ones, a fact that explains why the soldiers' takeover of Ba'ath marked the beginning of a restoration of Sunni control over the party, with Shi'a gradually removed from positions of authority. One must also take into account the role of familial and regional solidarities in the party's "Sunnization." For among Sunni officers, one group rapidly gained the upper hand. They consisted of people originally from the little town of Tikrit, in the northwestern part of the country, who were linked to one another by familial and tribal ties. It was from this group that Saddam Hussein came, and, following a second Ba'athist coup d'état in 1968, he ultimately reached the highest political offices.

Far from having corrected the unequal integration of Shi'a in state and nation, the advent of republican regimes thus perpetuated the religious divide in Iraq.[10] Indeed, the Shi'a were subjected to extensive persecution under these republican regimes. This persecution reflected not just the legacy left by the inegalitarian process of national construction begun under the monarchy but also the tense relations with Iran. For under the Pahlavi monarchy, Iran pursued an aggressive foreign policy toward its neighbors, making many territorial demands on Iraqi territory and actively supporting the opposition to the regime, particularly Kurdish guerilla fighters as well as, as we have seen, a large part of the Shi'a Islamist opposition (see chapter 3). The main waves of Shi'a deportation to Iran thus reflected tense moments in the bilateral relations between Iraq and Iran. Starting in the late 1960s, thousands of Iranian citizens were expelled, soon followed by most of the Shi'a Kurds (the Feylis) and, with the onset of the Iran-Iraq War in 1980, thousands of those holding category B citizenship.

The Shi'a Reduced to Their Sectarian Identity

The failure of the republican experience fueled Shi'a Islamist protest, which, as we have seen, was at first focused mainly on the fight against communism rather than any project to overthrow military regimes by revolution. Though secularization and the spread of nationalist ideas had opened up many other identity prospects, the elimination of the Iraqi Communist Party and subsequent Sunnization of the Ba'ath Party ultimately drove the Shi'a back to their sectarian identity. What's more, the ruling elites' hostility toward the Shi'a, whether under the monarchy or the republic, was without specifically religious foundation. The main problem, in their eyes, was the real or supposed links between the Iranian state and the Shi'a. For them, it was a question of eradicating Iranian influence in Iraq rather than fighting a form of religious deviance.

This explains why, starting in the mid-1960s, Shi'a Islamism became the main form of organized protest against the regime among Shi'a. Its strength resided in its organic ties with the Shi'a religious institution. The regime could arrest and assassinate militants and outlaw al-Da'wa and the Message Movement, but it was much more difficult to act against the authority of the great clerics and the institutional power of the *marja'iyya*, which extended well beyond Iraq via a dense tangle of transnational networks linking religious seminary professors, students, and prominent merchants. This is why, despite the initial reservations of the Americans, the Shi'a Islamist movements and the *marja'iyya* of Najaf, with the Iranian Ali Sistani at its head, emerged as major actors in the political transition as soon as Saddam Hussein was ousted in 2003. Yet tensions rapidly emerged among the Shi'i religious actors, proof that a number of problems swept under the rug during the authoritarian period had not been resolved.

Significantly, one of the first internal fault lines among Shi'i religious actors once again raised the old question of authentic Iraqi identity. Emerging much weakened from the 1991 Gulf War, Saddam Hussein's regime sought to develop new forms of governance to compensate for the deterioration of the state apparatus and the collapse of oil revenue (the result of an international embargo) as well as to contain the endemic revolts in the Shia South. To that end, it among other things sought to shore up its control over society via a network of Sunni and Shi'i tribal chiefs, an effort to reformulate loyalty to the regime in terms specific to the tribal world. Promoting them as the incarnations of an authentic Arab identity, it made these chiefs the intermediaries of the central state.[11] For the Shiʿa population, the stakes were high since these measures also sought to weaken the Iranian clerical elites.

In searching for allies to help establish this new mode of governance among the Shiʿa population, Saddam Hussein turned to Muhammed Sadiq al-Sadr (d. 1999), a cousin of Muhammad Baqir al-Sadr, the founder of al-Daʿwa. Although he was never an even match for Sistani, this man— known to his supporters as "the second Sadr," in reference to his famous cousin—needed no coaxing to embrace the regime's Arab and Iraqi nationalist discourse. He actively sought to mobilize Shiʿa Arabs, particularly in tribal circles, against the Iranians of Najaf. Muhammad Sadiq al-Sadr quickly succeeded in organizing around his person a large Shiʿa social movement that soon came to be known as the "Sadrists." Alongside tribal circles, it mainly had a foothold in the lower classes—less in the holy places than in the outskirts of other large towns, particularly Baghdad. Muhammad Sadiq al-Sadr also rapidly sought to win independence from the regime, profiting from his popularity to publicly criticize it and mobilize the Shiʿa. The result came soon enough: in 1999 he was assassinated with several of his sons in a bomb attack.

In the wake of Saddam Hussein's fall in 2003, Muqtada al-Sadr, al-Sadr's only surviving son, took the helm of the movement his father had created in spectacular and controversial fashion, violently clashing with all representatives of what he called the "silent *marjaʿiyya*"—that is, *marjaʿ* like Sistani and his predecessor Khuʾi, who had accepted the Baʿathist regime's persecution in silence and not said a word following his father's assassination. After having one of Khuʾi's sons lynched outside Imam Ali's mausoleum in Najaf following his return from London, where he had for years lived in exile, al-Sadr sent his supporters to attack Sistani's house in the aim of expelling him to Iran. Immediately afterward, al-Sadr positioned himself as the spearhead of the fight against the American occupation, calling on Sunnis and Shiʿa to join forces against the invader in a ruthless guerilla war. Hunted by the Americans, he was ultimately rescued after many twists and turns by Sistani himself. In what was at once a gesture of magnanimity and show of strength, Sistani arranged for him to be reintegrated into the institutional political process by giving him a place in the United Iraqi List, the great coalition of Shiʿa Islamist movements he had assembled in anticipation of the parliamentary elections of 2005. Divided among several factions, the Sadrists came out of the elections with the largest number of seats in Parliament.

An only slightly ideological movement, Sadrism was above all uninterested in the doctrinal quarrels that characterized Shiʿa Islam in the preceding decades—quarrels over the true nature of the Islamic state, the clergy's role in government, and the transferability of the Iranian political model. Actually, the Sadrists were above all the heirs of Arab and Iraqi nationalism as it had been constructed over the decades by the Sunni Iraqi ruling elites. This is an indication that, while it failed to adequately integrate the Shiʿa, the Iraqi state had at least succeeded in creating a feeling of collective belonging among Iraq's Arab inhabitants. As a result, what is at issue today is no longer so much the (broadly accepted) idea of an Iraqi nation as it is the antagonistic manner in which Sunnis and Shiʿa respectively represent it.[12]

The Unequal Integration of Sunnis

Following the fall of Saddam Hussein, the United States relied mainly on the Shiʿa opposition in exile, with which it had established contacts beforehand. These exiles had a profound influence on its initial perception of Iraq. Most were Shiʿi Islamists who had long ago lost contact with life in Iraq and thus lacked any real social base there, particularly when compared with the Sadrist movement's capacity for mobilization. It is their influence that explains why the Americans at first opted for a system of ethnosectarian quotas in the organization of the provisional government, where the distribution of seats reflected their understanding of the country's sectarian demography: with thirteen members, most of whom were Islamist members of exile organizations, the Shiʿa held a large majority there and were well ahead of the Sunni Arabs and Kurds, who had five members each.

Rejected by the Constitutional Assembly as well as most political actors, including the Shiʿi Islamists and the *marjaʿiyya*, the quota system was ultimately not institutionalized. Yet in politically rallying around Sistani and creating the Unified Iraqi List, whose posters bore his portrait, the Shi'a showed that they saw themselves in sectarian terms: despite their factional, ideological, and sociological differences, they had to join forces to become a united political actor. If they could succeed in doing so, the simple fact of their demographic preponderance would allow them to control the state apparatus. It was unnecessary to enshrine a quota-based principle of representation within the constitution. Their gamble only partly paid off: starting in 2005 discordant voices began to make themselves heard. For while the Sadrists were absorbed by the centripetal sectarian dynamic orchestrated by the *marja'iyya*, a significant number of Shi'a preferred to support nonsectarian movements, particularly Ayad Allawi's Iraqi National Accord, which came in third in the 2005 elections behind the main Kurdish list.

Ayad Allawi was one of the Shi'a who had supported the Ba'ath Party, where he held a number of important posts before breaking with it in the 1970s and being forced into exile in Great Britain. In the 1990s he participated in planning several attempted coup d'états against Saddam Hussein in collaboration with the British and American intelligence agencies as well as dissident Iraqi officers. He represented the type of person whom the United States would have liked to lead Iraq: a liberal and secular Shi'a who might have united Sunnis and Shi'a alike by emphasizing a nonsectarian Iraqi national identity. After four years of government by a coalition of Shi'a Islamist parties—a period marked by civil war, Shi'a militia violence, and the collapse of the central state—the Shi'a alliance split in the 2010 elections. This created a window of opportunity for Ayad Allawi, whose list, which succeeded in including most of the Sunni-based parties, won the majority of votes thanks to broad support from the Sunni population.

Yet despite his victory, Ayad Allawi did not succeed in having himself named prime minister. For after months of scheming and negotiations of all types, Nuri al-Maliki, a member of al-Da'wa and the outgoing prime minister, was given a second mandate. This marked a turning point in Sunni relations with the new regime, confirming their feeling that Iraq's democracy was rigged against them and that there was no legal way for them to integrate its political institutions. In fact, while the first al-Maliki government had made several overtures to the Sunnis under pressure from the United States, which understood that peace could be restored only if the latter were integrated into the political process, his second mandate, marked by the withdrawal of American troops in 2011, was characterized by a policy of near systematic marginalization of Sunni political elites. In addition to an intensified campaign of de-Ba'athification, the prime minister refused to institutionalize the Awakening Councils— Sunni tribal militias whom the Americans had trained to fight al-Qaida— thereby throwing them into the arms of the Sunni insurrection. He also set about prosecuting some Sunni figures who held official political office, including Vice President Tariq al-Hashimi, leader of the Iraqi branch of the Muslim Brotherhood. Reelected for a third term in 2014, Nuri al-Maliki had previously alienated the other Shi'a Islamist organizations and succeeded in shattering the Sunni-Shi'a alliance established by Allawi. Yet this political fragmentation did not put an end to the dynamic of sectarian polarization. Though their slogans all exploited Iraqi nationalism, the various political organizations depended on electoral bases that were either homogenous or at least heavily skewed toward particular sectarian or ethnic (in the Kurdish case) groups. Not surprisingly, this political context completely transformed the Sunnis' relationship to the state as well as to themselves. Before the change of regime, the Sunnis saw themselves neither as a sectarian community nor as a minority.[13] For the old regime had been at pains to sweep the issue of the sectarian demographic equilibrium under the carpet. In a general way, it did not emphasize a Sunni confessional identity but rather presented itself as a government representing the true Iraqis in contrast to foreigners. In this context, the refusal of communitarianism, which the Sunnis perceived as a typically Shi'a attitude, was one of the state's dominant political values. Moreover, the Sunnis saw themselves in a space larger than Iraq— that of the Arab nation and the Muslim world—in which they constituted a dominant majority. In contrast to the Shi'a, they also lacked powerful sectarian institutions capable of constructing, mobilizing, and representing their religious identity.

In reality, it was under the impact of the brutal and sudden encounter with a state power now profoundly anchored in Shi'a sectarian reality that the Sunnis became Sunnis, as it were. Their first reflex was to reject this new reality in its entirety, in particular by overwhelmingly refusing to participate in the first elections and becoming directly or indirectly involved in guerilla warfare. It is significant that this violence was immediately directed not just at the Americans and members of the government but also at Shi'a more generally, with the latter regularly targeted by blind attacks that took aim at them as a community. At the same time, political and religious entrepreneurs sought to construct the Sunnis into a sectarian community and in so doing extensively borrowed from Shi'i forms of organization and discourse.

They created religious institutions seeking to unify and represent the Sunnis. The most active of these was the Association of Muslim Scholars, which was founded in 2003 by an al-Azhar graduate who had been forced into exile in the late 1990s for his opposition to the Ba'athist regime.[14] The association sought to explicitly position itself as the Sunni equivalent of the Shi'a *marja'iyya*—that is, as a unified religious authority that occasionally intervened in politics. It also officially positioned itself against participation in the 2005 elections and as the spokesman of those it described as the armed Sunni "resistance." The members of this association appropriated the discourse of victimization traditionally embraced by the Shi'a, explaining that Sunnis were the target of systematic sectarian discrimination on the part of the new regime. Like the Shi'a, whose rich poetic tradition and equally rich popular iconography were peopled by an entire pantheon of heroes and saints, they made heroes of the companions of the Prophet, particularly those most despised by the Shi'a, such as Umar, the second caliph.

It is with this background in mind that one must examine the emergence of the Islamic State of Iraq and the Levant (Daesh). Directly originating in al-Qaida after the death of Abu Musab al-Zarqawi in 2006, Daesh redefined the priorities of the Sunni insurrection: in addition to fighting the Americans, it was necessary to create an Islamic state. As early as 2006 this had been done, but the little Islamic emirate was dismantled by Awakening Council militias in 2010. Many members of these Sunni tribal militias had earlier participated in guerilla warfare, but the Americans had convinced them to fight alongside them to eradicate al-Qaida in exchange for full integration into the security apparatus. Public subsidies for developing their regions were also established. In 2013 Daesh reemerged in a context marked by the anti-Sunni authoritarian radicalization of Nuri al-Maliki and civil war in Syria. By summer 2014 it had succeeded in establishing its domination over a large portion of Iraq's Sunni regions as well as eastern Syria.

In contrast to al-Qaida, which was dominated by foreigners and had been unable to maintain its alliances with Iraqi guerilla organizations over the long term, Daesh established an Iraqi leadership well embodied by "caliph" Abu Bakr al-Baghdadi and recruited well outside jihadist Salafist circles among the many Sunnis unhappy with the government's policy. Its officers, particularly those who had cleverly orchestrated its impressive military successes, were for the most part drawn from the ranks of Saddam Hussein's army, men who had been dismissed from their posts as part of the de-Ba'athification campaign. Daesh is thus less a consequence of the massive spread of jihadist Salafist ideology in Iraq than a symptom of Iraq's failed political transition.

Chapter 7

BAHRAIN

THE LEGACY OF A CONQUEST

Bahrain is a small archipelago of some 700 square kilometers wedged between Saudi Arabia and Iran. Like Iraq, it is located on the old fault line
separating the Ottoman and Safavid Empires, its population is majority
Shi'a, and the regime is dominated by the Sunni minority. There, too,
Sunni-Shi'a polarization is the legacy of a process of nation-state formation that placed Shi'a in a position of inequality and kept them there. In
contrast to Iraq, Bahrain's tense relationship with its Iranian neighbor did
not immediately play a role in social stratification, which initially developed on the basis of a pronounced dichotomy between conquerors and
conquered.

Conquerors and Vanquished

In ancient texts, the term "Bahrain" referred to the Arabian shore of the
Persian Gulf extending from the present-day port of Basra in southern
Iraq to the Qatar Peninsula. The inhabitants of this region were known
as the Baharna (sing. Bahrani), a name that is today used only to refer
to the Shi'a Arabs of the contemporary state of Bahrain. This region of
ancient Bahrain was very early on invaded by Alid politico-religious
movements. In the tenth century the Qarmatian Ismailis created a powerful state there (see chapter 1), and this was followed by various Ismaili
political entities. Starting in the thirteenth century a class of Twelver Shi'a
ulama in direct contact with the Shi'i clerical centers of southern Iraq
emerged, with some of its members holding important official positions
under the Ismaili governments.[1]

After falling under the domination of Sunni tribal powers as well as the Portuguese, who, among other things, were seeking to gain control of the spice route, ancient Bahrain found itself sitting directly on the border between the Ottoman and Safavid Empires: in the mid-sixteenth century what is today the Eastern Province of Saudi Arabia fell under Ottoman control, and in 1602 the Bahrain Archipelago was integrated into the Safavid Empire. Even before Bahrain was incorporated into Iran, close ties had developed between the Safavid regime and the archipelago's Shi'i ulama, some of whom had participated in efforts to establish Shi'ism as the state religion in Iran. As a major commercial crossroads, Bahrain grew prosperous during the Safavid period. The Shi'i ulama obtained prestigious institutional positions as judges, mosque imams, and administrators of mortmain goods. Most of them came from the latifundian and merchant notability and were also involved in the pearl trade, one of the region's main sources of wealth. After several decades of political instability that had emptied it of a large share of its inhabitants, in the late eighteenth century Bahrain came under the domination of the Al Khalifa, the dynasty that still governs it today.

What happened next is a matter of intense political controversy that both reflects and helps shape the division between Sunnis and Shi'a. The Al Khalifa, who professed Sunnism, found themselves at the head of a small emirate located a few cable lengths into the Qatar Peninsula. In the final decades of the eighteenth century Iranian power had begun to decline as a result of internal wars, leaving the Persian Gulf largely autonomous. Various Arab tribes, some of which had established emirates straddling the Arabian and Iranian coasts, engaged in incessant warfare to expand their dominions. It was in this context that, at the head of a coalition of Sunni tribes, the Al Khalifa defeated the Sunni Arab tribe that autonomously governed the Bahrain Archipelago but had sworn formal allegiance to the Iranian state. The Al Khalifa then annexed the islands, placing them under their domain.

One aspect of the contemporary political debate concerns the sectarian demography of Bahrain at the time of its conquest by the Al Khalifa. Was the archipelago entirely or at least principally populated by Shi'a?

Did all the Sunnis arrive in Bahrain in the wake of the Al Khalifa conquest? Who were the original inhabitants of Bahrain?

The various responses offered to these questions define antagonistic
conceptions of citizenship and visions of national identity, which themselves delimit political positions. Many Sunnis believe that the peopling
of Bahrain by Shi'a resulted from the archipelago's integration into the
Safavid Empire and that Bahraini Shi'ism is thus a pure product of Iranian expansionism. With this in mind, the Al Khalifa legitimate their conquest in Arab nationalist terms: their assumption of power restored a
parcel of its territory to the Arab nation. The Shi'a, for their part, tell a
much different story: at the time of the quarrels of succession that followed the death of Muhammad, the Baharna were among the first to
embrace the cause of Ali. Shi'ism is thus a reality deeply rooted in the
country's history. The Baharna Shi'a, in this view, were the "original inhabitants" of Bahrain, and the Al Khalifa conquest established a form of
intrinsically illegitimate foreign rule. The period preceding the conquest
is often presented as a sort of golden age during which the Shi'a lived a
simple but happy life under the sober and just government of the ulama.

The debate over sectarian demography also concerns the respective
share of Sunnis and Shi'a in the national population of contemporary
Bahrain.[2] The only census to have taken account of membership in the
various currents of Islam took place in 1941, when Bahrain was still a
British protectorate.[3] It showed that the Shi'a constituted 53 percent of
the population.[4] In the 1990s, publications on Bahrain, some of them
produced by academics, claimed that the Shi'a represented 70 percent
of the national population, a figure widely embraced by the Shi'a themselves. However, as a result of a policy to naturalize massive numbers of
Sunni foreigners—particularly the Saudi members of certain tribes
straddling the border between Saudi Arabia and Bahrain and members
of the security services (army and police)—the Shi'a share of the population has significantly diminished since the late 1990s. The government
carried out this policy with the aim of narrowing the demographic gap
between Sunnis and Shi'a. At the time of this writing, Sunnis and Shi'a
may represent roughly equal shares of the population.

This policy of selective naturalization also aimed to defuse one of the main themes of Shi'a Islamist mobilization: that their status as the demographic majority justifies a greater share of power and wealth than what they actually possess. In general, it is widely believed among Shi'a that the Al Khalifa systematically favor their coreligionists in the distribution of resources, including posts in the administration and government, and that theirs is thus a regime governed by a demographic and political minority. These debates over history and sectarian demography suggest that, in Bahrain, tension between Sunnis and Shi'a stems less from religious dynamics than from the fact that sectarian division has been overlaid on the social divisions that originated with the Al Khalifa conquest—specifically, the division between conquerors and vanquished and the directly related division between foreigners and natives.

As might be expected, the conquest profoundly disrupted established social relations. The conquerors, a category consisting of the Al Khalifa and their various Sunni tribal allies, rapidly claimed for themselves the better part of the archipelago's resources, including its pearl and palm grove operations. They established a system of serfdom based on the debt owed by Baharna Shi'a peasants to large landowners, most of whom were members of the Al Khalifa family. For their part, the regime's Sunni tribal allies tended to become involved in pearl diving and were granted broad autonomy in the management of their affairs. Only some Shi'i families who had collaborated with the Al Khalfa during the conquest were allowed to keep their land. In the pearl economy, the Baharna Shi'a above all worked as merchants, with the most prosperous of them investing in maritime trade.[5]

Over the course of history, various social categories were incorporated into this structuring division between Sunni conquerors and vanquished Shi'a. Many Sunni and Shi'i merchants thus established themselves on the archipelago and in the 1930s were joined by oil industry workers. Most came from the Iranian shore of the Persian Gulf. In the context of this constant circulation, other categories of Sunnis and Shi'a added to the complexity of the country's sectarian demography. They included the Huwala (sing. Huli), a city-dwelling community of Sunni Iranians claiming Arab tribal descent. Today the wealthiest Bahraini business-men are drawn from this category. There are also the 'Ajam (sing. 'Ijmi), Shi'a Iranians mainly living in towns who were extensively employed in the oil industry in its early days.

The Politics of Sectarian Membership

The division between Sunnis and Shi'a long remained unpoliticized. Con-fronted with the pressure exerted on them, the Baharna Shi'a opted for strategies of avoidance rather than opposition. When the pressure was too great, particularly during the many intertribal conflicts affecting Bah-rain over the course of the nineteenth century, many Baharna chose to migrate, giving rise to a diaspora that is today established throughout the Persian Gulf region. It was only in the 1920s that the Baharna mobilized politically for the first time—not in order to rise up against the Al Khal-ifa but rather to wield influence in a factional struggle between the crown prince and the emir centering on the implementation of reforms initiated by the British to facilitate the administration of economic life on the archipelago. These reforms were intended to diminish the preroga-tives of the great landowners and pearl merchants, most of whom came from the conquerors' group, and thus relieve some of the pressure exerted by tribal lords on the Shi'a population. The struggle took a violent turn, with opponents of the reforms attacking several Shi'i villages. While the sectarian identities of the assailants and victims alike were clearly defined, religion was not immediately at issue in the conflict, although it did oc-casionally supply both sides with mobilizing themes and symbols.

Starting in this period, Barharna and Iranian Shi'a regularly joined forces to mobilize around various social and economic issues. This in-cluded oil industry labor strikes that mainly sought to improve working conditions. Although they constituted a majority of the population, the Shi'a never mobilized on their own but always alongside Sunnis, in-cluding Arab expatriate workers (particularly Egyptians and Iraqis), socioprofessional solidarities taking precedence over religious identity. In this period religion seems to have in reality served more as a tool of countermobilization than of mobilization. This is illustrated by the political events of 1954–1956.

They began with a series of violent sectarian clashes. For reasons that continue to be debated by political activists, Sunni spectators attacked some of those participating in the procession of Ashura, the annual commemoration of the martyrdom of Imam Hussein. The rioting between Sunnis and Shi'a that followed led to the creation of an intersectarian network of activists and notables that sought to restore civil peace and demand reforms, including the election of a legislative assembly. The network was rapidly formalized via the creation of a National Union Committee, whose leadership was selected with the aim of respecting strict sectarian parity. These mobilizations took place in a context marked by the ascendance of anti-establishment Arab nationalist political ideologies. They were above all supported by young Sunnis and Shi'a educated in Lebanon and Egypt who emphasized the need to fight sectarianism in order to achieve national unity. The committee was very much a product of this. Whether Sunni or Shi'a, most opposition activists today blame the events of Ashura on the royal family: they are said to have stoked sectarian division to their advantage in order to destroy national unity between Sunnis and Shi'a. In fact, in 1955 the ruling dynasty openly supported the creation of an institution meant to be an alternative to the National Union Committee: the National Convention Committee. Exclusively consisting of Shi'a, its leadership was in equal parts Baharna and 'Ajam (Arab and Iranian Shi'a) and included several ulama. What this series of events shows is that, when confronted with the emergence of an opposition organized around essentially political issues, the regime sought to position itself as the guarantor of traditional values, throwing its support behind those members of the Shi'a merchant and religious notability who did not identify with the nationalist project.

Following independence in 1971, the first parliamentary elections were held. With left-wing movements (which recruited as heavily among Sunnis as among Shi'a) seemingly poised to take control of Parliament, the Al Khalifa continued to support the traditional Shi'i notabilities. It was in this vein that they welcomed the Shi'i Islamists who had in the late

1960s begun to organize as part of the transnationalization of Iraqi Shi'a Islamism (see chapter 3). Mainly recruiting its members from rural areas and particularly among the clergy, the Bahraini chapter of al-Da'wa had as its foremost objective not to take power but rather re-Islamization and the fight it entailed against communist and Arab nationalist ideologies. The same held for the Shirazists, who entered the scene in the early 1970s. Hadi al-Modarresi, the nephew of Muhammad al-Shirazi, was well-received by the ruling family thanks to his contacts with proregime members of the Shi'a merchant nobility. Among other things, this allowed him to rapidly obtain Bahraini nationality, a clear indication that the regime was not then as obsessed with the issue of sectarian demography as it is today.

In these conditions, the Parliament of 1973 was structured around the division between a People's Bloc created by elected members of the National Liberation Front, a Marxist movement secretly organized by Sunni and Shi'i activists in 1955, and a Religious Bloc consisting of al-Da'wa activists. Despite the regime's expectations and their apparently irreconcilable ideologies, however, these two blocs joined forces to oppose some reform projects championed by the emir, including a state security law restricting civil rights. This unusual alliance had a lasting effect on the oppositional field: though sometimes characterized by extreme dynamics of sectarian polarization, it also witnessed the emergence of coalitions between Shi'i Islamists and a portion of the left on the basis of shared objectives.

Confronted with this parliamentarian revolt, in 1975 the emir decided to dissolve Parliament, marking the start of a wave of repression that above all hit the left-wing opposition but simultaneously contributed to radicalizing Shi'a Islamism. This included the Shirazists, who in 1976 announced the creation of a new organization, the name of which perfectly summarized its program: the Islamic Front for the Liberation of Bahrain (IFLB). A few years later the Iranian Revolution of 1979 once and for all pushed the Shi'i Islamist movements into the opposition's camp. Al-Da'wa and the IFLB proclaimed their support for Ayatollah Khomeini, with the IFLB becoming the principal agent of efforts to export the revolution to Bahrain, ultimately resulting in the failed coup d'état of 1981.

By the 1980s the Shi'i Islamists had become the hegemonic actors of the opposition. Their ascendancy transformed what had been a merely societal Sunni-Shi'a divide into a major political one, rapidly reshaping the political landscape. Shi'a identity was now explicitly mobilized in opposition to the regime. What's more, Shi'i Islamists propagated a sectarian vision of relations between state and society and, more generally, of issues relating to democratization: the point of the political struggle was no longer so much democratization and justice as it was the need to liberate the Shi'a majority from the domination of a Sunni-minority regime. Such a perspective, which one also encounters in Iraq, involved closely superimposing the notions of demographic and political majority. Furthermore, this way of framing the issue changed the manner in which the threat was seen within the regime: henceforth the very presence of Shi'a on the country's territory was perceived as a threat to the regime's security.

This dynamic, which had also prevailed in Iraq, developed only belatedly in Bahrain: the Shi'a were depicted as an Iranian fifth column just waiting for the right moment to seize power. Though the Al Khalifa had always looked on Iran with suspicion, they had not developed their Iraqi counterparts' irrational fear of their powerful neighbor's intentions. Moreover, the Al Khalifa had always enjoyed excellent relations with the Iranian merchant notability (Sunni and Shi'a alike) residing in Bahrain, who had regularly replenished the emirs' coffers before the oil revenue had begun flowing. Shortly after Bahrain gained independence in 1971, Shah Mohammed Reza Pahlavi had called for Bahrain's incorporation into Iran, arguing that the archipelago had formerly been an Iranian province. The United Nations held a consultation with the population to determine the position that was to be adopted: it revealed that most Bahrainis, both Sunni and Shi'a, wanted their country to have the status of an independent state, forcing the shah to officially renounce any irredentist claims. Without the advent of the Islamic Republic of Iran, things would have perhaps stayed there. While it never officially called for Bahrain's absorption into Iran, the Iranian policy of exporting the revolution was only a variation on the shah's irredentism in the eyes of the Bahraini regime. From that time on, it became difficult to trust the Shi'a, particularly in what concerned the defense of the state and regime. Following the attempted coup d'état of 1981, the security apparatus was for this reason gradually emptied of its Shi'i elements, with the regime increasingly relying on foreign Sunni mercenaries, particularly Arabs and Pakistanis, many of whom, as we have seen, were naturalized in the 1990s.

The Sunnis: A Captive Sect

Even as it continued to be solidly supported by elements of the Shi'a population—in particular, the merchant notability and the Akhbari clergy,[6] who are hostile to Shi'a Islamism—the regime sought to convert the Sunnis into a captive political base so as to counter this new threat. To that end, the Al Khalifa sought to strengthen their ties with the various Sunni religious identity entrepreneurs, whether clergy or Sunni Islamist movements. Under the leadership of students fresh from the University of Cairo and, above all, several members of the Al Khalifa dynasty, the Muslim Brotherhood was the first of these movements to gain a foothold on the archipelago. Far from being an opposition organization, it has thus always been closely linked to the government and is today said to be largely financed by the king's cabinet, which consists of the sovereign's closest advisers. Following the restoration of Parliament in 2002, the Muslim Brotherhood formed a political movement, al-Minbar (the Tribune), which won several seats. Also represented in Parliament, the Salafists first appeared on the scene in the 1980s and positioned themselves as supporters of the regime. They are quick to emphasize that one must in all cases support the existing government in order to preserve the political order without which it is impossible to implement the religion, especially when the destabilization of this order threatens to put the *rawafidh* (Shi'a) in power.

The regime also sought to neutralize those forces possessing an undefined identity, that is, those capable of altering the correspondence between religious and political identity. These mostly consist of nonsectarian political opposition movements. Mainly the heirs of communist and Arab nationalist organizations, they draw their recruits from among Sunnis and Shi'a alike. Promoting a vision of national identity in which the sectarian question would no longer be a problem, their political program is mainly centered around the need for democratization. Although their audience is very small, their identity narrative presents a problem for the regime, especially given their occasional alliances with Shi'i Islamists. Al-Wa'd (the Promise) is a case in point. Though its leading figures are Sunni, it contains both Sunni and Shi'i members. In the 2006 and 2010 elections al-Wifaq, a large party bringing together all currents of Shi'a Islamism, sought to win all the seats in Shi'a-majority districts while supporting a handful of al-Wa'd candidates in Sunni-majority districts, hoping in this way to assemble a parliamentary majority. None of the al-Wa'd candidates were elected, however. According to the opposition, this was the result of systematic fraud on the part of the government, which was willing to relinquish Shi'i districts but not Sunni ones.

The manner in which the regime handled the mobilizations of the Arab Spring casts light on another aspect of its strategy vis-à-vis the Sunni population. As we have seen, in February 2011 all the country's opposition currents mobilized for democratic reform, seizing a traffic circle in the country's capital, Manama, after the model of Cairo's Tahrir Square. As elsewhere in the Arab world, the first actors of these mobilizations consisted of largely unorganized groups of young men who made no secret of their rejection of existing political organizations. Yet the protesters were soon joined by Shi'a Islamist movements and those closely associated with the Shi'a population—al-Haqq (the Right), for example, a movement that had split away from al-Wifaq. This lent the protests a Shi'a sectarian hue. Thus while the mobilization's actors were not exclusively Shi'a—the crowds waved Bahraini flags and proclaimed a form of Bahraini patriotism that made equal place for Shi'a and Sunnis alike (or, as a popular slogan put it, "Not Sunni, not Shi'a, just Bahraini")—the vast majority of them were. Many Sunnis were alienated, what's more, by the omnipresence of Shi'a Islamist activists, clerics, and symbols—so many reminders that, in the demographic and political context that had for several decades prevailed in Bahrain, complete democratization would amount to handing control of the government over to Shi'i Islamists.

It was in this context that a counterrevolutionary movement mobilizing Sunni sectarian identity was created under the leadership of a group of Sunni ulama: the National Unity Gathering. In highly symbolic manner, its creation was announced during a counterdemonstration that took place on the grounds of the great al-Fatih (the Conqueror) mosque, an imposing building in the country's capital where only Sunnis pray and that was named in memory of the conquest of Bahrain by the Al Khalifa. The movement was led by Abdullatif al-Mahmud, an al-Azhar trained former professor of religious studies at the University of Bahrain. Addressing the crowd assembled for the counterdemonstration, he denounced the protesters as vengeful Shi'a solely motivated by a project to monopolize power for themselves and impose a political regime inspired by the Islamic Republic of Iran under which the Sunnis would be marginalized.

The creation of the National Unity Gathering was the final act in the sectarianization of mobilizations—that is, their reorganization around the Sunni-Shi'a divide. What's more, it was evidence of a reflexive process of community construction that, carried through to its conclusion, would have polarized the political scene even more deeply along sectarian lines. For, more than a counterrevolutionary movement, the Gathering was above all a project seeking to unite Sunnis in the same way that al-Wifaq had largely succeeded in uniting the Shi'a. When al-Wifaq was created in 2001, a new emir had just come to power and launched a phase of political liberalization. Al-Wifaq rapidly succeeded in federating the various tendencies of Shi'a Islamism and establishing close links with the Shi'a clerical institution. In this, it particularly benefited from its ties to the Council of Ulama, an institution responsible for coordinating the position of Shi'i clergy on a whole range of social, religious, and political issues in order to provide the community with a hegemonic (if not unique) authority. Al-Wifaq was also active beyond religious circles, bringing together notables, academics, and a variety of civil society actors for whom Shi'ism was less a political ideology than an inherited social identity. Its principal objective was thus very much to present itself as a community political actor.

In the same way, the National Unity Gathering sought to position the Sunni clergy as the community's leader and incorporate a broad array of

Sunni public figures. The first objective required that internal power re-lations among Sunni religious actors be reorganized to the benefit of al-Azhar graduates as well as Sufis—marginal players in the political and religious field who had seized on this opportunity to assert themselves on the public stage.[7] While they were also brought into the movement, the Muslim Brothers and Salafists did not occupy a dominant position within it. The movement's second objective explains why it included ac-tivists of vague ideological identity, including former Nasserists attuned to Islamist ideas, former communist revolutionaries, and labor unionists. Sunni identity constituted a minimal point of commonality among these heterogeneous actors. Two things allowed the movement to serve as a rallying point: the perception that there was an imminent threat that the Shi'a would take power and a desire to find a third way between the rul-ing dynasty and al-Wifaq. For many of its members had long ago reached the conclusion that the Al Khalifa had resigned themselves to some form of power sharing with al-Wifaq, recognizing its dominant position in the Shi'a population but in exchange seeking to remain the leading power among Sunnis and thereby prevent the possible emergence of a Sunni voice critical of the regime. The main project of those who had come to-gether in the National Unity Gathering was to subvert the balance of power within the Sunni population and, in particular, challenge the po-sition of relative dominance held by the Muslim Brotherhood and the Salafists. The movement's leader, moreover, had in the past been part of the opposition. In the 1990s he had participated alongside Shi'i Islamists and other opposition currents in a petition movement calling for the res-toration of Parliament and had been briefly arrested for his trouble.

This desire to create a critical Sunni voice explains why, once the op-position mobilizations were finally put down, the leader of the Gather-ing, Abdullatif al-Mahmud, distanced himself from the regime, insisting on the need to expand the powers of Parliament and—a more sensitive demand—inviting the prime minister, a member of the Al Khalifa dy-nasty who had been in office since 1971, to make room for a younger generation. Significantly, it was at this time that tensions began to in-crease within the movement, leading to the departure of the Muslim

Brotherhood and the Salafists. When the movement subsequently split, it was doubtless at the instigation of the regime itself. After a few months, the National Unity Gathering ultimately ceased all significant political activity, failing even to elect deputies in the 2014 elections. Its failure is yet another example of the difficulties that Sunnis face in organizing themselves as a minority community.

Chapter 8

PAKISTAN

FROM MUSLIM STATE TO ISLAMIC STATE

As we have seen, South Asian Islam has always been characterized by its syncretism (see chapter 2). In an Islam dominated by Sufi brotherhoods and in which popular worship of the Prophet's family was deeply anchored, Sunnis and Shi'a coexisted quite peacefully. Many studies have shown how this syncretism found particular expression in the rituals of Ashura, which commemorates the martyrdom of Imam Husayn. Shi'a, Sunnis, and Hindus jointly participated in these ceremonies, making them a crucial moment during which the various religious categories of the population could come together. Since the 1990s, however, Pakistan has been the theater of sectarian violence on the part of radical Sunni and Shi'i organizations, resulting in thousands of deaths. How did we get here?

From Syncretism to Sectarianism in Colonial India

The first major tensions between Sunnis and Shi'a date from the colonial period. The Muslim elites associated with the deposed Moghul government had entered a period of decline, as much the result of British mistrust of the country's former rulers as it was of the Hindus' greater ability to adapt to the social and economic changes brought about by colonization. Like their coreligionists in the Arab world, the Indian Muslims of the time responded by seeking to strengthen and reform Islam. Several types of actors participated in this revival, with a number of them drawing on the great historic figures of Muslim reformism in India, Shah Waliullah (d. 1762) and his son, Shah Abdul Aziz (d. 1824). Shah

Waliullah had spent time in Arabia, where he met and came to admire Muhammad ibn Abd al-Wahhab and his disciples. His son penned (in Arabic and Persian) one of the earliest and most unforgiving anti-Shi'a polemics of colonial India.[1] In fact, all Indian Sunni Muslim revivalist movements were at one time or another involved in anti-Shi'a polemics. It was as if colonization had provoked introspection, inciting ulama and Sufi masters to embark on a quest for authentic Islam. This, in turn, led them to reject the religious syncretism that had been central to South Asian Islam.

One of Shah Waliullah's earliest followers was Syed Ahmad Barelvi (d. 1831), a member of the Sufi Naqshbandi brotherhood, which always stood apart in India by virtue of its strong attachment to Sunni identity. Barelvi was a native of Awadh state, which had since the eighteenth century been ruled by a Shi'a dynasty, and had used violence to oppose the Shi'a ritual of publicly insulting the first three caliphs and the Prophet's companions in the state's capital, Lucknow.[2] In what we would now describe as typically "Salafist" fashion, another revivalist movement, Ahl-i Hadith, drew on the hadith to move beyond all schools of law, which it maintained had deformed original Islam. Finally, the Deobandi school movement—named after the small town of Deoband, near Delhi— sought to fight Westernization by modernizing religious instruction on the European model. Without disowning the contributions of Sufi mysticism, the Deobandi were hostile to many of the brotherhoods' practices, including their pilgrimages to the tombs of saints, and sought to fight what they saw as the disproportionate power that Sufi masters wielded over the lower classes. Like the Ahl-i Hadith, they were very anti-Shi'a. As we shall see, contemporary Pakistani anti-Shi'a organizations, particularly the most violent of them, are often associated with these two schools.

It was in this context that some Shi'i ulama, starting in the state of Awadh and then gradually expanding to India's other Shi'i population zones, sought to create their own Islamic revivalist movement. Whereas Shi'i ulama and rulers had until the late nineteenth century tended to encourage their coreligionists to travel to Iraq and Iran to receive instruction, the emergence of a Sunni religious movement based on the creation of new educational institutions encouraged greater localization of Shiʻa religious instruction, leading to the establishment of a network of dozens of new seminaries encompassing a large number of Indian Shiʻa communities. This movement went hand in hand with a reaffirmation of the ulama's role as the guides of Shiʻi communities and their representatives vis-à-vis the colonial authorities. This effort was coupled with a project to unite the Shiʻa of colonial India into a single community despite their dispersion between different ethnolinguistic communities across several regions.[3]

This emergence of separate instructional systems contributed to hardening what had in the past been relatively fluid Sunni and Shiʻa identities. The fate of one of the very small number of attempts to create an organization that would bring together all Indian Muslim currents and movements in order to present a united front vis-à-vis rising Hindu power says much about the deep gulf that had developed in this period. Created in 1894, Nadwatul Ulama (the Ulama Club) had to abandon its ecumenical aspirations after just three years, faced with criticism from Barelvi ulama (followers of Syed Ahmad Barelvi), and ultimately came to present itself as a Hanafi Sunni organization.[4] Beginning in the final two decades of the nineteenth century, an identical process of separation took place in the popular rituals of Ashura. Reacting to the introduction of new practices by some aristocratic Shiʻi families who wished to reinforce their status, the Sunni inhabitants of a growing number of towns set about protesting what they felt was a corruption of Ashura, especially after Shiʻa began to rediscover their penchant for publicly insulting the first three caliphs and the companions of Muhammad. This ultimately resulted in a series of riots, which in some cases lead Sunnis and Shiʻa to hold separate ceremonies.[5]

While Sunni and Shiʻi religious actors for the most part mobilized separately against the colonial order, many Shiʻa joined the movement that would ultimately lead to the birth of Pakistan in 1947. It was not spared sectarian tensions, with some segments of the Shiʻa clerical and lay notability seeing it as another example of Sunni domination. Yet because the movement was dominated by a new secular bourgeoisie seeking to unite Indian Muslims beyond their differences and achieve a synthesis between Islam and Western modernity, it succeeded in recruiting educated people from both populations. The movement's founder, Syed Ahmad Khan (d. 1898), was a member of the Sunni Muslim high aristocracy. In contrast to the actors of the religious mobilization, he had always supported the British, saying that he preferred their rule to that of the Hindus. Khan founded a school modeled on Cambridge University in the town of Aligarh, near Delhi. In doing so, he aimed to overcome Muslims' reservations regarding modern education and thereby supply them with the resources needed to level the playing field with the Hindus. For in contrast to the Muslims, many Hindus had entered the modern education system created by the British, where, among other things, they had learned English, facilitating their integration into the new economic and political order. In 1906 Khan's movement led to the creation of the Muslim League. Although most of its cadres consisted of Sunni Muslims, the movement also included important Shiʻi figures. Of these, the best known was Muhammad Ali Jinnah (d. 1948), who became its president in 1916 and was the first governor of Pakistan. Pakistanis look on him as the father of the nation. Born into a *khoja* family, an Ismaili merchant caste, he studied law in Great Britain and later became an attorney. Although committed to defending the interests of Indian Muslims, he was not religious, freely consuming alcohol and going so far as to marry a Parsi woman from the Iranian-origin Zoroastrian minority.[6] Shortly after returning from Great Britain, he chose to convert to Twelver Shiʻism, apparently on the grounds that the Twelver community was less strictly organized than the Ismailis.[7]

A Muslim State or an Islamic State?

At first Pakistan was not a religious project but rather a national one. In other words, it sought to preserve the interests of Muslims as a community by forming them into a nation in its own right. It was thus not a question of creating a state based on Sharia but rather of creating one that would bring together Muslims and where the rights of religious minorities would be respected. In this sense, Pakistan was created in 1947 as a Muslim national state in the same way that Israel had been created as a Jewish national state:[8] religion was meant to function there as a form of secularized national belonging. This nationalization of religion was based on a disjunction between religion as national identity and religion as belief in specific dogmas. It moreover entailed an open conception of religious identity—that is, one relatively blind to the differences between the various currents of Islam.

Very rapidly, however, religion recaptured the nation in Pakistan. An example of this can be found in the events surrounding the death of Pakistan's first governor, Muhammad Ali Jinnah, in 1948, just a few months after the official birth of Pakistan. Much like the father of Muslim reformism, Jamal al-Din al-Afghani (see chapter 2), Jinnah had for much of his life cultivated ambiguity as to his sectarian membership. He had always taken pains to avoid publicly presenting himself as a Shi'a and dodged any questions he was asked in this regard. As chief of state, he did not want to be identified with a minority Muslim denomination but rather aligned himself with a generic Muslim identity. Yet his death lent specific content to the nationalized generic Islam he had advocated throughout his life. For Shi'a and Sunnis practice different funerary rites. Which rites would be observed for the father of the nation? Explaining that he was Twelver Shi'a, his family privately opted for Shi'i rites. The public rites, for their part, were Sunni.[9] While it was possible as a matter of rhetoric to evoke a generic Islam shared by all, at the critical time of his death, this inclusive Islam was revealed to be that of the Sunni majority.

In an effort to identify national heroes who might be offered as examples for young Pakistanis, the government also promoted religious figures like Shah Waliullah—a model, as we have seen, for all Sunni reformist currents. Far from promoting an inclusive vision of Islam, however, their quest for a purified version of Islam led Waliullah and his followers to differentiate between good and bad Muslims and be unsparing in their criticism of Shi'a. Largely unfamiliar with the doctrinal subtleties of the ulama's world, most Pakistanis did not immediately perceive the problems entailed by this decision to highlight religious figures. Indeed, Pakistani schoolbooks, which were put together by historians faithful to the ecumenical spirit of Muslim nationalism, insisted on their action on behalf of the unity of all Muslims.[10]

Yet the first tensions to appear within this nationalized Islam were not sectarian in nature but rather ethnolinguistic and regional. Most of Pakistan's founding elites came from the Muslim high castes of northern India and were Urdu speakers. Owing to its proximity to Persian and Arabic, Urdu was in their view the language best suited to anchor Pakistan in the Muslim world and should for this reason be the country's only official language. What's more, it should be one of the main vectors for creating the nation. The founding fathers of Pakistan generally exhibited a pronounced taste for political centralization and were distrustful of cultural diversity and even more so of autonomist demands. For, in addition to sectarian demands, Indian Muslims had always been divided between several regional, ethnic, and linguistic groups, to say nothing of the division between high and low castes, which they shared with the Hindus, or the divisions between tribes. Alongside these preexisting forms of diversity, the partition of India in 1947 added a distinction between *mohajir*—the "migrants" who had formerly resided in territories remaining under Indian sovereignty before moving to Pakistan—and natives. Many *mohajir* had supported the Muslim League and unsurprisingly came to dominate the executive branch and upper ranks of the administration in the state's first years. They were gradually supplanted by the Punjabis, who came from one of the most prosperous and populous regions of the country and who were also very well represented within the administration, especially the army, which had become an influential actor in the Pakistani political equation.[11]

The centralizing desire of the state's founding elites soon came up against the issue of regional separatism. The case of Bengal is the most telling example in this regard. Located east of the other regions that formed Pakistan and separated from them by the northern part of India, Bengal was also more populous than the other regions, with most of its people speaking a distinct language, Bengali. It immediately expressed its desire for a federal state in which the regions would be granted extensive autonomy. Government elites refused this demand. At the same time, Bengalis faced many obstacles to integrating the state apparatus. The result was a fratricidal war that ended with the creation of the sovereign state of Bangladesh in 1971.

Focused on the threat of separatism in peripheral regions, the elites did not initially consider the potential problem posed by intra-Muslim divisions of a sectarian and doctrinal nature. It was religious actors who, starting in the 1970s, first identified this issue. The latter had never shared the national and secularized vision of religion promoted by the founding elites. The ulama mobilized in the Barelvi and Deobandi networks thought that Islam was fundamentally transnational and that the nation-state was a Western invention completely contrary to Islam. For their part, the Islamists, with Abul Ala Maududi at their head, held that Pakistan should not simply be a Muslim state but rather an Islamic one based on Sharia (see chapter 3). Maududi took a more active role than any other figure in the controversies regarding the nature of the Pakistani project, leading him to be incarcerated on several occasions starting in 1948 and even sentenced to death in 1953.[12]

A few compromises were proposed in response to the religious actors' mobilization. In addition to officially changing the nation's name to the "Islamic Republic of Pakistan," the constitution of 1956 specified that only Muslims could hold the office of president and that state laws were not to contravene "the Koran and the Sunna."[13] While the other articles left open the question of the specific content that was to be associated with Islam, this final article had already created a breach in ecumenism by explicitly referring to the Sunna—that is, the Sunni tradition. Shi'i sectarian organizations immediately insisted on the inclusion of a provision specifying that the expression "Koran and Sunna" be understood in keeping with the particular teachings of each denomination or school of law.[14]

With the adoption of a new constitution in 1973, yet another threshold was crossed. In addition to making Islam the state religion, it allowed freedom of expression only on condition that it not run counter to the interests of Islam and committed the state to promoting religious instruction. It also conferred more specific content on the category of "Muslim" by establishing a list of non-Muslim Pakistanis: the Christians, Hindus, Buddhists, Parsis, and Ahmadis. In 1974 an amendment to the constitution even explicitly declared the latter to be apostates. The Ahmadis were the disciples of a certain Mirza Ghulam Ahmad (d. 1908), who was born into a Sufi family in Punjab and presented himself both as a prophet in the tradition of Muhammad and Jesus and as an avatar of the Hindu deity Krishna. Though most ulama immediately considered the movement heretical, the Ahmadis saw themselves as Muslims. It was his participation in an initial wave of anti-Ahmadi agitation in the 1950s seeking to have the Ahmadis declared apostates that resulted in Maududi's death sentence. By the 1970s, however, the political context had changed and the government assented to this demand on the part of religious groups. Rivalries among political leaders and the secession of Bangladesh had produced a crisis situation: in this context, Pakistan's rulers now sought the support of religious parties and, under their influence, had even embarked on a policy of Islamization.

This was also led by Zulfikar Ali Bhutto (d. 1979), the country's president at the time of the new constitution's adoption and of the amendment categorizing the Ahmadis as apostates. Yet Bhutto was a typical representative of the nation's secularized intelligentsia. In 1967 he created a socialist party, the Pakistan People's Party, and, upon coming to power in 1971, he initiated a movement to expand the state's role in the economy. Born into an important family of Shi'i landowners in the southern region of Sind, as a Shi'a he had reasons to be wary of this first step toward supplying a religious definition of the "Muslim" category. For tactical reasons, however, he renamed his party's doctrine "Islamic socialism" and became involved in the policy of Islamization. In doing so, he sought to counter the religious parties on their own ground, consolidate support for his party among Sufi masters, and assert a shared basis of identity in the framework of the country's confrontation with India, which had given military assistance to Bengali separatists during the war that preceded the creation of Bangladesh.[15] In 1977 a military coup d'état orchestrated by army chief Muhammad Zia ul-Haq (d. 1988) put an end to the power of Bhutto, who was hung in 1979. General Zia ul-Haq accelerated the policy of Islamization, as much for reasons of personal conviction as for those of legitimization, like his predecessors. What's more, his mandate coincided with the war in Afghanistan. Encouraged by Saudi Arabia and the United States, Pakistan agreed to support the anti-Soviet jihadists, providing them with a rear base that allowed them to expand their influence in the country. Under Zia ul-Haq, the law was Islamized, prohibiting the adoption of any law that contravened Islam as it had been defined by commissions of ulama. The domain of education suffered the same fate, with among other things the creation of a large network of religious schools. While many of these schools were state funded, others were financed by Saudi Arabia, including all of those associated with the Salafist current of Ahl-i Hadith, or the People of Hadith (see chapter 5).[16]

The policy of Islamization gave rise to the first major conflicts with the Shi'a. Until then, the Pakistani project had promoted secularized Shi'i political leaders who had taken care to leave their sectarian identity ambiguous. In this, Bhutto had imitated Jinnah. Under ulama leadership, however, a portion of the country's Shi'a formed a pressure group in keeping with the dynamic of separation that had begun during the colonial regime. In 1907, one year after the Muslim League was founded, a coalition of Shi'i ulama and laypeople established the All-India Shi'a Conference, a name intended to present a Shi'a alternative to the Muslim League, the full name of which was the "All-India Muslim Conference." The Shi'a Conference ultimately joined Gandhi's Congress Party, which militated for a united India in which the Shi'a Conference intended to defend Shi'i community interests. Though linked with the Shi'a Conference, the Punjab Shi'a Conference nevertheless decided to support the Muslim League.[17]

Whatever their position regarding the Pakistani project, these organizations were above all devoted to defending the specificity and interests of the Shi'a community. A few years before Pakistan was created, the Shi'a Conference wrote a letter to Muhammad Ali Jinnah voicing its fears regarding the Shi'a position in any future Muslim state and requesting certain guarantees. Among other things, the letter expressed concern regarding the demands of some Sunni religious actors that Pakistan model itself after the state of the first well-guided caliphs. It also mentioned the anti-Shi'a behavior of some Sunni candidates in local elections: when running against a Shi'a opponent, these candidates did not shy away from denouncing Shi'a as non-Muslims. Among the Conference's demands was that no law should deprive Shi'a of religious freedom or give offense to their beliefs and that Shi'a representation in government be determined on a proportional basis.[18]

Once Pakistan had been created, other Shi'i community organizations picked up where the Shi'a Conference had left off. The Shi'a Political Conference, in particular, saw itself as the latter's heir. By announcing that, in its view, the best way to preserve the rights of Shi'a was for all Pakistani Muslims to be seen as belonging to a single community, it aligned itself with the position taken by the nation's dominant political elites. This provoked the ire of conservative circles, especially ulama, who wished to preserve a separate form of community existence for the Shi'a. In reaction, they created the Organization for the Defense of Shi'a rights, which was for several years led by Mufti Jafar Hussein (d. 1983). He was a rather apolitical, sixty-year-old ulama trained in Najaf who had established himself as one of the leading representatives of the Shi'a. In this capacity, he had since the 1960s sat on the Council of Islamic Ideology, an institution created under the 1962 constitution that was responsible for issuing recommendations relating to the promotion of Islam and for verifying that laws were in conformity with it. Mufti Hussein represented the Shi'a perspective in the council. In 1979 he resigned in protest against Muhammad Zia ul-Haq's decision to appoint a majority of ulama affiliated with the notoriously anti-Shi'a Deobandi school and Ahl-i Hadith.[19] In the wake of his resignation, a great Shi'a convention elected Mufti Jafar Hussein "leader of the Shi'a community." Hussein then announced the creation of a new Shi'a sectarian organization, the Movement for the Implementation of Ja'fari Law (i.e., Shi'a religious law). He was soon leading a movement to protest the policy of Islamization and, more particularly, the Islamization of the tax system. Adopted in 1979, this policy transformed the zakat—a Muslim tax distributed to the poorest segment of the population—into a legal obligation. Henceforth all Muslims had to pay this tax directly to the state through the intermediary of a Central Zakat Fund. Shi'i sectarian organizations immediately mobilized to reject this new tax law on the grounds that Shi'a religious law required them to pay the zakat directly to the poor people of their choice rather than to the state. Moreover, it seems that the Central Zakat Fund had, on Saudi insistence, extensively financed Sunni religious school networks associated with Ahl-i Hadith.[20] In 1980 Mufti Jafar Hussein led a major demonstration against the new tax law in Islamabad, placing the government under virtual siege in defiance of martial law. The government was ultimately obliged to exempt Shi'a from the *zakat* tax. This was doubtless the first time that the government agreed to exempt Shi'a from the general law. Until then, all demands for the establishment of special measures had gone unheeded.

Following Hussein's death in 1983, his movement split in two. A traditionalist tendency continued to follow the deceased leader's practice of seeking compromise with the regime. A more radical tendency directly modeled itself on Iranian revolutionary Islam. Its supporters organized themselves within the Ja'fari Movement of Pakistan under the leadership of a young ulama, Arif Hussein Al-Husseini (d. 1988). The latter had studied in Najaf in the 1960s, where, among other things, he had regularly met with Khomeini. He subsequently spent several years in Qom in Iran before returning to Pakistan a few months before the Iranian Revolution. He quickly became a major focal point of Shia political mobilization. Elected as leader of the Shi'a community in 1984, like Mufti Jafar Hussein before him, al-Husseini was recognized by Khomeini as his official representative.

Radicalizations

As its name indicates, the Movement for the Implementation of Ja'fari Law created by Mufti Jafar Hussein had a much larger project than simply opposing the Islamization of the tax system. In addition to defending Shi'i community interests, it sought to Islamize the Shi'a. The emergence of such a demand is clear illustration of the manner in which domestic Pakistani issues interacted with regional developments. In 1979 the Iranian Revolution, the resulting rivalry between Saudi Arabia and Iran for leadership of the Muslim world, and the onset of the anti-Soviet jihad in Afghanistan all profoundly affected the Pakistani domestic equilibrium.

General Zia ul-Haq's policy of Islamization must also be understood in this regional context. For it also resulted from the rapprochement between Saudi Arabia and Pakistan, both of which were worried about the Iranian revolutionary dynamic, as well as from the fact that Pakistan—now also officially an "Islamic Republic" presenting itself as a model Islamic state—was engaged in a dialectic of competition with Iran. In this context, Saudi Arabia heavily financed Pakistani Sunni religious movements, including Ahl-i Hadith and the Deobandis. With Pakistani and Saudi support, moreover, armed groups affiliated with these Sunni movements became actively involved in the Afghan jihad. Like other Shiʻi populations of the region, Pakistani Shiʻa were for their part targeted by Iran's policy of exporting the revolution. And Iran had also become involved in the Afghan jihad by way of its own armed Shiʻi groups. As a result, the war in Afghanistan became the theater for a rivalry among regional powers, each seeking to present itself as the hero of the anti-Soviet struggle on the basis of clearly differentiated Sunni and Shiʻa identities. Once Afghanistan was liberated from the Soviets, the members of these armed groups returned to Pakistan, where they continued to fight one another. In these conditions, the Shiʻa question was no longer an ultimately minor community problem for the Pakistani state but rather a major political one.

The great demonstration against the *zakat* had already given the military regime an opportunity to take stock of the manner in which the Shiʻa question had been transformed. During the demonstration, Shiʻa Islamist student union activists had chanted particularly aggressive slogans identifying Zia ul-Haq with the figure of Yazid, the caliph responsible for killing Imam Hussein. They had also held a rally outside the Iraqi Embassy to protest the assassination a few months earlier of Muhammad Baqir al-Sadr, the founder and leader of the Iraqi Shiʻa Islamist party al-Daʻwa, showing that regional issues had found their way into the debate. Moreover, Khomeini himself had pressured Pakistan to exempt the Shiʻa from paying the *zakat*, threatening Zia ul-Haq with the same fate as the shah of Iran should he refuse.[21]

While he had to capitulate, doing so left a bitter taste in Mohammed Zia ul-Haq's mouth and the conviction that Iranian—and thus Shiʻa—influence in his country had to be contained at all costs. Sunni religious movements were just as concerned about the Shiʻa mobilization. The

massive funding supplied Sunni religious schools as part of the Islamization policy helped them more broadly spread their ideas and conception
of Islam in the population. Despite the process of Sunni-Shi'a separation that had begun in the colonial period, popular Islam had largely
remained syncretic. In a country that to this day continues to be marked
by high rates of illiteracy, many Muslims did not have a clear idea of what
distinguished a Sunni from a Shi'a. In practice, Islamization policy helped
spread the clerical Islam of anti-Shi'a Sunni movements, particularly
among the lower classes. It presented Sunnism and Shi'ism as clearly
distinct—and even mutually exclusive—entities. Domestic political developments and particularly the vicissitudes of the democracy movement also played a key role in exacerbating the divide between Sunnis
and Shi'a. In 1983 the Ja'fari Movement of Pakistan thus allied with the
Pakistan People's Party, which had been created by Zulfikar Ali Bhutto
and was led by his daughter, Benazir, following his execution. Well established throughout the country, the party presented itself as the main
opposition to Zia ul-Haq's military regime. Its program called for a return
to democracy and promised to stand up for the poorest members of the
population. The Pakistan People's Party was already very popular among
Shi'a, partly due to the Bhutto family's Shi'a identity and partly to the fact
that many Shi'a were receptive to its secular discourse favoring state neu-
trality in regard to religious differences. Support by the Ja'fari Movement
of Pakistan for the party deepened the Shi'a sectarian undertones of opposition to Zia ul-Haq and the democracy movement more broadly.[22]

In 1983 a series of anti-Shi'a riots took place in Karachi. They were orchestrated by a radical Sunni organization that later took the name Sipah-e Sahaba Pakistan (Army of the Prophet's Companions). Founded
in 1985 by Haq Nawaz Jhangvi (d. 1990), this organization—part militia,
part political party—was linked to the Deobandi-aligned Jamaat-e
Ulema-e-Islam (Assembly of Islamic Clerics), which had been created
in 1945. Significantly, Jhangvi, like other Sipah-e Sahaba figures, had
begun his career as an activist in the anti-Ahmadi movement of the 1970s.
This movement was particularly well established in his home region of
Jhang, the center of the Ahmadi movement. Jhangvi was also among the
first to demand that the Shi'a suffer the same fate as the Ahmadis—that

is, be declared non-Muslims and apostates in the constitution. There thus exists a direct link between anti-Ahmadism and anti-Shi'ism. Both were initially advocated by the same actors and in keeping with the same intellectual frameworks.[23] In the region of Jhang, where Sipah-e Sahaba was born, the social structure was moreover propitious to anti-Shi'a mobilization, with the divide between Sunnis and Shi'a partly coinciding with that between a dominant class of Shi'i large landowners and a *mohajir*-origin Sunni urban middle class eager for social advancement and subject to Deobani influence.[24] Even as it continued to engage in militia violence, in the late 1980s Sipah-e-Sahaba with some success threw itself into electoral politics. When Sipah-e-Sahaba and the Ja'fari Movement of Pakistan moved to disassociate themselves from sectarian violence in the early 1990s, the result was not less violence but rather schism, with extremist factions splitting off from both movements. Among Sunnis, this led to the creation of Lashkar-e-Jhanjvi (Army of Jhangvi, so named for the founder of Sipah-e-Sahaba, who had been killed in an attack) and other armed organizations. Among Shi'a, Sipah-e-Muhammad (Army of Muhammad) emerged as an armed response to the violence of Sunni groups. Like its founder, Allama Syed Ghulam Naqvi (d. 2016), most of this organization's cadres had served in the anti-Soviet jihad in Afghanistan in the ranks of armed Shi'i groups financed by Iran.[25] Sipah-e-Muhammad proved just as violent as its Sunni counterpart, Sipah-e-Sahaba, targeting Sunnis for attack where the latter targeted Shi'a. A murderous dialectic developed between the two organizations, which employed the same methods and rhetoric.

It is interesting to note that Sipah-e-Sahaba and, later, Lashkar-e-Jhangvi imitated many of the symbols and techniques of Shi'a mobilization, very much after the fashion of the dialectic that emerged in Iraq between Sunni guerilla warfare and Shi'a Islamist movements (see chapter 6). For example, they promoted genuine worship of the Companions of Muhammad, figures reviled by the Shi'a. Just as the Imams and the "People of Muhammad's House" were objects of genuine worship among the Shi'a, particularly for Sipah-e-Muhammad, the Companions of Muhammed were a central part of Sipah-e-Sahaba's identity.[26] This dynamic of confrontation and imitation produced thousands of victims.

At first, the targets of this violence were limited to militants and high of-fice holders in the state apparatus, who were killed in targeted assassina-tions likely involving various Pakistani, Iranian, and Saudi intelligence services. From the mid-1990s, however, the violence increasingly took the form of mass attacks against ordinary civilians. To this day, Pakistan is one of the main scenes of anti-Shi'a sectarian violence.[27]

Chapter 9

PRAGMATIC SECTARIANISM?

SUNNIS AND SHIʿA IN SAUDI ARABIA AND IRAN

As we have seen, Saudi Arabia and Iran present themselves as the champions of Sunni and Shiʿa Islam, respectively. Since 1979 they have been involved in a cold war that has contributed to radicalizing sectarian affiliations and fueled violence on the part of extremist groups. In what concerns their relations with their respective Shiʿa and Sunni minorities, however, Saudi Arabia and Iran exhibit a high degree of pragmatism. Combining compromise and discriminatory practices, each has adopted a case-by-case approach for managing the minority question in which the desire to maintain internal stability prevails over the uncompromising ideology projected abroad.

Sunnism on the Margins of Iranian Territory

As the heir of a great multicultural empire, contemporary Iran is characterized by a high degree of ethnic, linguistic, and religious heterogeneity. While at least 80 percent of the population practices Shiʿism, the country also includes several sectarian minorities: Jews, Christians of various denominations, Zoroastrians, Bahaʾis, Mandaeans, and Sunni Muslims.[1] The Sunnis are by far the country's largest religious minority, comprising between 8 and 20 percent of the total population.[2]

Under the Safavids, however, Sunnism was subjected to a systematic policy of eradication. Alongside propaganda, this involved pressure of all kinds, including the use of violence to subjugate the most recalcitrant. In the Safavid period, as we have seen, the issue was less a matter of revering Ali and the Prophet's family, as they were central to many types of popular worship before the arrival of the Safavids. Rather, it was a matter of being willing to unflinchingly listen to and possibly repeat in unison the ritual imprecations directed against the first three caliphs, the companions of the Prophet, certain of his wives (Aisha and Hafsa, who are believed to have been hostile to Imam Ali), and some Umayyad and Abbasid caliphs. Invented by the Safavids, these rituals were spread by groups of zealots who were more generally responsible for the ideological surveillance of the population.[3]

The fight against Sunnism was also an aspect of the struggle against the Sufi brotherhoods, which embodied the dominant form of Islam. It covered two aspects: for the Safavids, who were themselves a Sufi brotherhood, it was necessary to supplant their competitors; for the Shi'i ulama, it was necessary to eliminate those who promoted esoteric doctrines incompatible with their rationalist orthodoxy. This is why, though the Safavid sovereigns sometimes exhibited a tolerant attitude toward the Shi'i brotherhoods, the ulama fiercely fought them.[4]

The policy of eradication did not succeed in totally eliminating Sunnism. Significantly, it persisted on the empire's fringes, in border zones where the central government functioned poorly, intermittently, and through the intermediary of what were often autonomous local potentates sometimes able to seek protection from powerful neighboring empires.[5] In these regions, Sunni affiliation coincided with minority tribal, ethnic, and linguistic affiliations vis-à-vis the dominant Turco-Persian group. Since the ninth century, Turks and Persians had occupied a position of political dominance, with the territory corresponding to present-day Iran most often finding itself under the domination of Turkish dynasties (including the Safavids). The Persians, for their part, who today mostly live on the central plateau and constitute a relative majority of the population (46 percent),[6] were linked with the government and played a key role in shaping elite culture, particularly through their language.

The peripheral character of Sunnism persists to this day. Balochistan is one of the country's principal Sunni population centers. Bordering Pakistan and Afghanistan to the south, it constituted a frontier zone between the Safavids and their successors, the Qajar, and the Mughal

Empire. Speaking a language that resembles Persian, the Baloch people today straddle Pakistan and Iran. In both countries, there are endemic Baloch irredentist movements, making the Baloch question an important security issue. Another one of Iran's Sunni zones is Kurdistan. This region is part of an ethnoregional entity straddling Iran, Iraq, Turkey, and Syria and possesses a firmly established nationalist movement that has for decades made headlines and threatens these states' territorial integrity. In both Kurdistan and Balochistan, the dominant form of Islam is that of the Sufi brotherhoods. Finally, a word should be said regarding the coastal regions of the South. Populated by an Arab minority, a large portion of whom are Sunni, the people are the heirs of the Arab tribal chiefdoms that dominated the Persian Gulf after the fall of the Safavids in the eighteenth century. There are autonomist movements here, too. Since the region holds Iran's hydrocarbon reserves, these movements—formerly manipulated by the nation's neighbor Iraq—appear all the more threatening to the Iranian state.

As we have already seen in the Iraqi and Bahraini cases, this territorial and ethnolinguistic fragmentation only further exacerbates the intrinsic difficulty facing Sunnis in representing and organizing themselves at the national level as a minority group. In Iran, it was thus long impossible to speak of the Sunnis as a community in the sense of a group possessing a shared collective consciousness with its own more or less developed institutional existence and an at least occasional capacity for collective action. This is only reinforced by the fact that ethnolinguistic affiliation typically prevails over sectarian affiliation in the expression of collective identities, particularly when the former has been politicized. Both the monarchy and the republic have witnessed the emergence of separatist movements in non-Persian-speaking regions, including those with a mainly Shi'a population. The most widely studied case is that of Iran's northern Azerbaijan region, which is inhabited by a Turkic-speaking population practicing Shi'ism. Though closely associated with the enterprise of state construction, the region's ethnolinguistic identity has since the 1990s become politicized, a trend particularly reflected in the promotion of the Turkic language.[7] Sunni populations are no exception to this rule and have principally drawn on an ethnic and regionalist repertoire to denounce the policies of the central state.

Yet the sectarian question has never been entirely absent, particularly once Shi'a affiliation became the basis for implicit or explicit discrimination in accessing some high political and administrative offices under the Islamic Republic. An example of this may be found in the debates surrounding the adoption of the first constitution in 1979, during which a Sunni Baloch deputy publicly expressed his surprise at the fact that the text officially recognized Jews, Christians, and Zoroastrians but not Sunnis.[8] Indeed, these three minorities, which already enjoyed institutional recognition under the monarchy, retained it under the republic. Counted by the census, they possessed a quota of deputies in Parliament—three for the Christians, one for the Jews, and one for the Zoroastrians out of a total of 290—and had their own family courts that handed down judgments on the basis of their respective religious laws.

This decision to recognize non-Muslim communities while refusing to recognize Sunnis only appears to be paradoxical. For it is in keeping with the best tradition of Muslim states. In basing themselves on the Koran, which calls for protecting the "people of the Book"—that is, followers of the revealed religions—most of these states granted Jews, Christians, Zoroastrians, and also (in the case of the Mughal Empire) Hindus institutional recognition and autonomy in the management of their religious affairs. This recognition was always accompanied by an inferior status. In a way that varied from one period to the next, these communities were subject to various restrictions and taxed at significantly higher rates than their Muslim counterparts.

By their nature, these measures were applied to certain non-Muslim minorities only; religions originating in Islam such as Bahaism and the minority Muslim communities thus never benefited from them. Since it appears to be post-Islamic in that it calls into question the central tenets of Muhammad's religion, Bahaism was long persecuted in Iran and is today banned there. Sunnis, for their part, are only implicitly recognized. While the constitution recognizes the four schools of Sunni law (Hanafi, Maliki, Shafi'i, and Hanbali) and Sunnis possess their own mosques, religious education establishments, and religious courts, they tend to be invisible. For in addition to the fact that the constitution chose to dissolve Sunnism in a generalized recognition of law schools, Sunnis possess no quota of deputies in Parliament and are not counted by the census.

Moreover, the Sunnis are subjected to multiple forms of discrimination and administrative strategies intended to dilute their existence as a community and limit their influence. In addition to the fact that being Sunni makes it impossible to rise to high positions in the bureaucracy and army, the administrative division of the provinces was conceived so as to prevent the Sunnis from appearing to constitute a majority at the local level. This has been used as justification for the refusal to apply a constitutional measure that would allow them to establish local legislation on the basis of one or more Sunni law schools in regions where non-Shi'a represent a majority of the population.[9] In addition, impediments are often put in the way of constructing Sunni mosques. Despite having a large Sunni population as a result of internal migration, Tehran thus does not possess a single Sunni mosque.

Accommodating Wahhabism

Because the eastern part of Saudi Arabia was long part of ancient Bahrain, a bastion of Ismailism and, later, Twelver Shi'ism, the kingdom contains a large Shi'a minority, estimated at between 8 and 20 percent of the national population. Though the position of Shi'a in Saudi Arabia in some ways resembles that of Sunnis in Iran, it also differs from it in many ways. One such difference is the territorial concentration and ethnolinguistic homogeneity of Saudi Shi'a, who are of Arab extraction like the rest of the Saudi national population. With the exception of a small minority of Twelver Shi'a who have long resided in Medina and an Ismaili minority in the region of Najran along the Yemeni border, the Shi'a all live in the eastern part of the kingdom, where its hydrocarbon resources are concentrated. On several occasions, this region witnessed wars between the Al Saud and the Ottomans, who first incorporated it into their territory in the sixteenth century.

At the time of the Al Saud's final conquest of the region in 1913, its Shi'a were distributed between two large subregions: Hasa and Qatif. Centered on the towns of Hufuf and Mubarraz, Hasa has always had a mixed sectarian profile, with Shi'a and Sunnis cohabiting in urban zones as well as the surrounding villages at times. Over the course of the various chapters of the Saudi state's formation, many of Hasa's Shi'a fled Wahhabi exactions, establishing a diaspora that extends throughout the Persian Gulf region. They are especially present in Kuwait, where the Hasawis are a prosperous and influential community. A major trading port and pearl-diving zone, Qatif was an entirely Shi'a town surrounded by many religiously homogenous villages. In both Hasa and the region of Qatif, the Shi'a were an exclusively sedentary and detribalized population of merchants, artisans, farmers, and fishermen. They also possessed a relatively large clerical class connected to the religious centers of Iraq and Iran and playing a central role in the organization of the population's community life.

As in Bahrain, the history of the Shi'a in Saudi Arabia is a highly politicized matter. The same questions arise, particularly those relating to the origin of Shi'ism and the time frame of its introduction, as well as the circumstances of the Al Saud's conquest of Shi'a-populated areas. Far from having exhibited a fierce spirit of resistance, the vast majority of Shi'i notables chose to submit to the new authority without a fight. As the first to be contacted by the Al Saud's emissaries, the Shi'i notables of Hasa—ulama, merchants, and landowners together—chose to imitate their Sunni neighbors and submit. They sent messages to their coreligionists in Qatif to encourage them to do the same. A great debate took place among the port's notables, with the majority deciding to stay out of the conflict between the Al Saud and the Ottomans. Seeing this, the small Ottoman garrison chose to abandon the place and were followed by a small group of diehards who had favored armed resistance. Many of them left for Bahrain or Iraq.[10]

It is interesting to consider for a moment the reasons advanced by those who favored surrender. In addition to their belief in the unlikelihood of Ottoman victory and Britain's refusal to intervene in order to halt Saudi expansion—Britain had protectorates all along the coast—they thought the Al Saud might bring stability to a region that had for many years been exposed to the violence of certain Bedouin tribes. A few years earlier a particularly violent conflict between these tribes and the inhabitants of Qatif and its surrounding villages had resulted in the death of dozens of Shi'i peasants and pearl divers. In determining the advantages and disadvantages of submitting to the new power, the matter of the Al Saud's religious affiliation had clearly been judged of secondary importance.

As in Bahrain, the Al Saud and their allies initially behaved like conquerors in the eastern region, as they also did in the other regions taken from the Ottomans or autonomous tribal powers. There, too, the Sunni-Shi'a divide was immediately superimposed on a division between conquerors and vanquished, foreigners and natives. That being the case, the first problem encountered by the Shi'a under the new authority was economic in nature, with the confiscation of much arable land and the imposition of a high level of taxation forcing many Shi'i to flee for Bahrain. At the religious level, by contrast, the notables had succeeded in negotiating the right to continue practicing their religion in exchange for political loyalty to the new rulers.

While Shi'i doctrines have always been condemned by the official curricula of Saudi religious instruction, Shi'i religious practices have thus been tolerated in these circumstances. This tolerance has varied over time with historical and social circumstances. To this day, Shi'a in the religiously mixed areas of Hasa thus comport themselves discreetly in public in keeping with a more or less tacit agreement: they can practice and teach their religion only in the closed space of the home, mosque, and *hussainiyya*, the buildings reserved for the commemoration of the martyrdom of Imam Hussein. In the region of Qatif, by contrast, the ceremonies of Ashura and other commemorations of the birth and death of the Imams have long been carried out in public places, with the muezzins delivering the call to prayer according to the Shi'a formula, which specifies that "Ali is the representative (*wali*) of God."

In both regions, the Shi'a were also able to maintain their own religious courts based on Shi'a law and overseen by Shi'i ulama, most of whom had been trained in Najaf. Starting in the 1970s, these jurisdictions were placed under the authority of the Ministry of the Interior, which, among other things, was responsible for paying judges' salaries. In a context marked by fears of a generalized Shi'a uprising provoked by regime change in Iraq (see chapter 5), this system was reformed and extended in 2005. In general, the maintenance of Shi'a courts has allowed a group of Shi'i notables loyal to the Saudi government to consolidate their position.[11] It has also institutionalized the existence of a Shi'a community distinct from the Sunni community, one that is mainly represented in its dealings with the state by the ulama and notables. This represents another major point of difference vis-à-vis the Sunnis in Iran: the Saudi Shi'a rapidly succeeded in forming themselves into a community. Lacking a parliament or political participation, the question of quotas has never arisen in Saudi Arabia. That said, ever since a Consultative Council appointed by the king was created in 1992, the authorities have always made sure to include a few Shi'a in this body, which presents itself as representative of the country's various regional, tribal, and social components.

This pragmatic policy toward the Shi'a has not gone without creating tensions between the Al Saud and the Wahhabi clerical establishment, which has regularly exerted pressure to bring these supposedly heretical populations back into the fold of orthodoxy. Significantly, however, the Al Saud have only rarely given way to this pressure, going so far as to put down by force the most fervent and dangerous supporters of the Wahhabization of the Shi'a and other "deviant" Muslims. In 1930 King Abdulaziz thus decided to massacre most leaders of the Ikhwan, a group of elite Bedouin warriors who had recently been sedentarized and indoctrinated in Wahhabism. As the avant-garde of the Al Saud's army, the Ikhwan displayed particular religious zeal and were guilty of many acts of violence, particularly against the Shi'a. They regularly disobeyed the Al Saud and were thus as much a source of destabilization as a military asset. Once the conquest had been carried to completion, it was inevitable that they would be eliminated. Though useful in the conquest phase, their ideological zeal became a problem once the state set about attempting to consolidate itself.

In practice, the Saudi regime's efforts to manage its Shi'a minority have always consisted of a series of reasonable compromises with Wahhabi norms. This shows that, contrary to the manner in which the Safavids looked on Sunnism, the Al Saud did not initially see Shi'ism as a counterideology capable of jeopardizing the state's stability. The Shi'a were not generally perceived as a subversive element. Additional evidence of this may be found in the large-scale integration of Shi'a in the petroleum industry. A strategic economic sector if there ever was one, petroleum has since the 1930s supplied a large portion of the state's income and is today the main source of government revenue. Since the oil wells are located in the Eastern Province, the Shi'a were among the first Saudis recruited by Aramco (Arabian-American Oil Company). Starting in the 1950s and 1960s, they extensively benefited from the company's training policy and came to occupy key positions, a major source of social promotion that resulted in the emergence of a Shi'a middle class and petite bourgeoisie.

Comparing these accommodations with the Safavids' policy of eradicating Sunnism reveals different modes of state construction: whereas the Safavids sought to religiously homogenize the populations under their control and thought that adherence to Shi'ism was the foundation of loyalty to the state, the issue of conversion was never a priority for the Al Saud, who looked on the loyalty of conquered populations as a matter distinct from their religious beliefs. At the time of the Saudi state's construction in the early twentieth century, the Al Saud saw the main danger as consisting in the nomadic Bedouins, a major source of instability as indicated by the attitude of the Shi'i notables of Qatif. Creating the state was above all a matter of eradicating Bedouin culture.[12]

The Emergence of a Sunni Community in Iran

Under the Islamic Republic, the religious sociology of the Sunni regions of Iran rapidly evolved as a result of their integration into mainly South Asian transnational political and religious networks. In addition to changing the nature of the equilibrium between the two main Sunni regions of Kurdistan and Balochistan, this social and political transformation contributed to the emergence of a feeling of Sunni sectarian affiliation that, for the first time, seemed to successfully transcend regional, ethnic, and linguistic differences.[13] Since the 1990s this has, among other things, been reflected in the emergence of a Sunni communal vote inasmuch as the Sunnis are now characterized by electoral behavior distinct from that of the Shi'i Muslims, overwhelmingly casting their ballots for reformist or secular candidates.[14]

This transformation first began in the early twentieth century as a result of the diffusion of reformist ideas, particularly in Kurdistan and Balochistan. It must be emphasized that this phenomenon occurred in a context marked by the eclipse of tribal elites in both regions, the result of a Pahlavi policy to reduce the power of tribal chiefs. As in all peripheral regions, what's more, these zones witnessed an influx of Shi'a, themselves internal migrants from the central plateau. This further exacerbated feelings of religious difference among the Sunnis. In this context, religious leaders of all stripes stepped in, including the leaders of traditional Sufi brotherhoods and young ulama trained in the networks of reformist religious seminaries or attuned to the militant Islam of the Muslim Brotherhood and other antiestablishment religious movements.

In Balochistan, these new religious actors were largely drawn from Deobandi networks (see chapter 8). In the first half of the twentieth century, Baloch student networks developed in the Deobandi seminaries of India and, later, Pakistan. In 1970 this led to the creation of Darul Ulum (House of Knowledge), a large Sunni religious seminary located in Zahedan, the capital city of Sistan and Balochistan Province. Born into a line of religious figures with ties to a powerful Baloch tribe known for its struggle against the British, Mawlana Abd al-Aziz Makki was the seminary's founder and served as its director until his death in 1987. Following the 1979 revolution, he became famous for his public protests against the new regime, rejecting the constitution by refusing to recognize the validity of the doctrine on which it was based: *wilayat al-faqih*, or government by specialists of religious law. The regime's response was all delicacy. In a context marked by the simultaneous emergence of a more radical opposition among the Sunni religious leaders of Kurdistan, Mawlana Abd al-Aziz's willingness to negotiate established him as one of the government's regular interlocutors.[15]

The nascent religious revivalist movement in Kurdistan was primarily the work of the Muslim Brotherhood. Unlike elsewhere in the Arab world, it was not former al-Azhar students who introduced their ideas to the region but rather an influx of Iraqi political refugees during the Iran-Iraq War.[16] Among their guiding figures was Ahmad Moftizadeh (d. 1993). Born into a family of ulama, Moftizadeh decided against pursuing a clerical career. His religious and ideological culture reflected the eclecticism of this period, a time when the sectarian issue, in particular, had yet to become central. In addition to Sunni Islamist thinkers, he was also a great reader of the Shi'a intellectual Ali Shariati (see chapter 3).

In 1978 Moftizadeh founded Maktab-e-Quran (School of the Koran), which quickly grew into a network of Sunni religious seminaries and charitable associations. A supporter of the Islamic Revolution, Moftizadeh promoted the idea of an autonomous Iranian Kurdistan. Following adoption of the constitution, he was among the foremost critics of the religious discrimination that the Islamic Republic's markedly Shi'a character clearly entailed. In 1980 Moftizadeh participated in the creation of the Sunni Central Council, an institution that sought to unite and represent the Sunnis. His various activities earned him ten years in prison. Following his death shortly after being released, he was held up as a model by his followers, half-militant religious intellectual, half-Sufi master.[17]

The central government long looked on these Sunni religious movements as a threat. Since the 2000s, however, the regime has adopted a new attitude, a reflection of its ascendant reformist and pragmatic factions and of the spread of Sunni Islamist guerilla movements. In 2002 the activists of the Muslim Brotherhood network received authorization to officially organize under the name of the Society for Preaching and Reform. As a result, the country now officially hosts a branch of the Muslim Brotherhood devoted to defending the rights of Iranian Sunnis, in Kurdistan and beyond. The society eventually expanded beyond Kurdistan, and its network today covers the entire Sunni population of Iran. In Balochistan, the Deobandi networks and Zahedan's Dar al-Ulum also claim to speak for all Sunnis and benefit from the same type of recognition on the part of the central government, which sees them as a counterweight to radical movements. Since the 2000s this objective has only become more urgent with the rise of the Jundallah (Soldiers of God) movement and, more recently, Jaish al-Adl (Army of Justice), whose activities have been a source of endemic instability in the region. These movements have carried out numerous attacks, particularly against representatives of the Pasdaran, the regime's powerful paramilitary institution. Believed to be supported by Pakistan and Saudi Arabia, they also have ties to radical anti-Shiʻa movements in Pakistan and Afghanistan.

These developments helped make Balochistan the main hub of Sunni religious activity in Iran, to the detriment of Kurdistan. This reflected the central role that Zahedan's Dar al-Ulum had assumed in the area of religious instruction. There, the lessons were given in Persian, a lingua franca that allowed it to attract students from all Sunni regions of Iran, including Kurdistan and the Arab population zones of the South. What's more, this religious studies institute attracted a growing number of Persian-speaking foreign students from Central Asia, particularly Afghanistan and Tajikistan, making it a magnet for the region. With its spokesmen exclusively reliant on Urdu, the Deobandi current had formerly had little influence over these Persian-speaking populations. Thanks to its use of Persian, however, Dar al-Ulum was able to spread its message to all of them. Mawlana Abd al-Hamid, the present director of Dar al-Ulum and the son-in-law of its founder, has become one of the most popular preachers among the region's Persian-speaking Sunni populations.[18]

The emergence of Balochistan as the magnetic pole of Sunnism in Iran is clearly inseparable from its regional influence. It cannot be understood without also taking account of the changing attitude of the authorities in Tehran. The latter are now willing to treat the actors of the Sunni religious revival as interlocutors and representatives of a nascent Sunni community. Though they protest and challenge state authority, these religious actors have favored reformist solutions to the problems facing Iran's Sunni population. Cultivating them thus seems a good way to counterbalance the influence of radical, separatist, and/or jihadist movements. But the regime also understood that its Sunni population could provide a tool of regional influence extending well beyond the Persian-speaking populations of Central Asia. For Zahedan's Dar al-Ulum also influenced religious actors in the Arab-speaking regions of southern Iran. With long-standing ties to the religious actors and institutions of the Arabian Peninsula, these actors in their turn became poles of influence vis-à-vis the Iranian-origin Sunni populations now residing in the Gulf monarchies, Qatar in particular.[19]

Saudi Shi'a: An Ethnic or Religious Minority?

In Saudi Arabia, the Shi'a were already structured as a community before the emergence of reformist and Islamist religious actors. As was the case of Iran and its Sunni Islamists, the regime initially looked on the emergence of Shi'i Islamists as a threat, particularly given their adoption of a revolutionary agenda in the immediate aftermath of the Iranian Revolution of 1979. In the late 1980s, however—a context marked by the ascendance of pragmatic actors within the Iranian regime and the marginalization of their radical counterparts—Saudi Arabia's main Shi'a political organization, the Organization for the Islamic Revolution in the Arabian Peninsula (see chapter 4), gradually shifted to a reformist agenda. This allowed it to become the Saudi regime's main interlocutor in what concerned Shi'a issues in the kingdom and thus the Shi'a community's foremost representative.

This process was at first fully reflected in the drastic transformation of the organization's rhetoric, beginning with a wholly unambiguous change of name: in 1991 the Organization for the Islamic Revolution in the Arabian Peninsula became the Reform Movement (a name reminiscent of that adopted by the Muslim Brotherhood in Iran), at the same time choosing to become autonomous of its Iraqi patrons. Formerly exiled in Iran, its cadres left for Syria, Great Britain, and the United States. Not surprisingly, the movement's various mouthpieces also changed their names: the *Islamic Revolution* magazine became *Arabian Peninsula*, and a new journal named *Oasis* was created. Significantly, none of these new names referred to religion.

The content of these publications exhibited an interesting effort to redefine not just the terms of Saudi political debate but also the identity of the kingdom's Shi'a. In this, it was the reverse image of what had taken place among the Sunnis of Iran. To move beyond the head-on conflict between Wahhabism and Shi'ism, which seemed to lead nowhere, the Reform Movement attempted to include the Saudi Shi'a identity within a broader cultural identity distinguished by its own language, regional affiliation, and way of life, thereby defining the Shiʿa as more of an ethnolinguistic minority than a religious one. To this end, the movement's publications turned their attention to the history of the eastern region, insisting on the zone's long-standing Shiʿa presence and the autochthonous character of its inhabitants, depicted as members in full standing of the Baharna people (see chapter 7). Like the Arabs of the Arabian coast of the Persian Gulf, the Baharna speak an Arabic dialect distinct from that of the inhabitants of the central Arabian Peninsula from whom the Al Saud family were drawn. In contrast to the nomadic or recently sedentarized Bedouin, who are similarly associated with the ruling dynasty and its allies, they are also distinguished by their long-sedentarized way of life. In addition to its regional complexion, Shiʿism in Saudi Arabia was thus said to correspond to a distinct civilizational affiliation. This redefinition of Shiʿa identity was associated with the formulation of a political agenda based on a demand for increased political participation and thereby dovetailed with the demands of other, more or less organized opposition currents consisting of Sunni Islamists and liberal intellectuals. The Reform Movement claimed that, in this framework, the kingdom's Shiʿa were ready to accept the Saudi monarchy and even show real Saudi patriotism. They no longer demanded regime change but rather that the Shiʿa be recognized as full citizens on par with the Sunnis. In 1993 the Reform Movement's efforts paid off, leading to the signing of an agreement with the regime that allowed the movement's exiled cadres to return to the kingdom and become the government's privileged interlocutors. This process accelerated in 2003 as concerns over regime change in Iraq mounted—concerns that the Reform Movement skillfully manipulated. Following the fall of Saddam Hussein, the movement presented the kingdom's then-regent, Crown Prince Abdullah, with a petition entitled "Partners of the Nation." In it, some 450 Saudi Shiʿa figures reaffirmed their loyalty to the Al Saud but in exchange asked that the Shiʿa be recognized as a legitimate religious community. Having been publicly received by the sovereign, in June 2003 the petitioners subsequently participated in the first of a series of "National Dialogue Conferences" dedicated to the kingdom's various religious components. Shortly thereafter the various impediments that had been systematically put in the way of constructing new Shiʻi mosques and religious buildings in the Eastern Province were lifted, and in 2005 the Shiʻa personal statute court system was reformed, allowing the number of Shiʻi courts to be increased. That same year, municipal elections were held for the first time since 1950, with the Reform Movement winning the vast majority of seats on Shiʻa-majority municipal councils.

Throughout the 2000s the Reform Movement consolidated its position as the regime's privileged interlocutor for Shiʻa affairs. At the same time, however, it experienced growing internal dissension, with some criticizing the lack of ambition shown by its leaders. At a time when mass unemployment had increasingly become a reality for Saudi young people, they continued to focus on the issue of religious recognition rather than such crucial problems as public-sector labor discrimination. The Arab Spring accelerated this process, bringing to the fore new opinion leaders from the Message Movement. More radical in their demands, the latter became key figures in the riots that roiled the region of Qatif in 2011 and 2012. Based in the region of Hufuf, where Shiʻa and Sunnis live alongside one another in the same urban neighborhoods, Tawfiq al-Amer thus sought to further extend the dynamic of religious recognition by organizing public Shiʻi rituals despite a rule banning them. In February 2011 he crossed another red line by publicly demanding that the monarchy be made constitutional. His arrest shortly thereafter triggered the first demonstrations in the Shiʻi zones. In the region of Qatif, Sheikh Nimr al-Nimr was simultaneously establishing himself as the most aggressive critic of the Reform Movement's strategy, stating that the Eastern Province should secede if an end was not put to anti-Shiʻa discrimination. His execution in January 2016, as we have seen, prompted Iran and Saudi Arabia to break off diplomatic relations.

Chapter 10

YEMEN

ZAYDISM BETWEEN SUNNISM AND SHIʿISM

Today the Zaydis mainly reside in Yemen, where they may represent as much as 40 percent of the population. Most Yemenis practice the form of Sunni Islam associated with the Shafiʿi school of law. The Zaydis are commonly classified as Shiʿa, including by Middle East experts. There is a simple reason for this: historically, the Zaydis were initially supporters of Imam Ali. The Yemeni Civil War, which began in 2004 and intensified in 2014 in the context of the Arab Spring, is most often treated as part of a larger regional conflict between Sunnis and Shiʿa. Since the eighteenth century, however, Yemeni political leaders have for various reasons encouraged a process of rapprochement between Sunnism and Zaydism. This process was facilitated by the "lack of doctrinal rigidity"[1] that characterizes Zaydism, an orthodox form of which has never been established.

Political Radicalism and Doctrinal Openness

Supporters of one of the fourth Imam's sons, Zayd ibn Ali, the Zaydis split off from those who would become the Twelver Shiʿa over a disagreement as to the appropriate attitude to adopt toward the caliphate. While the sixth Imam, Jaʿfar al-Sadiq, took the path of peaceful coexistence with the Abbasids and redefined the imamate as an essentially religious and communal authority, the Zaydis by contrast asserted that the struggle against unjust government must continue. Like the Ismailis, the Zaydis fomented many rebellions against the caliphs during the Middle Ages.

Over time, Zaydism split into several doctrinal currents and factions, particularly once the Zaydis had succeeded in establishing states of their own in the ninth century. One of these was in present-day northern Iran, its inhabitants mainly switching to Twelver Shi'ism under the Safavids. The other, located in northern Yemen, lasted until 1962. Moreover, owing to the great emphasis it placed on the individual practice of religious exegesis, the history of Zaydism has been regularly punctuated by the emergence of independent ulama who sometimes expressed contradictory views, particularly with regard to the manner in which the imam was to be chosen and the status of reason in religious exegesis. In these debates, the various Zaydi currents sometimes positioned themselves closer to the Shi'a and sometimes closer to the Sunnis. Some of them thus refused to unilaterally condemn the first three caliphs while others thought that, contrary to the Mutazilite idea that would eventually become a pillar of Twelver Shi'ism, humankind was not free but rather in everything subject to divine will.[2]

The stance ultimately adopted by most Zaydi ulama regarding the question of the imamate was broader than that of the Twelver Shi'a. After Hussein, in their view, the imam was no longer appointed by God but rather had to be chosen by consultation among the descendants of Hassan and Hussein who were willing to stand up against injustice—if necessary, by force. Nor did the Zaydis agree with the Twelvers in attributing extraordinary qualities of infallibility to the Imams. Some currents of Zaydism even claimed that the imam need not necessarily be the best of his generation. Others went so far as to promote the idea of a totally open imamate from the point of view of heredity, with any candidate who stood up against unjust government capable of aspiring to the imamate. To the degree that its representatives claim (with a few exceptions) that political authority must be exercised by the descendants of Ali, Zaydism clearly belongs to the Alid current. In its insistence on the idea that the imamate must be transmitted by consultation, however, Zaydism proves to be just as close to Sunni thinking.

The case of the Yemeni imamate casts particular light on the arrangements that this back and forth between Shi'ism and Sunnism made possible. The imamate was founded in 898 in a mountainous region neighboring the town of Saʿda in present-day North Yemen. Local tribes there invited the first imam to arbitrate their conflicts as a neutral third party with no affiliations to the local tribal order. Known as al-Hadi ila al-Haqq (that is, "he who guides toward law/justice"), Yahya ibn Husayn al-Rassi (d. 911) was the son of one of the most prestigious Zaydi ulama. From Saʿda, he helped spread Zaydism, defining several major characteristics of its dominant "Hadawi" current (in reference to the imam's nickname, al-Hadi). While this doctrine recognizes Ali's rightful claim to govern after Muhammad, it nevertheless depicts the first three caliphs as good leaders. It also presents the imam as a religious and political leader who the community's notables choose from among the descendants of Ali and Fatima for his skills in religious exegesis and physical bravery—that is, his ability to make war against unjust powers (the *khuruj*). He is not infallible in religious terms but must be obeyed as long as he actively promotes virtue and fights vice.[3] As was also the case of Twelver Shiʿism, the Hadawi doctrine adopted a Mutazilite theology.[4]

Doubtless because the Yemeni imamate covered a territory dominated by large tribes with unstable and often conflictual relationships, Hadawi Zaydi doctrine has always been characterized by a high degree of political pragmatism. It thus allows that, in some periods, there may be no candidate who meets religious and political standards of excellence. In such cases, a "less excellent" imam may be recognized, or even two such imams reigning over separate territories. These imams may be given the duty of defending and protecting their territory but cannot lead Friday prayers or claim to collect the *zakat*. In practice, the territory actually controlled by the imams has varied over the course of history. On some occasions—when tribal chiefs have refused to give their allegiance to the imam, for example—it has been restricted to urban zones. On others, as when the imam had succeeded in negotiating relative peace among the tribes, it has extended to tribal rural zones. Since the Zaydis occupied it alongside Sunni followers of the Shafiʿi school of law, this territory was never religiously homogenous. When the territory was particularly large and included portions of present-day southern Yemen, it happened that the majority of the imamate's population was Sunni.

Imam al-Hadi brought around fifty companions with him, all descendants of Imam Ali. Together with their descendants, they rapidly formed a distinct status group—the *sada* (sing. *sayyid*)—within the tribal notability and are still known as Hashemites owing to their membership in the Prophet's family. They were the imamate's aristocracy and backbone. Representing the imam's government in the tribal territories, it was their duty to spread the doctrine, arbitrate conflicts, and collect the Koranic tax.

Convergence between Sunnis and Zaydis

In the eighteenth century, the government of the imams underwent profound change as the imamate was gradually transformed into a classic kingdom in which the imams no longer corresponded to the ideal model of the ulama-warrior posited by Zaydi tradition.[5] The imams thus began to succeed one another within the same dynasty and in the absence of any consultative process. The imamate also gradually took the form of a state, changing the relationship between government and society. Inspired by the Ottomans, the imams created an administration that included ministers and other high-ranking officials. They also established an independent army distinct from the unstable tribal coalition upon which the imamate had traditionally depended. Many of these new soldiers were slaves. In these circumstances, many Zaydi ulama refused to acknowledge their leaders as full-fledged imams and could potentially call on the population to revolt against them. In search of religious legitimization, the sovereigns thus turned to ulama who, though born into families in the Zaydi tradition, were closer in their thinking to Sunni Islam.[6] Although they did not constitute a majority, such ulama had existed since the fifteenth century. What chiefly distinguished them was their reliance on the canonical hadith of Sunnism in practicing religious exegesis. This sometimes led them to significantly stray from the fundamental principles of Zaydism as they had been defined by Imam al-Hadi, which as we have seen were similar to those of Twelver Shi'ism. Furthermore, they refused to employ rational thought in exegesis, tending instead to solely rely on scriptural sources, a practice that also drew them away from Twelver Shi'ism and toward Sunnism. One such Sunni-leaning Zaydi ulama was Muhammad al-Shawkani (d. 1834). Born into a line of Zaydi ulama, al-Shawkani pushed rapprochement with Sunnism the furthest, to the point of abandoning most of the foundations of Hadawi Zaydism. For this reason he is often seen as having actively contributed to the "Sunnization of Zaydism."[7] Among other things, his ideas have been integrated into contemporary Salafism (see chapter 5), particularly his call to move beyond all schools of law. Like his contemporary Muhammad ibn Abd al-Wahhab, the founder of Wahhabism, al-Shawkani was a proponent of literalist exegesis and claimed that it was forbidden to revolt against political leaders who were unjust or failed to respect Islam. Nor did he believe it necessary for the imam to be versed in religious studies. In all these respects, he clearly broke with the pillars of traditional Zaydi doctrine.[8] As might be expected, his ideas perfectly fit the needs of imams in search of religious legitimization, and Muhammad al-Shawkani made a career in their bureaucracy, where he served, among other things, as head of the judicial administration.

The Zaydi imamate had intermittently been part of the Ottoman Empire since the sixteenth century. In the nineteenth century it found itself confronted, like most of the region's political entities, with European colonial expansion. In 1839 the British occupied the Port of Aden in the South and there established a protectorate that threatened to encroach on the lands of the imamate. It was in these conditions that a new dynasty of Imams came to power, the Hamid al-Din. Determined to unite the tribes in order to fight foreign influence, they accelerated the imamate's transition toward a modern state. A product of this dynasty, Imam Yahya Hamid al-Din aspired to create a greater Yemen under his leadership but came up against the British in the South and the Al Saud in the North.

Starting in the 1930s the Imams were confronted with a many-sided wave of internal protest that was formalized in 1944 by the creation of the Free Yemeni Movement (see chapter 4). The movement was a heteroclite coalition consisting of various social categories of Zaydis and Sunnis, young Arab progressive and nationalist officers, intellectuals, *sada* who felt they had a claim on the imamate, tribal chiefs, supporters of the imamate, and also some who toyed with the idea of a republic. This religiously mixed coalition was jointly led by a Zaydi and a Sunni. Strongly influenced by the Egyptian Muslim Brotherhood, its religious ideology urged that sectarian affiliation be subordinated to a generic Islam in which Zaydis and Sunnis could both recognize themselves.[9] As we have seen, while this perspective was perfectly in keeping with the reformist and Islamist ideas that were spreading everywhere at the time, it was far from being foreign to Yemeni Islam.

After Imam Yahya was assassinated in an aborted coup attempt in 1948, his successors were unable to reestablish the regime's legitimacy. Growing protests ultimately led to a coup d'état in 1962, putting in power a military junta that was allied with several notables and established an Arab nationalist republican regime heavily inspired by the Nasserian model. A civil war ensued with supporters of the imamate, resulting in the latter's defeat seven years later. In 1968 the Yemen Arab Republic was established in the country's North on the territory of the former imamate[10] and accelerated the rapprochement between Zaydism and Sunnism. In the hope of bridging the sectarian divide—a goal already embraced by the Free Yemeni Movement—the new regime sought to promote the "Sunnized" version of Zaydism, in practice raising it to the level of orthodoxy. In this context, Muhammad al-Shawkani was posthumously awarded the status of organic intellectual to the republican regime.

More broadly, the republic's official religious discourse systematically obscured the differences between Zaydism and Sunnism. This intentional effort to blur boundaries was particularly implemented in the educational sector through textbooks and the presence of the Egyptian, Syrian, and Sudanese teachers—many of them affiliated with the Muslim Brotherhood—who had been recruited to make up for the paucity of skilled personnel.[11] In the 1970s this process of convergence accelerated with the rapid spread of new, Saudi-financed schools to fight communism on the basis of a Hanbali-Wahhabi curriculum. It must be underscored that convergence did not uniquely concern the Zaydis; the Sunnis for their part abstained from stigmatizing Zaydism, in particular ceasing to identify it with Shi'ism. Today many Yemenis thus believe Zaydism to be among the Sunni schools of law. As part of this process of convergence, the markers of Zaydi and Sunni identity did not disappear but rather were minimized. In what concerns some ritual practices, for example, Zaydis and Shiʿa continue to have much in common: they celebrate the festival of Ghadir Khumm commemorating Muhammad's nomination of Ali just before his death, pray with their arms at their sides, and include the phrase "hurry to the best of deeds" (*hayy-a ʿala khayr al-ʿamal*) in their call to prayer.[12]

Zaydi Revivalism and Rapprochement with Shiʿism

Though it had been promoted by the political authorities since the eighteenth century, this Sunni-inflected Zaydism did not for all that wipe out Zaydi currents faithful to the position established by Imam al-Hadi or rejecting what they saw as the dilution of Zaydi identity in Sunnism. Moreover, some members of the former imamate's elites had always shown nostalgia for the old regime—a nostalgia stoked by the distrust with which the central government unfailingly looked on the Zaydi regions that fiercely resisted the republicans after the fall of the imamate in 1962. Never defeated in battle, they were integrated into the republic only after much negotiation. As a result of this distrust, Zaydi regions benefited less than others from the redistribution of resources, and their economy came to depend on cross-border contraband in drugs, weapons, and medicine.[13] The creation of a united Yemeni state in 1990 allowed some Zaydi actors to politically organize and thereby speak for these formerly central but now peripheral regions. Baptized the Republic of Yemen, this state was born of the union of North Yemen (Yemen Arab Republic) and South Yemen (People's Democratic Republic of Yemen). To create a political system that would allow the respective elites of these two former states to peacefully coexist, the new state established a democratic regime under which the various influence groups could create political parties.

It was in this context that, in 1990, several Zaydi-based parties were created, including al-Haqq (the Party of Truth). Founded by Zaydi ulama and *sada*—members of the imamate's old aristocracy—al-Haqq sought, not to reestablish the imamate, but rather to reaffirm Zaydi identity and adapt it to republican modernity. Among other things, this took the form of critically reinterpreting the imamate's transformation into a traditional dynastic power starting in the fifteenth century. To that end, al-Haqq clearly positioned itself against the Sunni-inflected current of Zaydism embodied by Muhammad al-Shawkani, whom party activists accused of being merely a Salafist and Wahhabi who legitimated the rulers' limitless power and forgot the primacy of the law. In their eyes, established regimes had used his ideas to minimize the historic importance of Zaydism in Yemen and fool people into thinking that Salafism had similarly deep roots in the country. In contrast to al-Shawkani, al-Haqq cadres eagerly reasserted the rationalist Mutazilite foundations that characterized the Zaydism of Imam al-Hadi and Twelver Shi'ism alike.[14]

Al-Haqq's project also aimed at fully integrating Zaydism into the republic, as is indicated by the 1990 publication of a manifesto by Zaydi ulama associated with the party, including its secretary general. The manifesto claimed that the imamate was a historically obsolete regime; while it may have been valid in earlier periods, it could no longer exist in modern times. Today the imamate could only consist of a spiritual and community authority. In the political domain, Muslims had to choose a leader solely on the basis of his ability to govern well and without consideration of whether he descended from Ali and Fatima. For this reason, it was perfectly legitimate to support the republican regime. The revolt against unjust government—the other foundational principle of Zaydism—was now to take place, not by force of arms, but via participation in the electoral process.

Another objective of al-Haqq was to combat the expansion of Salafism at a time when the government had given free rein to the various actors engaged in propagating this doctrine, including in the Zaydi population zones of the country's North. One factor that favored the spread of Salafism in these regions was that Yemen's leading Salafist, Muqbil al-Wadi'i (d. 2001), himself had come from a large Zaydi tribe. In the 1980s, he established Dar al-Hadith (House of Hadith), a religious studies institute that quickly became Yemen's leading Salafist institution, choosing for its location a village very close to Sa'da, the historic bastion of

Zaydism. What's more, Muqbil al-Wadi'i had studied at Saudi Arabia's Islamic University of Medina, and his reputation extended beyond the frontiers of Yemen. In his writings, he readily criticized the rigidity of the social hierarchy within the Zaydi population and maintained that he had been denied access to religious knowledge in Yemen because he was not from a family of *sada* or ulama. This helped him become aware of the sclerotic character of the social system on which Zaydism was based, and he became one of its most savage critics. Together with an entire generation of his students, he established several Salafist institutions in Yemen, thereby helping reactivate what had become a largely latent sectarian division between Zaydis and Sunnis.[15]

Over the course of the 1990s, the al-Haqq Party politically allied itself with the country's dominant political forces, including the Yemeni Socialist Party, an offshoot of South Yemen's former ruling party. Though this allowed it to obtain a few ministerial posts, it later sided with the government when the South sought to secede and civil war broke out. In 1997 a group of party activists who had since 1990 formed what they called the "Young Believers" discussion group deserted al-Haqq. It seems that this group had existed at least informally since the 1980s, among other things as a forum to debate the Iranian Revolution.[16] In the 1990s it was gradually reorganized as an activist movement under the leadership of Hussein al-Houthi (d. 2004) and rapidly became known as the "Houthis." Elected as a deputy in 1993, al-Houthi was born into a *sada* family, and his father was a well-known ulama. At first the Young Believers forum mainly brought together religious studies students who wished to discuss how Zaydism might be internally reformed—that is, adapted to modernity but not merged with Sunnism—while combating the spread of Salafism in Zaydi circles in the region of Sa'da. They broke with the leadership of al-Haqq over personal disagreements that the regime exploited in the aim of dividing the political actors of the northern region into several factions. The regime had always seen this region as a potential source of contest and was quick to seize on this opportunity to simultaneously weaken al-Haqq and the Salafists. In this context, some Young Believers, including Hussein al-Houthi's brother, even joined the ruling party, the General People's Congress.[17]

.It was the geopolitical reconfiguration brought about by September 11, 2001, that, in complex circumstances, led the Young Believers to break with the government. It seems that Hussein al-Houthi had aspired to lead a broad-based popular movement uniting Zaydis and Sunnis around a critique of American policy in the Middle East and Yemen's new status as that country's strategic ally in the War on Terrorism. Refusing to obey the government's order to not publicly criticize American policy, al-Houthi urged his compatriots to utter the following slogan at the end of Friday prayer: "God is the greatest, death to America, death to Israel, curse the Jews, glory to Islam!" In the very anti-American and anti-Israeli context of the Middle East, this slogan merely reiterated what was a matter of consensus—if not politically then at least in what concerned the population's dominant values. At the same time, Hussein al-Houthi called on Muslims to no longer content themselves with religious learning and act against American imperialism. To that end, he widely drew on contemporary Shi'i examples, including the Iranian Revolution, the person of Khomeini, and Lebanese Hezbollah. Portraits of Hezbollah's secretary general, Hassan Nasrallah, are now commonplace in Houthi-controlled areas. At the same time that he drew on these figures of Shi'a resistance, Hussein al-Houthi took a clear stance against certain typically Shi'a doctrines, particularly *wilayat al-faqih*, or government by the specialist of religious law.[18] One of his leading ideas, moreover, was that Muslims should solely rely on the Koran as their reference without seeking a hidden meaning there, as doing so might lead them astray. For, in his view, every Muslim was capable of understanding the meaning of the Koran without the assistance of a guide.[19] Once again, this position ran counter to the doctrines of Twelver Shi'ism, which assigns a central place to the ulama and their work of exegesis.

After hundreds of young people who had regularly turned out to chant al-Houthi's slogans in Yemen's Zaydi-majority capital, Sana'a, were arrested in 2004, armed clashes broke out between the Houthis and government forces, leading to Hussein al-Houthi's death. This was the first phase of a civil war that continues to this day and that has seen various members of al-Houthi's family take up the struggle. The first to do so was Hussein's father, the old and very respected ulama Badr al-Din al-Houthi, followed by Hussein's brother, Abd al-Malik al-Houthi. In 2012, with the Arab Spring still in full swing, the government of Ali Abdallah Saleh fell. Saleh had been Yemen's president since unification in 1990 and was formerly president of North Yemen. With his departure, the alliances were reversed, allowing the Houthis to take control of a larger share of the country's North, including the capital city, starting in 2014 (see chapter 5).

Because it began in a regional context profoundly marked by the fall of Saddam Hussein's regime in Iraq, where a sectarian framework had already begun to broadly inform the interpretation of political events, the Yemeni Civil War had a major impact on the redefinition of Zaydi identity. This took place under the influence of several actors. On the one hand, the Houthis' adversaries immediately set about discrediting them as Shiʿa working for Iranian interests who sought nothing less than to re-establish the imamate. This perception rapidly took hold in Yemeni society, neighboring countries, and the international media, where the Houthis are (also for reasons of simplicity) presented as Shiʿa. In Yemen, the media and the various polemical publications devoted to Zaydism created a climate of stigmatization of Zaydis in general and the *sada* in particular, who are accused of having started the war in order to regain their formerly dominant position.[20] On the other hand, by mobilizing certain Shiʿa political references, the Houthis themselves helped "re-Shiʿize" Zaydism. This process is far from complete and will doubtless never be so. For beyond its multiple doctrinal particularities, what constitutes the specificity of Zaydism is precisely its interstitial position between Sunnism and Shiʿism. Depending on the social and political context, a Shiʿa- or Sunni-leaning tendency dominates. Yet neither has ever completely absorbed a Zaydi identity that is resilient even in its transformations.

Chapter 11

LEBANON

THE SEARCH FOR A NEW
SECTARIAN PACT

In Lebanon, religious identity supplies the foundation of the political system. Eighteen different communities are officially recognized, with political and administrative posts distributed among them on the basis of a quota system. There, the Sunni-Shi'a divide was long diluted by the broader question of relations between Christians and Muslims. This changed with the Lebanese Civil War (1975–1990). By shattering the Islamo-Christian pact and thrusting the Shi'a community to the center of the political equation, it turned the Sunni-Shi'a divide into an organizing principle of the political field.

A Multisectarian Political System

The region corresponding to contemporary Lebanon is a highly mountainous area and as such has long served as a refuge for numerous persecuted religious minorities. This explains the country's particularly splintered religious landscape. At the center of the Lebanese political equation are the Maronite Christians, followers of doctrines developed by the fourth-century monk Maron who were seen as heretics by the Byzantine state. Beginning in the twelfth century they developed very close relations with Europe, in particular France, leading them to recognize the pope's authority. In the 1920s these relations were to play a decisive role in the creation of a sovereign Lebanese state, conceived as a Christian national homeland.

Twelver Shi'a made their way to the mountainous areas of Lebanon for the same reasons. Hounded by Sunni Muslim powers and particularly the Ottomans, they mainly congregated in the Jabal Amel region of the country's South—the birthplace, as we have seen, of several ulama who helped establish Shi'ism as the state religion of Safavid Iran (see chapter 2)—as well as the Becca Valley in the East, which is today located on the frontier with Syria. In addition to the Shi'a, the Lebanese mountains have since the eleventh century sheltered a large Druze community. The latter, it is to be recalled, are an offshoot of Ismailism (see chapter 1). Although Lebanese sectarian nomenclature today categorizes them as "Muslims," their status within Islam is a matter of debate among Druze and non-Druze alike.

Having given up on directly administering this hard-to-access region, beginning in the sixteenth century the Ottomans delegated control over it to Druze emirs, a move that some historians see as prefiguring the contemporary Lebanese state. In a framework characterized by unstable alliances between clans of different religious persuasions, the emirate had authority over a population with multiple religious identities, including Maronites, Sunnis, and Shi'a. For political reasons, the great families that shared political and economic power often passed from one religion to the other, deliberately keeping their sectarian identity vague. Thus, upon the extinction of the first line of Druze emirs in the late seventeenth century, a family of Sunni emirs took over, several of whom converted to Maronite Christianity one after another.

In this landscape populated by heterodox sectarian communities and where religious identities were relatively fluid, the Sunnis were above all concentrated in Mediterranean coastal towns (Beirut, Tripoli, and Sidon, in particular) and were mainly involved in trade. The divide between representatives of the Ottomans' official Sunni orthodoxy and the main minority religions was thus also largely a divide between town and country, mountain people and coastal dwellers.

The modern Lebanese state is for the most part a Maronite project. Indeed, it was pressure from Maronite elites and particularly the clergy that persuaded France, which had received the mandate over Syria and

Lebanon in 1920, to oppose the Arab nationalist project championed by
the future king of Iraq, Faysal, to establish a "Greater Syria" uniting Syria
and Lebanon. At the urging of its Maronite allies and with the aim of
weakening the Arab nationalists, France became involved in the creation
of a "Greater Lebanon" that included not just the region's mountainous,
Maronite-Druze center but also the surrounding, majority-Sunni and
Shi'a areas. The new entity gave Christians a slight demographic advantage over the Sunni, Shi'a, and Druze Muslim communities.

As elsewhere, the Sunni Muslims who were incorporated into Greater
Lebanon saw themselves as the majority and for the most part supported
the Arab nationalist project of creating a Greater Syria. Whereas the latter would have perpetuated Sunnism's dominant, majoritarian status,
Greater Lebanon placed this population in the position of a minority
community on an equal footing with others. As early as 1922, moreover,
France set about transforming Muslims into just such a minority community, first by institutionalizing Sunni religious representation via the
creation of Dar al-ifta (the House of fatwa), which was responsible for
managing Sunni religious affairs, and then by establishing (in 1932) the
office of *mufti* of the republic, whose occupant became president of Dar
al-ifta. The Christian communities already possessed such institutions
of their own, which had been inherited from the Ottoman system of allowing non-Muslim religious communities to autonomously organize.
In contrast to the Christian institutions, however, Dar al-ifta was placed
under the authority of the state and, despite various reforms, was never
able to free itself from the tutelage of institutional political authorities,
particularly that of the prime minister.[1]

The Shi'a, for their part, proved much more reluctant vis-à-vis the project for a Greater Lebanon. While most Shi'a, like their Sunni counterparts, supported the Arab nationalists, the community's notables were
more divided. On the one hand, they were receptive to nationalist discourse and could see themselves as part of a Greater Syria; on the other,
they were aware that Faysal was the representative of a Sunni Islam that
did not necessarily respect their specificities. Following the official birth
of the Lebanese Republic in 1926, most Shi'i notables quickly threw their
support behind the Lebanese cause. It is important to note here that, as

part of their effort to undo the Arab Muslim nationalist bloc, the French for the first time offered the Shi'a the possibility of existing as a distinct community. Under the Ottoman Empire, their freedom of religion had often been restricted and they were subject to the Sunni Hanafi school of law, which was that of the empire. The new republic, by contrast, authorized them to create their own religious courts on the basis of Shi'a law. As a community, the Shi'a thus acquired an institutional existence distinct from that of the Sunnis.

The Lebanese Constitution of 1926 established an original political system in Lebanon that is still operative today. It consists of a democratic system in which political power is nevertheless distributed between the various religious communities in keeping with their demographic weight as revealed by a 1932 census. At that time the Maronites were the largest group, followed by the Sunnis and the Shi'a. Upon independence in 1943, the National Pact laid the foundations for a "historic compromise"[2] between the Maronite and Sunni elites, who shared most institutional political power among themselves. In particular, they decided that the president of the republic and commander in chief of the armed forces would always be chosen from among the Maronites, while the prime minister would be chosen from among the Sunnis. The Shi'a, for their part, received the presidency of Parliament, a less important institution—recognition, in its way, not just of their lesser demographic weight but also of their marginal territorial and economic position. For the Shi'a were a mainly rural population inhabiting peripheral zones and often living in great poverty. In contrast to the Sunnis, whose community leaders came from the urban commercial bourgeoisie, the Shi'a community was dominated by great landowners.

To this day, no new census has been conducted, with the result that the distribution of power does not conform to the country's changing sectarian demography. Yet the Shi'a very likely became Lebanon's majority population as early as the 1960s, a fact that should have led to a new distribution of institutional powers. Only the number of seats in Parliament was revised after the Civil War (1975–1990), with the number of Shi'i deputies being increased as part of a general revision of the Islamo-Christian equilibrium. Before the war the Christians had insisted on a

60 percent Christian–40 percent Muslim distribution of parliamentary seats and administrative posts. After the war this distribution was revised in the direction of strict Islamo-Christian parity.

The sectarian pact strengthened the country's religious communities by laying the foundation of a weak state. To this day, economic policy is laissez-faire in nature, and, in the absence of a welfare state, social protection has been delegated to community-based charitable institutions. Most of these are run by members of the clergy and notables, who have used them to consolidate their client networks. In the absence of a strong and disciplined army, militias linked to notables or community-based political parties proliferated in every community. In contrast to the Shi'a, the Maronite and Sunni communities possessed their own institutions for supervising the population. Among the Sunnis, the most important of these was the Philanthropic Islamic Association of Beirut, or Maqasid. Founded in 1878 in reaction to Christian missionary activities, its activities focused on education and health care. It possessed an entire network of schools that primarily sought to educate the children of Beirut's poor Sunni families as well as the city's best hospital, an orphanage, a retirement home, and exclusive control over burials in the city. The association's board members were drawn from Beirut's merchant and religious notability. In the framework of the new Lebanese state, Maqasid also set about operating as a pressure group to defend the interests of the Sunnis of Beirut.[3]

Like other countries in the region, Lebanon embarked on a period of rapid social change starting in the late 1950s. These changes simultaneously affected intra- and intercommunity relations, thereby modifying the political landscape. The choice of an open, trade-based economy that neglected agriculture and favored large landowners resulted in a rural exodus that drove thousands of small peasants into the cities, among other things creating a belt of poverty around Beirut. The emergence of this new subproletariat weakened the relations of clientelist interdependence linking community leaders to the lower classes and favored the emergence of (often militarized) antiestablishment political movements in all communities. Though they wished to preserve Christian domination in Lebanon, the Maronite Phalanges sometimes showed themselves to be violently antiestablishment after the fashion of European fascist movements. Discontented Sunnis, meanwhile, mainly rallied to the ideologies of Nasserism and the Palestinian cause. The community's principal antiestablishment movement, the Nasserist-aligned al-Murabitun (the Sentinels), was led by a Beirut gang boss very popular among the lower classes who was bankrolled by Yasser Arafat's Fatah Party and Muammar Gaddafi's Libya.

Feelings of frustration were particularly intense within the Shi'a community, which had been marginalized in the national political compromise and heavily affected by the decline of agriculture and the rural exodus. Its mobilization (and transformation from marginal actor to pillar of the political equation, at the Sunnis' expense) is the most salient political phenomenon of Lebanon's recent history and civil war. While Nasserism and the Palestinian cause were also popular among the Shi'a, large numbers of whom were to be found in the ranks of al-Murabitun, the world of Shi'a protest was above all dominated by left-wing parties. Prominent among them was the Communist Action Organization in Lebanon, whose leaders conceived of the Shi'a as a "class-community"—that is, as a population combining sectarian identity with the social characteristics of the proletariat[4]—that should by rights be at the forefront of the revolution.

As in Iraq, Iran, and Bahrain, the attraction exerted over Shi'a by revolutionary and secular ideologies provoked a reaction on the part of the ulama. In Lebanon, this reaction centered on the figure of Musa al-Sadr (d. 1978). Educated in the religious seminaries of Najaf and Qom, he also had a degree in law and economics from the University of Tehran. Though born in Iran, he was a distant relation of the main Shi'a authority in the town of Tyr, Abd al-Hussein Sharaf al-Din (d. 1957), famous for his anti-French activities under the mandate. Having remarked on Musa al-Sadr's charisma and political commitment while visiting his family in Iran, al-Din had asked al-Sadr to succeed him.

Drawing on a discourse that called on all the "disadvantaged" to unite, Musa al-Sadr's activities in Lebanon mainly consisted of renewing the Shi'a community's leadership and strengthening its foundations. The first of these activities took the form of promoting a new type of clerical leader modeled on himself and of encouraging the political emergence of new lay elites (many of them from the liberal professions) not born into the families of the notability. By creating many institutions, Musa al-Sadr also consolidated the underpinnings of the Shi'a community. They included schools, an orphanage, and a religious seminary financed by the Lebanese Shi'a diaspora that had enriched itself in Africa and the United States.[5] He also put the finishing touches on the institutional separation of Shi'a and Sunnis, actively working for the adoption of a 1967 law creating the Shi'a Higher Council. In addition to being responsible for overseeing Shi'a religious affairs on the basis of Ja'farite law, this body represented the community in its dealings with the state. The Shi'a had formerly been included on the Islamic Higher Council, an institution created in 1955 to administer the religious affairs of Sunnis and Shi'a alike. It was also for this reason that, in 1973, al-Sadr created the Amal Movement, which is today one of the main Shi'a political parties. The aim was to provide Shi'a with a structure of political mobilization that would facilitate their participation in the state and sectarian politics. Helping place Shi'a in important positions in the state bureaucracy has thus always been one of the movement's objectives. It today controls the main Shi'a channels for accessing high government positions.

While he sought to mobilize the community so that it could take its future into its own hands and assert itself on the national political stage, Musa al-Sadr was fundamentally a legalist. In other words, his objective was not to overthrow the existing order but rather to better integrate the Shia community within it. Some believed he even sought to substitute the Shi'a community for its Sunni counterpart as the second pillar of the sectarian pact. For he was always careful to maintain good relations with the Maronite ruling class and was a fervent supporter of Islamo-Christian dialogue. This attitude sharply contrasted with the antiestablishment radicalization of left-wing organizations and earned him Lebanese nationality in 1963, just a few years after arriving in the country. For some, the creation of the Shi'a Higher Council was a means for the Maronite ruling class to separate the Shi'a from the Sunnis and thereby frustrate the efforts of left-wing organizations to unite all Muslims behind the Palestinian cause.[6]

The Civil War: Rising Shi'a Power and Sunni Decline

The Civil War that broke out in 1975 was the result of a conjunction of internal and external strains. There was thus persistent disagreement within the Maronite-Sunni couple, with the president of the republic doing everything in his power to reinforce Christian dominance despite the country's changing sectarian demography while successive prime ministers hoped to revise the distribution of power in favor of Muslims. These various positions regarding the distribution of powers were more-over coupled with disagreements over the Israeli-Palestinian conflict.

Lebanon fought against Israel during the first Arab-Israeli War (1947–1949). When the war ended, it had to come to terms with the fact that some 100,000 Palestinian refugees were now present on its soil, most of them residing in camps near Shi'a population zones in the country's South. The presence of these Palestinians threatened Lebanon's fragile politico-sectarian balance in two ways. First, the great majority of the refugees were Sunnis. Christians feared that their prolonged and even permanent presence would reinforce Muslim demography, feeding demands for a revision to the sectarian pact in favor of Muslims and Sunnis in particular. Second, the emergence of the Palestinian Liberation Organization (PLO) over the course of the second half of the 1960s had set in motion the militarization of Palestinian refugees. Starting in 1970, Lebanon had even become the main rear base for Palestinian guerilla activities, leading to Israeli reprisals on Lebanese soil. This further intensified the rural exodus of Shi'a to the southern suburbs of Beirut and also radicalized large swaths of the Muslim population, which, in contrast to the Christians, wanted Lebanon to become more deeply involved in the struggle against Israel. In general, the Palestinian cause was unanimously supported by the discontented, who wanted to change the status quo in the distribution of power. Palestinian resistance organizations intentionally stoked this phenomenon, seeking to establish interdependent relations with the Muslim opposition in order to create a sanctuary for themselves in Lebanon.[7]

Following months of escalation, war finally broke out in April 1975 after militiamen from the Christian Phalanges Party machine-gunned a bus transporting Palestinians. The Phalangists were seeking to avenge the death of several of their own, shot by Palestinian gunmen a few hours earlier as they participated in the inauguration of a church. At first the war was conducted along relatively clear, Muslim versus Christian lines. On one side were the various armed Muslim groups (Palestinians, Sunni Lebanese, Shi'a, and Druze) united under the banner of the National Movement. Created in 1970 by Kamal Jumblatt (d. 1977), the leader of the Druze community, the movement presented itself as "progressive"— that is, Arab-nationalist and socialist leaning. On the other side were the Christians, who in 1976 joined forces in the Lebanese National Front, which had been created by former president of the republic Camille Chamoun (d. 1987). With the National Movement seemingly on the point of victory, in 1976 the president of the republic officially called on neighboring Syria to intervene, its soldiers crossing the border to prevent Lebanon from falling into the hands of revolutionary organizations. While Syria had always formally supported the Arab nationalist and Muslim currents, the war brought the realization that any victory on the part of its traditional allies would drag Lebanon and, with it, Syria into open war with Israel—a conflict the Syrians knew they had no chance of winning. The arrival of Syrian troops on Lebanese soil, where they would remain stationed until 2005, gradually reshuffled the balance of political forces between religious groups. The first victim was the National Movement, particularly with the departure of the Amal Movement, which immediately rallied to the Syrian side. This was partly a strategic choice: with this move, Amal became Syria's main ally in the country, which it to a great extent remains to this day. A few years earlier, moreover, Musa al-Sadr had done a favor for Syrian president Hafez al-Assad by declaring that the Alawites were Shi'a and therefore Muslim. This allowed the regime in Damascus to counter the arguments of its Sunni Islamist opposition, which never missed an opportunity to denounce the heretical nature of the Alawites (see chapter 5). But the Amal Movement's decision to align itself with Syria also reflected the deteriorating relations between Amal and the Palestinian organizations. Prior to this moment, the two had conducted joint military operations in southern Lebanon, with the Palestinians extensively assisting in training and arming the Shi'i militias. Yet Amal could not ignore the fact that Israeli reprisals against Palestinian resistance activities, which severely affected the Shiʻi populations of the South, had increasingly led them to reject the Palestinians. Israeli Army raids in these areas only compounded their endemic poverty, persuading the local population that, obsessed with their own struggle against the Jewish state, the Palestinian organizations had little interest in their problems. Large swaths of the South, moreover, found themselves under the de facto control of the PLO, particularly Yasser Arafat's Fatah Movement, which, in addition to interfering in local governance to protect its own interests, was also suspected of secretly negotiating with the Christian militias. The mysterious disappearance of Musa al-Sadr in 1978 during a trip to Libya was probably due to an agreement between the regime of Muammar Gaddafi and the Palestinian organizations, which were eager to rid themselves of a man who had become one of their leading adversaries.

Between 1985 and 1987 the conflict between Amal and the Palestinians culminated in the "War of the Camps," during which Amal laid siege to several Palestinian camps with help from the Syrian Army. In addition to wanting to continue being seen as the protector of Shiʻa interests, the Amal Movement sought to influence national political negotiations by rhetorically presenting itself as a key actor in the preservation of national independence and Syria's main ally. The War of the Camps, in turn, strengthened the ties between Palestinian and Sunni organizations, particularly al-Murabitun, which continued to heavily depend on Fatah's support. But this alliance was no match for the Shiʻi militias of Amal, which in 1985, as part of the War of the Camps, laid siege to and destroyed the headquarters of al-Murabitun and established their dominance over most of Beirut's Sunni neighborhoods. For the Sunnis, this was a traumatic episode that embodied their defeat as a community and the apparently unstoppable rise of their Shiʻi counterparts.[8] One consequence of the defeat of the Palestinians and their Sunni allies was the eclipse of the Sunni's most well-established revolutionary organizations, with notables reemerging as the community's principal representatives. The latter, however, had little purchase among the lower classes and suffered from internal divisions as a result of the intense rivalries between individuals and clans, badly diminishing their ability to control the population.

Al-Murabitun's enfeeblement set the stage for the emergence of new religious actors, most of whom were aligned with the Muslim Brotherhood. Particularly divided along lines of local identity, however, the latter were unable to build a hegemonic political movement at the level of the entire community. In general, the Sunnis were much more fragmented during the war than was the case of the other major communities, where strong leadership emerged in the form of political movements associated with charismatic figures. There were rivalries between the towns where the majority of Sunnis lived as well as within these towns, with different neighborhoods competing against one another. The situation was much the same in the North, where Sunni-populated towns found themselves confronting a handful of Sunni-populated villages.[9]

Whereas the Sunnis exited the war profoundly weakened as a community, the Shi'a were its main winners. In practice, the conflict accelerated the process of Shi'a community mobilization begun by Musa al-Sadr, putting it in a position to negotiate a redistribution of representation in Parliament and the administration. At the same time, it conferred the status of defender of the nation on Hezbollah (the Party of God). The latter was born around 1982, during the war, from the gradual union of various Shi'i movements and militias dissatisfied with the direction taken by Amal and eager to advance the cause of exporting the Iranian Revolution. Some rejected the idea that the movement should abandon the struggle against Israel and turned against the Palestinians. Others regretted that, following the death of Musa al-Sadr, Amal had been taken over by a lay leadership that had neither political scruple nor any real interest in issues of re-Islamization. Nabih Berri was very much its personification. Born into Lebanon's African diaspora, this lawyer was perfectly representative of the rising classes in search of social and political recognition that Amal had helped promote. He continues to lead Amal to this day and has held the presidency of Parliament since 1992.

The Iranian Revolution acted as a catalyst to unify these various sources of discontent into a single movement initially characterized by two main objectives: to continue the struggle against Israel, which in 1982 permanently installed its troops in southern Lebanon to create a buffer zone allowing it to protect the northern portion of its own territory; and to antiestablishment, an Islamic republic on the Iranian model in Lebanon. Resolutely antisystem, Hezbollah thus revived the political radicalism that Amal had tried to eradicate from the Shi'a community. In keeping with the Islamic Republic's pan-Islamic philosophy, what's more, this movement, though exclusively recruiting from the Shi'a community, sought to reduce the widening sectarian divide between Sunnis and Shi'a by creating joint organizations bringing together ulama from both communities. In 1982 it thus supported the establishment of the Union of Muslim Ulama in Lebanon, a body that included Sunni and Shi'i ulama who were well disposed toward Tehran. The objective was twofold. On the one hand, it sought to weaken the two communities' traditional lay notables, especially among the Sunnis. On the other, it aimed to reduce the sectarian divide and thereby construct a united Muslim front.[10] Neither these efforts to unite the country's Muslims nor Iranian influence over Lebanese Sunni circles were to last long. From the 1990s onward, as we shall see, Saudi patronage gained the upper hand among Sunnis.

From the Islamo-Christian Equation to the Sunni-Shi'a Divide

Though rising Shi'a power reconfigured the Islamo-Christian equation during the Civil War, it remained central to the political calculus. Evidence of this can be found in the Taif Agreement ending the war, which was signed by the belligerents in 1989 under the patronage of Saudi Arabia. The agreement recalibrated the distribution of political and administrative posts on the basis of strictly equal representation for Christians and Muslims. Although it increased the Muslim share, however, it did not bring the distribution of power into line with the reality of sectarian demography. For according to all estimates, the Muslim communities were by that time far larger than their Christian counterpart, with the most recent estimates putting the Shi'a population at between 30 and 40 percent of the national total. Whatever the case, the Shi'a are now the country's largest community, followed by the Sunnis and Maronites in descending order. In keeping with the Taif Agreement, Shiʻa representation in Parliament has increased from 18 to 21 percent, putting them at parity with the Sunnis but far behind the Maronites, who have kept what is by far the largest number of seats despite their shrinking share of the population.[11] What's more, the manner in which the posts of president of the republic, prime minister, and president of Parliament were distributed in no way changed. The relative reconfiguration of Islamo-Christian relations was accompanied by a reconfiguration of Sunni-Shiʻa relations. The Shiʻa exited the war dominated by an alliance between Amal and Hezbollah. It is altogether remarkable that the existence of two powerful Shiʻi political organizations did no damage to the process of unifying the Shiʻa community, which is an essential condition for wielding influence over the sectarian compromise at the highest reaches of the state.[12] In 1988, with the war drawing to a close, several months of clashes broke out between Amal and Hezbollah in the South, with Hezbollah winning a clear advantage on the ground. Significantly, the fighting stopped after Syria and Iran orchestrated an agreement between the two militias. It will be recalled that the two countries had been strategic allies since the early 1980s. The good relations they enjoyed by virtue of their shared interests and the influence they respectively wielded over Amal and Hezbollah contributed to establishing a functional partnership between the two organizations based on a division of tasks. Having lost much of its following to Hezbollah over the course of the war, Amal concentrated on what was already Musa al-Sadr's objective: to win institutional representation and steer public resources toward the Shiʻa community in order to consolidate clientelist networks. Hezbollah, for its part, sought to construct an irreproachable moral reputation for itself, in part by capitalizing on its role in the struggle against the Israeli occupation of South Lebanon and in part by saying that it refused to participate in Lebanese politics so as to avoid being associated with petty political dealings and the corruption of political staff.

Shattered by the war, the Lebanese Army never took the lead in the struggle against the Israeli occupation of the South, which lasted from 1982 to 2000. This job was left to Hezbollah fighters, who presented themselves as defending the entire nation on their own. This enabled

Hezbollah to successfully negotiate an exception to the clause of the Taif Agreement that provided for militias to be disarmed. It was thus allowed to keep its weapons in order to continue the fight against the Israeli occupation. Though claiming that it wanted nothing to do with Lebanese politics, Hezbollah nevertheless gradually took part in it. Like other Shi'a Islamist movements linked with the Islamic Republic of Iran, it officially abandoned its efforts to export the revolution to Lebanon and establish an Islamic state there. Since 1991 the slogan "the Islamic revolution in Lebanon" no longer figures on its famous yellow flag of a fist brandishing an AK-47 assault rifle (iconography borrowed from the Iranian Pasdaran). In other words, Hezbollah had also embarked on a process of deradicalization, something the group itself referred to as "Lebanonization." This was reflected in its transformation into a full-fledged political party: it participates in local and national elections, generally in an alliance with Amal, and has adapted to the Islamo-Christian religious compromise, which, though representing a community that can legitimately lay claim to a greater share of institutional political power, it has never challenged. The leaders of Hezbollah explain that, even though they still believe that an Islamic state on the Iranian model represents the best political system, it cannot be established in a multidenominational society like Lebanon, where it is imperative to preserve the Islamo-Christian balance as well as the feelings of other Muslim communities.

Having come to terms with the limitations of the institutional political system, Hezbollah thus established itself as a quasi-state actor, with the result that it was regularly denounced as a "state within the state." In addition to its powerful militia, which had more than enough resources to confront the Lebanese Army should that be necessary, Hezbollah developed an entire network of institutions that crisscrossed the Shi'a community, including hospitals, schools, orphanages, telecommunication networks, television, radio, and charitable institutions. In Shi'i population zones, it very effectively substituted itself for the state, something that was far from unusual in the Lebanese context. As we have seen, the structure of the Lebanese state was weak by design, with the country's ruling elites seeing it as an arena of negotiation among community representatives rather than a supplier of public services.

The process of unification took time to take hold among the Sunnis, who left the war particularly divided owing to the military defeat of their political organizations (including the Palestinian militias), the factional divisions among their notables, and the absence of any external patronage that might foster unity. During the war and the years leading up to it, the Sunnis and Palestinians had received political and financial support from several states: Syria, Egypt, Iraq, Libya, and Saudi Arabia. Each of them had its own champions and agenda, a fact that fueled the fragmentation of the community and its Palestinian allies. It was only at war's end that it reorganized itself as a cohesive actor. Unlike the Shiʿa, however, this did not take place via ideologized mass political organizations but rather was centered on the figure of an individual who embodied a new type of notability: the billionaire businessman Rafiq al-Hariri (d. 2005), who between 1992 and 2004 held the post of prime minister almost without interruption.

The son of a small fruit producer from the port city of Sidon, Hariri did not belong to the traditional Sunni notability from which prime ministers had always been drawn since the National Pact. Nor was he among the warlords who had won political power by force of arms. Like so many other Lebanese, al-Hariri emigrated to Saudi Arabia in the 1960s, where he became a real estate entrepreneur and also built bridges of trust with the royal family. Starting in 1982 he began to play an increasingly important role in Lebanon thanks to his involvement in various real estate projects and the creation of a charitable organization, the Hariri Foundation. At first, the foundation's activities were limited to awarding educational grants. Starting in the 1990s, however, it began to develop a vast network of schools and hospitals, supplanting the old Maqasid association on which the traditional Sunni notability had formerly relied to construct their leadership. Owing to his close ties with the Saudi government, including King Fahd (d. 2005), Rafiq al-Hariri also became Saudi Arabia's principal intermediary in Lebanon. After the war, he consolidated his position by becoming the leading player in the effort to reconstruct downtown Beirut.[13]

Hariri's growing power provoked opposition within the Sunni community among both the old notability and religious actors. In contrast to what had taken place among the Shi'a, Sunni Islamists were unable to establish themselves as the Sunni community's hegemonic leaders and representatives—in part because the war had done nothing to heal the preexisting divisions within the community, but in part also because the Syrian regime, which set the terms of Lebanese politics from its arrival in 1976 until its departure in 2005, sought to prevent Sunni Islamists from uniting. The organization responsible for managing the religious affairs of the Sunni community, Dar al-ifta, for its part remained under the close control of the prime minister—that is, Rafiq al-Hariri. The latter also strove to present himself as a religious philanthropist by sponsoring the construction of several mosques across the country.

Hariri's assassination in 2005 did not radically change the situation in the Sunni community, with his son Saad assuming leadership of the Future Current founded by his father. It did, however, deepen the Sunni-Shi'a polarization: for the first time in Lebanon's history, this divide took the place of the Islamo-Christian equation as the main factor structuring the political landscape. It is to be recalled (chapter 5) that the assassination was carried out by Hezbollah at Syria's request after al-Hariri assumed leadership of a broad anti-Syrian front demanding the withdrawal of Syrian troops from Lebanon and the disarming of Hezbollah. The "martyr" and his family (especially his son Saad) provided figureheads for the vast mobilization that followed. Known as the Cedar Revolution, it ultimately led to the Syrian Army's departure. But the power of Syria's traditional allies—chiefly, the Amal-Hezbollah couple—was not to be discounted. Finding themselves wrong-footed by the Syrian withdrawal, on March 8, 2005, they held a large demonstration in Beirut to "thank Syria." Less than one week later, on March 14, the anti-Syrians mobilized in their turn to reiterate their demands for a sovereign Lebanon.

These two great demonstrations resulted in the emergence of two totally unprecedented coalitions, the March 8 Alliance and the March 14 Alliance—coalitions defined as much by the Shi'a-Sunni divide that structured them as by their pro- or anti-Syrian stance (matters of conviction or circumstance, depending on the case). For these two communities were respectively the largest members of each coalition and were inseparably associated with them at the level of their identities. The Christians, for their part, were historically uncoordinated: evenly divided between the two coalitions, they occupied a clearly subordinate position within each of them. For the Sunnis, the Syrians' departure opened up the prospect of regaining the upper hand vis-à-vis the Shi'a and taking back their historically dominant position among Muslim communities and also on the political scene. For the Shi'a, by contrast, the end of Syrian tutelage jeopardized the gains they had made during the war.

In Beirut and the northern city of Tripoli, the two camps came to blows on a number of occasions, sometimes under arms. The largest such clash took place in 2008 when the government, now dominated by the March 14 Alliance, attempted to deprive Hezbollah of its parallel telecommunications network. In response, Hezbollah forces attacked Beirut, where they literally "took" the western, majority-Sunni neighborhoods of the capital. Unable and unwilling to intervene, the army looked on in impotence. As this show of force unfolded, the offices of the Future Current and some organizations associated with it were ransacked or destroyed with explosives, with some Amal militiamen apparently shouting anti-Sunni insults.[14] Though Hezbollah had only sought to flex its muscles and withdrew after a few days, the incident further stoked Sunni feelings of impotence and humiliation vis-à-vis Shi'a hegemony.

The regional context is another aggravating factor of Sunni-Shi'a polarization in Lebanon. Prior to the assassination of Rafiq al-Hariri, the influence of Iran and Saudi Arabia had grown in parallel (that is, within the confines of distinct communities); they now found themselves on conflicting sides. Saudi Arabia became the largest patron of the Sunni community in Lebanon, with the Future Current heavily depending on its money to perpetuate the policy of clientelist distribution upon which Hariri's leadership was based. For the Saudis, Lebanon became another site of confrontation with Iran, whose influence (via the intermediary of Hezbollah) they wished at all costs to contain.

A new threshold was crossed in 2011 with the start of the Syrian Civil War. As we have seen, in order to weaken Iran, Saudi Arabia and other Gulf monarchies decided to support the Syrian opposition. Hezbollah and Iran, meanwhile, intervened militarily on the side of the regime, doing much alongside Russia to save Bashar al-Assad from the fate of Tunisia's Zine El Abidine Ben Ali and Egypt's Hosni Mubarak. Hezbollah's direct involvement in the Syrian conflict reinforced the link between Lebanon's domestic balance of power (and thus that between Sunnis and Shi'a), Syria's internal situation, and the regional rivalry between Saudi Arabia and Iran.

CONCLUSION

Several lessons may be drawn from this book. I shall discuss two of them here. The first is that the Sunnis and Shi'a have often been joined in a mimetic rivalry. Their rivalry, in other words, has not simply been a cause of differentiation but also of imitation. The emergence of the ulama as a distinct group is an example of this phenomenon. When Ja'far al-Sadiq transformed the imamate into an institution of religious exegesis and community leadership in the eighth century, he was participating in a more general process that ultimately resulted in the emergence of a body of religious scholars among those who would later become known as the Sunnis. While the methodology of religious exegesis differed from that of the Sunni schools of law by virtue of its reliance on rational argument, it was initially modeled on that of the Sunnis, particularly regarding the central place accorded the Hadith. Another example of this mimetic rivalry may be found in the development of the Safavid state as the mirror image of its Ottoman counterpart. If it was the rationalist Shi'ism of the ulama rather than the esoteric Alidism of the first Safavids that was established as the state religion of Iran, it is because the Safavid sovereigns wished to have an official religion that might respond point for point to the official Sunnism of the Ottomans.

Multiple examples of this mimetic relationship may also be found in the Sunni-Shi'a relations of contemporary national contexts. In particular, it is striking to see how, when in a position that might allow them to organize themselves as a minority community, the Sunnis tend to take the Shi'a as their model or regret their inability to form the same type of cohesive community. As the case of Bahrain shows, this temptation would appear to be particularly great among the Sunni clergy, whose fascination with the leadership ability of Shi'i ulama is only compounded by the immense difficulties they face in asserting their own authority, particularly vis-à-vis the Islamists. In Iran, the development of a Sunni community has depended, in typically Shi'a fashion, on the recognition of Sunni clerics as their community's main representatives.

Ultimately, the remarkable resilience of traditional Shi'a clerical authority partly stems from the great continuity that has always existed in Shi'ism between the world of the ulama and that of the Islamists. The relationship of mimetic rivalry with Shi'ism might reinforce the emergence of a hybrid Sunni religious authority that couples the figure of the ulama with that of the Islamist militant. Indeed, such figures have existed since the 1980s. Yusuf al-Qaradawi, for example, is an Egyptian Muslim Brother who became a very popular transnational ulama thanks to the support of Qatar, where he lives. Until now, however, these figures have remained relatively isolated. Yusuf al-Qaradawi himself is without ties to any activist organization and is heavily reliant on the Qatari state.

It is interesting to note that the "caliph" of the Islamic State (Daesh), Abu Bakr al-Baghdadi, also embodies this fusion of figures: a religious studies graduate, he can legitimately lay claim to the status of ulama even as he is the leader of an Islamist political organization. His emergence might also be interpreted as the result of mimetic rivalry with his Shi'i adversaries. Though basing himself on the great Sunni myths, he embodies a figure who has until now existed only among the Shi'a. His existence is also an indication that the aspiration one encounters among certain currents of Sunni and Shi'a Islamism to return to the earliest forms of Islam has led to a convergence of Sunni and Shi'a conceptions of legitimate political power, which in both cases was initially based on the theocratic fusion of political and religious authority characteristic of the first centuries of the caliphate.

Another major lesson that may be drawn from this book is that relations between Sunnis and Shi'a exhibit several classic characteristics of minority-majority relations. Much more than an arithmetical question, the sociological notion of minority refers to the condition of a discriminated group. In most cases, as we have seen, the national configurations into which Sunnis and Shi'a are incorporated reflect the global characteristics of the Sunni-Shi'a relationship: the Shi'a are a demographic minority and, when they are the majority, they are often in the minority politically since they are placed in a marginal position in the institutions of government or even excluded from them altogether.

For these reasons, the history of Sunni-Shiʻa relations in the contemporary period has often been marked by Shiʻa mobilization in protest of their subordinate position. This has taken place in a context in which the creation of nation-states in place of former empires has everywhere been accompanied by the spread of egalitarian ideas that make it more difficult to tolerate inequality between individuals and communities. By propagating the idea, doctrinal differences notwithstanding, of Muslim unity in the struggle against imperialism, Muslim reformism and Islamism have actively contributed to promoting these egalitarian ideas.

One of the specificities of the relationship between Sunnis and Shiʻa understood as a classic minority-majority relationship is doubtless the difficulty experienced by Sunnis in structuring themselves as a community when they find themselves a demographic minority. It may be hypothesized that this difficulty stems from the historical experience of Sunnis, who were the demographic and political majority prior to the era of nation-states. They inherited from this past a representation of themselves as a universal norm from which all other Muslims—and Shiʻa, in particular—have necessarily deviated. This is yet another classic characteristic of the majority-minority relationship: majorities tend to conceive of their specificities as universal and somehow neutral, whereas they see minorities as the embodiment of difference and even deviance.

This is particularly well illustrated by attempts to promote generic forms of Islam in the context of nation-state construction. Thus when the republican regime in Yemen wanted to integrate Zaydis and Sunni Shafiʻi into a single nation, it was in reality promoting a profoundly Sunni Islam, ultimately provoking a reaction on the part of the former elites of the Zaydi imamate, who refused to allow their specificity to be diluted. One observes the same thing in Pakistan. Conceived and constructed by secularized elites for whom Islam was first and foremost a matter of national belonging, this state immediately had all kinds of problems in accepting doctrinal diversity. An example of this is the funeral of the father of the nation, Muhammad Ali Jinnah, a Twelver Shiʻa publicly buried as a Sunni.

In practice, majority-Muslim nation-states, like many states in other geographical and cultural contexts, seem above all to have found it difficult to conceive and manage diversity in general. The issue of Sunni-Shiʻa relations is thus only one aspect of the problem posed by citizenship in the contemporary nation-state. What is the place of difference? To what degree can the state accommodate community-based demands? How is it to embody the nation?

Unsurprisingly, these states generally exhibit a high degree of pragmatism. While discrimination against minorities takes many forms, deportation and ethnic cleansing have been the exception rather than the rule. Iraq is one of the exceptions in this respect. The planned state violence enacted against Shiʻa (and Kurds) is not encountered elsewhere. Most of the time, states authorize a form of separate institutional existence for minorities, even when that runs counter to their official ideology. This is what Saudi Arabia has done with its Shiʻa minority. In Iran, the state understood that allowing its Sunni minority to organize at the scale of the country could ultimately contribute to social stability and even help consolidate the regime's influence outside its borders and beyond the Shiʻi communities who are its traditional representatives.

CHRONOLOGY

❧ ❧ ❧

632: death of Muhammad

632–634: caliphate of Abu Bakr al-Siddiq

634–644: caliphate of Umar ibn al-Khattab

644–656: caliphate of Uthman ibn Affan

661: death of Ali ibn Talib

657: Battle of Siffin and start of *fitna*

660–680: caliphate of Muawiyah ibn Abi Sufyan

680–683: caliphate of Yazid ibn Muawiya and beginning of the Umayyad caliph dynasty

680: martyrdom of the third Imam, Hussein Sayyid al-Shuhada, at Karbala

685–705: caliphate of Abd al-Malik ibn Marwan

740: death of Zayd ibn Ali, founder of Zaydism

750: Abbasid revolution, beginning of the Abbasid caliph dynasty

762: death of Ismail ibn Ja'far, who the Ismailis follow

765: death of sixth Imam, Ja'far al-Sadiq

767: death of Abu Hanifa, founder of the Hanafi school of law

795: death of Malik ibn Anas, founder of the Maliki school of law

820: death of al-Shafi'i, founder of the Shafi'i school of law

833: death of Abbasid caliph al-Ma'mun

855: death of Ibn Hanbal, founder of the Hanbali school of law

868–905: reign of the Turkish Tulunid emirs (Egypt, Palestine, Syria, and Iraq)

874: death of the eleventh Imam, Hassan al-Askari; start of the Minor Occultation of the twelfth Imam, Muhammad al-Mahdi

898: foundation of the Zaydi imamate in North Yemen by Yahya ibn Hussein al-Rassi al-Hadi ila al-Haqq

900: foundation of the Qarmatian Ismaili state in Bahrain

909–1171: Fatimid state in the Maghreb and then Egypt

941: start of the Major Occultation of the twelfth Imam

945–1055: reign of the Buyyid emirs in Baghdad (Iraq and Iran)

1021: death of the Fatimid caliph al-Hakim bi Amr Allah and foundation of Druzism

1038–1063: Turkish Seljuk Empire, founded by Tughril Beg

1058: death of Abu al-Hassan al-Mawardi, theoretician of the caliphate

1258: Mongol capture of Baghdad and end of the Abbasid dynasty

1328: death of Taqi al-Din ibn Taymiyyah in Syria

1453: conquest of Constantinople by the Ottomans

1501: rise to power of the Safavids and establishment of Shi'ism as state religion in Iran

1722: fall of the Safavids in Iran; foundation of the Shi'a state of Awadh in India

1744: foundation of the first Saudi state in central Arabia

1757: start of the British colonization of India

1762: death of Shah Waliullah in India

1783: conquest of Bahrain by the Al Khalifa

1792: death of Muhammad ibn Abd al-Wahhab in Arabia

1798: expedition of Napoléon Bonaparte to Egypt

1820: first British protectorates in the Persian Gulf

1830: start of French colonization of Algeria

1831: death of Sayyid Ahmad Barelvi in India

1834: death of Muhammad al-Shawkani in Yemen

1857: end of the Indian Rebellion

1858: end of the Mughal Empire in India

1867: foundation of the Deobandi school in India

1882: start of British colonization in Egypt

1897: death of Jamal al-Din al-Afghani

1898: death of Syed Ahmad Khan, inspiration of the All-India Muslim League

1905: death of Muhammad Abduh in Egypt

1906: creation of the All-India Muslim League

1907: creation of the All-India Shi'a Political Conference

1918: fall of the Ottoman Empire

1920: British and French mandates over the Arab provinces of the Ottoman Empire

1921: creation of Iraq

1923: foundation of the Republic of Turkey by Mustafa Kemal Ataturk

1924: abolition of the caliphate by Mustafa Kemal Ataturk

1925–1979: reign of the Pahlavi dynasty in Iran

1926: creation of the Republic of Lebanon

1928: foundation of the Muslim Brotherhood in Cairo by Hassan al-Banna

1932: foundation of the third Saudi state

1935: death of Rashid Rida in Syria

1936: Arab revolt in Palestine

1941: foundation of Jamaat-e-Islami in India

1943: National Pact in Lebanon

1946: foundation of the Devotees of Islam by Navvab Safavi in Iran

1947–1949: first Arab-Israeli War

1947: partition of India and creation of Pakistan, foundation of the Association for the Rapprochement of the Islamic Legal Schools in Cairo; foundation of the Ba'ath Party in Syria

1948: foundation of the State of Israel; assassination of Imam Yahya Hamid al-Din in Yemen; death of Muhammad Ali Jinnah in Pakistan

1952: Free Officers Movement seizes power in Egypt

1953: Mohammed Mosadegh's government in Iran overthrown

1958: Abd al-Karim Qasim's coup d'état in Iraq; foundation of Islamic Da'wa Party in Iraq

1959: recognition of Twelver Shi'ism as a fifth school of law by Mahmud Shaltut in Egypt

1961: foundation of the Islamic University of Madinah in Saudi Arabia

1962: fall of the Zaydi imamate in northern Yemen; Saudi Arabia founds the Muslim World League

1963: first Ba'athist coup d'état in Iraq; Ba'athist coup d'état in Syria

1965: foundation of the Message Movement in Iraq

1967: Six-Day War between Israel and its Arab neighbors; foundation of the People's Democratic Republic of Yemen

1968: second Ba'athist coup d'état in Iraq; foundation of the Yemen Arab Republic

1969: Saddam Hussein comes to power in Iraq

1970: death of Gamal Abdel Nasser in Egypt; death of the *marja'* Muhsin al-Hakim in Iraq; Hafez al-Assad comes to power in Syria

1971: independence of Persian Gulf emirates under British protectorate; partition of Pakistan and creation of Bangladesh

1973: Musa al-Sadr creates the Amal Movement in Lebanon

1975–1990: civil war in Lebanon

1976: Syrian invasion of Lebanon

1977: Ali Shariati dies in Iran; coup d'état of General Zia ul-Haq in Pakistan

1979: Iranian Revolution and foundation of the Islamic Republic of Iran; takeover of the Great Mosque of Mecca and Shi'a uprising in Saudi Arabia; Soviet invasion of Afghanistan and start of anti-Soviet jihad; Movement for the Implementation of Jafari Law created in Pakistan

1980–1988: Iran-Iraq War

1981: assassination of Anwar al-Sadat by the al-Jihad group in Egypt; failed Islamist coup d'état in Bahrain

1982: Hezbollah founded in Lebanon

1983: Arif Hussein al-Husseini founds Ja'fari Movement of Pakistan

1985: Haq Nawaz Jhangvi founds Sipah-e-Sahaba Pakistan

1987: al-Qaida founded; Iran and Saudi Arabia break off diplomatic relations

1987–1993: First Intifada in Palestine

1988: death of General Zia ul-Haq in Pakistan; death of Arif Hussein al-Husseini in Pakistan

1989: death of Ruhollah Khomeini; Ali-Akbar Hashemi-Rafsanjani elected president of the Republic in Iran; parties to Lebanese Civil War accept Taif Agreement

1993: Oslo Accords between Israel and the Palestinian Liberation Organization

2001: al-Qaida attacks in New York; fall of Taliban in Afghanistan

2003: fall of Saddam Hussein in Iraq

2004: start of Sa'da War in Yemen

2005: elections in Iraq bring Shi'a Islamists to power; Syrian troops leave Lebanon; assassination of Rafiq al-Hariri in Lebanon

2006: death of Abu Musab al-Zarqawi in Iraq

2006–2014: term of Prime Minister Nouri al-Maliki in Iraq

2011: start of Arab Spring; death of Osama bin Laden

2012: fall of Ali Abdallah Saleh's government in Yemen

2014: proclamation of the Daesh caliphate in Iraq and Syria

2015: Saudi intervention in Yemen begins

2016: execution of the Shi'a ulama Nimr al-Nimr in Saudi Arabia; attack on the Saudi Embassy in Tehran; Iran and Saudi Arabia break off diplomatic relations

NOTES

Chapter 1. Caliphate and Imamate

1. Patricia Crone and Martin Hinds, *God's Caliph: Religious Authority in the First Centuries of Islam* (Cambridge: Cambridge University Press, 2003), chap. 1.

2. Nabil Mouline, *Le Califat* (Paris: Flammarion, 2016), 39.

3. Mouline, *Le Califat*, 62.

4. Guillaume Dye, "Pourquoi et comment se fait un texte canonique? Quelques réflexions sur l'histoire du Coran," in *Hérésies: Une construction d'identités religieuses*, ed. Guillaume Dye, Anja Van Rompaey, and Christian Brouwer (Brussels: Université de Bruxelles, 2015), 103.

5. Mohammad Ali Amir-Moezzi and Christian Jambet, *Qu'est-ce que le shî'isme?* (Paris: éd. du Cerf, 2014), 31.

6. Amir-Moezzi and Jambet, *Qu'est-ce que le shî'isme?*, 53–54.

7. Saïd Amir Arjomand, "The Crisis of the Imamate and the Institution of Occultation in Twelver Shiism: A Sociohistorical Perspective," *International Journal of Middle East Studies* 28, no. 4 (November 1996): 492.

8. Marshall G. S. Hodgson, "How Did the Early Shí'a Become Sectarian?," *Journal of the American Oriental Society* 75, no. 1 (January–March 1955): 10.

9. Hodgson, "How Did the Early Shí'a Become Sectarian?," 12.

10. Arjomand, "Crisis of the Imamate," 494.

11. Kais M. Firro, *A History of the Druze* (Leiden: Brill, 1992), 7–8.

12. Yaron Friedman, *The Nusayris-Alawis: An Introduction to the Religion, History and Identity of a Leading Minority in Syria* (Leiden: Brill, 2010), chap. 1.

Chapter 2. Rivalry and Convergence

1. Mohammed Arkoun, *La Pensée arabe* (1975; reprint Paris: PUF Quadrige, 2015), 35.

2. Christian Décobert, "L'Autorité religieuse aux premiers siècles de l'islam," *Archives de sciences sociales des religions*, no. 125 (January–March 2004): 29–30.

3. John P. Turner, *Inquisition in Early Islam: The Competition for Political and Religious Authority in the Abbasid Empire* (New York: I. B. Tauris, 2013), chaps. 5 and 6; Dominique Sourdel, "La politique religieuse du calife abbaside al-Ma'mun," *Revue des études islamiques*, no. 30 (1962).

4. Mouline, *Le Califat*, 148.

5. Mouline, *Le Califat*, 142.

6. Mouline, *Le Califat*, 154–61.

7. Gilles Veinstein, "La question du califat ottoman," in *Le choc colonial et l'Islam*, ed. Pierre-Jean Luizard (Paris: La Découverte, 2006), 457–58.

8. Arjomand, "Crisis of the Imamate," 497.

9. Between the third century and the Arabo-Muslim conquest of 651, the Sasanian Empire dominated an area roughly corresponding to present-day Iran as well as a portion of the Arab world and contemporary Turkey.

10. Arjomand, "Crisis of the Imamate," 501.

11. Arjomand, "Crisis of the Imamate," 504.

12. Moojen Momen, *An Introduction to Shi'i Islam: The History and Doctrines of Twelver Shi'ism* (New Haven, CT: Yale University Press, 1985), 80.

13. Mohammed-Ali Amir-Moezzi, *Le Guide divin dans le shî'isme original: Aux sources de l'ésotérisme en Islam* (Lagrasse: Verdier, 2007), 43–44.

14. Constance Arminjon Hachem, *Chiisme et État: Les clercs à l'épreuve de la modernité* (Paris: CNRS, 2013), 29.

15. Arminjon Hachem, *Chiisme et État*, 30.

16. Liyakat N. Takim, *The Heirs of the Prophet: Charisma and Religious Authority in Shi'ite Islam* (Albany: State University of New York Press, 2006), 69.

17. Lawrence G. Potter, "Sufis and Sultans in Post-Mongol Iran," *Iranian Studies* 27, no. 1/4 (1994): 100.

18. Amir-Moezzi and Jambet, *Qu'est-ce que le shi'isme?*, 47.

19. Rula Jurdi Abisaad, *Converting Persia: Religion and Power in the Safavid Empire* (London: I. B. Tauris, 2004), 11–13.

20. Arminjon Hachem, *Chiisme et État*, 34–35.

21. Mohammed Ali Amir-Moezzi, "Le shî'isme doctrinal et le fait politique," in *Le Grand Satan et la Tulipe. Iran: Une première République*, ed. Mortéza Kotobi (Paris: Institut supérieur de gestion, 1983), 85.

22. Yitzhak Nakash, *The Shi'is of Iraq* (Princeton, NJ: Princeton University Press, 1994), 30–31.

23. Masashi Haneda, "Emigration of Iranian Elites to India during the 16–18th Centuries," *Cahiers d'Asie centrale* 3/4 (1997); Muzaffar Alam, "The Pursuit of Persian: Language in Mughal Politics," *Modern Asian Studies* 32, no. 2 (1998).

24. Juan R. I. Cole, *Roots of North Indian Shi'ism in Iraq and Iran: Religion and State in Awadh, 1722–1859* (Berkeley: University of California Press, 1989), 115–17, 229–33.

25. The former Arab possessions of the empire were placed under what was known as the international mandate regime by the League of Nations, ancestor of the United Nations. The administration of these territories was assigned to the British (Palestine, Iraq, Transjordan) and the French (Lebanon, Syria) with an official mission to prepare for their eventual independence.

26. Pierre-Jean Luizard, *Histoire politique du clergé chiite* (Paris: Fayard, 2014), 71.

27. Sabrina Mervin, *Un réformisme chiite: Oulémas et lettrés du Gabal 'Amil (actuel Liban-Sud) de la fin de l'Empire ottoman à l'indépendance du Liban* (Paris, Beirut, and Damascus: Karthala, CERMOC, and IFEAD, 2000), 275.

28. Rainer Brunner, *Islamic Ecumenism in the 20th Century* (Leiden: Brill, 2004), 55–60.

29. Brunner, *Islamic Ecumenism*, 94–95.

Chapter 3. Islam as Ideology: Sunni and Shi'a Islamism

1. Gudrun Krämer, *Hassan al-Banna* (London: Oneworld, 2010), chap. 1.

2. Richard Paul Mitchell, *The Society of the Muslim Brothers* (Oxford: Oxford University Press, 1993), 12–13.

3. Seyyed Vali Nasr, *The Vanguard of the Islamic Revolution: The Jama'at-i Islami of Pakistan* (London: I. B. Tauris, 1994), 3–19.

4. Vali Nasr, *Vanguard of the Islamic Revolution*, 21.

5. Vali Nasr, *Vanguard of the Islamic Revolution*, 12.

6. Vali Nasr, *Vanguard of the Islamic Revolution*, 115.

7. Today Shi'a may represent as much as 60 percent of the population.

8. Pierre-Jean Luizard, *La Question irakienne* (Paris: Fayard, 2002), 35.

9. Faleh A. Jabar, *The Shi'ite Movement in Iraq* (London: Saqi, 2003), 75.

10. Basim al-Azami, "The Muslim Brotherhood: Genesis and Development," in *Ayatollahs, Sufis, and Ideologues*, ed. Faledh A. Jabar (London: Saqi Books, 2002).

11. Bernard Haykel, "Al-Qa'ida and Shiism," in *Fault Lines in Global Jihad: Organizational, Strategic and Ideological Fissures*, ed. Assaf Moghadam and Brian Fishman (London: Routledge, 2013), 186.

12. Stéphane Lacroix, "L'islamisme au prisme des Frères musulmans," in *Islams politiques: Courants, doctrines et idéologies*, ed. Sabrina Mervin and Nabil Mouline (Paris: CNRS, 2017), 7.

13. Vali Nasr, *Vanguard of the Islamic Revolution*, 6.

14. Olivier Roy, "The Crisis of Legitimacy in Iran," *Middle East Journal* 53, no. 2 (Spring 1989).

15. Olivier Carré, *Mystique et politique: Lecture révolutionnaire du Coran par Sayyid Qutb, Frère musulman radical* (Paris: Presses de Sciences Po and Editions du Cerf, 1984), 4.

16. Olivier Carré and Gérard Michaud, *Les Frères musulmans: Égypte et Syrie (1928–1982)* (Paris: Gallimard/Julliard, 1983), 99.

17. Gilles Kepel, *Le Prophète et Pharaon: Aux sources des mouvements islamistes* (Paris: Seuil, 1993), 73–107, 207–39.

Chapter 4. An Islamist International?

1. Ziad Abu Amr, *Islamic Fundamentalism in the West Bank and Gaza: Muslim Brotherhood and Islamic Jihad* (Bloomington: Indiana University Press, 1994), 1.

2. François Burgat, "Le Yémen islamiste entre universalisme et insularité," in *Le Yémen contemporain*, ed. Rémy Leveau, Franck Mermier, and Udo Steinbach (Paris: Karthala, 1999), 231.

3. A. Z. al-Abdin, "The Free Yemeni Movement (1940–1948) and Its Ideas on Reform," *Middle Eastern Studies* 15, no. 1 (January 1979): 36–48.

4. Between 1967 and 1990 the southern portion of Yemen was under the sovereignty of a communist regime.

5. Laurent Bonnefoy and Marine Poirier, "The Yemeni Congregation for Reform (al-Islâh): The Difficult Process of Building a Project for Change," in *Returning to Political Parties: Partisan Logic and Political Transformations in the Arab World*, ed. Myriam Catusse and Karam Karam (Beirut: Lebanese Center for Policy Studies and Presses de l'IFPO, 2010).

6. Gérard Prunier (in collaboration with Marc Lavergne), "Les Frères musulmans au Soudan: un islamisme tacticien," in *Le Soudan contemporain*, ed. Marc Lavergne (Paris: Karthala/Amman, CERMOC, 1989), 360–63.

7. Hanna Bantatu, "Syria's Muslim Brethren," *MERIP* 12, no 110 (November–December 1982), http://www.merip.org/mer/mer110/syrias-muslim-brethren.

8. Myriam Benraad, "Irak: Le double échec des Frères musulmans dans un pays en voie de partition," in *Les Frères musulmans et le Pouvoir*, ed. Pierre Puchot (Paris: Galaade éditions, 2015), 283–87.

9. Malcolm H. Kerr, *The Arab Cold War: Gamel Abd al-Nasr and His Rivals, 1958–1970* (Oxford: Oxford University, 1965).

10. Stéphane Lacroix, *Les Islamistes saoudiens: Une insurrection manquée* (Paris: PUF, 2010), 50–52.

11. Lacroix, *Les Islamistes saoudiens*, 56–57.

12. Carine Lahoud-Tatar, *Islam et politique au Koweït* (Paris: PUF, 2011), 55.

13. Lahoud-Tatar, *Islam et politique*, 67–70.

14. David B. Roberts, "Qatar, the Ikhwan and Transnational Relations in the Gulf," *Project on Middle East Political Science*, March 9, 2014, https://pomeps.org/2014/03/18/qatar-the-ikhwan-and-transnational-relations-in-the-gulf#fn2.

15. Aurélie Daher, *Le Hezbollah: Mobilisation et pouvoir* (Paris: PUF, 2014), 83.

16. Nathan Brown, "The Muslim Brotherhood," congressional testimony, April 13, 2011 (Washington, DC: Carnegie Endowment for International Peace), 11, http://carnegieendowment.org/files/0413_testimony_brown.pdf.

17. Marie Vannetzel, *Les Frères musulmans égyptiens: Enquête sur un secret public* (Paris: Karthala, 2016).

18. Olivier Roy, "Islamisme et nationalisme," *Pouvoirs* 104/1 (2003: 45–53).

Chapter 5. From Pan-Islamism to Sectarianism

1. Wilfried Buchta, "Tehran's Ecumenical Society (Majma' al-Taqrib): A Veritable Ecumenical Revival or a Trojan Horse of Iran ?," in *The Twelver Shia in Modern Times: Religious Culture and Political History*, ed. Rainer Brunner and Werner Ende (Leiden: Brill, 2001), 334.

2. Emmanuel Sivan, "Sunni Radicalism in the Middle East and the Iranian Revolution," *International Journal of Middle East Studies* 21, no. 1 (February 1989): 5.

3. Buchta, "Tehran's Ecumenical Society," 346.

4. Sivan, "Sunni Radicalism in the Middle East," 12.

5. Palestinian uprising in the occupied territories (West Bank and Gaza).

6. It is to be recalled that the Oslo Accords provided for the establishment of the Palestinian Authority—in reality, an embryonic Palestinian state—in the West Bank and Gaza.

7. Quotation from the famous fatwa (religious opinion) of Taqi al-Din ibn Taymiyya (d. 1328), cited in Michel Seurat, *L'État de barbarie* (Paris: PUF, 2012) chap. 1, n. 19.

8. It is to be recalled that Israel has occupied a piece of Syrian territory, the Golan Heights, since 1967.

9. Olivier Roy, *L'Échec de l'Islam politique* (Paris: Seuil, 1992), 226.

10. Buchta, "Teheran's Ecumenical Society," 346.

11. I here translate the Arabic term *majus* by "mages," which is generally used to refer to the Zorastrians, followers of Iran's ancient religion, and by extension the Iranians and Shiʻa.

12. Haykel, "Al-Qaʻida and Shiism," 187.

13. Yitzhak Nakash, *Reaching for Power: The Shiʻa in the Modern Arab World* (Princeton, NJ: Princeton University Press, 2006), 45.

14. Raihan Ismail, *Saudi Clerics and Shiʻa Islam* (New York: Oxford University Press, 2016), 54–95.

15. Ismail, *Saudi Clerics*, 145.

16. A radically antirationalist theology that Henri Lauzière described as a form of fideism—that is, a position for which faith takes precedence over reason in achieving knowledge. Henri Lauzière, *The Making of Salafism: Islamic Reform in the Twentieth Century* (New York: Columbia University Press, 2016).

17. Bernard Haykel, "On the Nature of Salafi Thought and Action," in *Global Salafism: Islam's New Religious Movement*, ed. Roel Meijer (New York: Columbia University Press, 2009), 33–57.

18. Nabil Mouline, *The Clerics of Islam: Religious Authority and Political Power in Saudi Arabia*, trans. Ethan Rundell (New Haven, CT: Yale University Press, 2014), 19–20.

19. Lauzière, *The Making of Salafism*, 60–94.

20. Frank Griffel, "What Do We Mean by 'Salafi'? Connecting Muhammad Abduh with Egypt's Nur Party in Islam's Contemporary Intellectual History," *Die Welt des Islam* 55 (2005: 186–220).

21. Lacroix, *Les Islamistes saoudiens*, 99–121.

22. Lauzière, *The Making of Salafism*, 60–94.

23. Mouline, *The Clerics of Islam*, 42–60.

24. Stéphane Lacroix, "Sheikhs and Politicians: Inside the New Egyptian Salafism," Brookings Doha Center, *Policy Briefing*, June 11, 2012, https://www.brookings.edu/research/sheikhs-and-politicians-inside-the-new-egyptian-salafism/.

25. Thomas Hegghamer, "Abdallah Azzam, l'Imam du jihad," in *Al-Qaida dans le texte*, ed. Gilles Kepel et al. (Paris: PUF, 2005), 113–37.

26. Lacroix, "Ayman al-Zawahiri," 219–40.

27. Haykel, "Al-Qaʻida and Shiism," 189.

28. Mileli, "Abou Musab al-Zarqawi," 376.

29. Guido Steinberg, "Jihadi Salafism and the Shiʻis," in *Global Salafism: Islam's New Religious Movement*, ed. Roel Meijer (New York: Columbia University Press, 2009), 110.

30. Fabrice Balanche, "Géographie de la révolte syrienne," *Outre-terre* 29, no. 3 (2011: 437–58).

31. Thomas Pierret, "Syrie: L'islam dans la révolution," *Politique étrangère* (2011/4: 879).

Chapter 6. Iraq: On the Frontier of Sunnism and Shiʻism

1. Shiʻa amounted to 56 percent in 1932. Nakkash, *The Shiʻis of Iraq*, 25.

2. Nakkash, *The Shiʻis of Iraq*, 25–48.

3. Sami Zubaida, "The Fragments Imagine the Nation: The Case of Iraq," *International Journal of Middle East Studies* 34, no. 2 (2002): 212.

4. Hanna Batatu, *The Old Social Classes and the Revolutionary Movement in Iraq: A Study of Iraq's Old Landed and Commercial Classes and of Its Communists, Ba'thists and Free Officers* (Princeton, NJ: Princeton University Press, 1978), 244–318.

5. Toby Dodge, *Inventing Iraq: The Failure of Nation Building and a History Denied* (New York: Columbia University Press, 2003), 68.

6. Nakash, *The Shi'is of Iraq*, 17.

7. Fanar Haddad, *Sectarianism in Iraq: Antagonistic Visions of Unity* (London: Hurst, 2011), 38.

8. Pierre-Jean Luizard, "Le mandate britannique et la nouvelle citoyenneté irakienne dans les années 1920," in *Le Choc colonial et l'Islam*, ed. Pierre-Jean Luizard (Paris : La Découverte, 2006), 403.

9. Luizard, *La Question irakienne*, 74.

10. And the ethnic divide as well. Involved in various guerilla wars from the time of the monarchy, the Kurds were also refused the status of a legitimate component of the nation.

11. Amatzia Baram, "Neo-Tribalism in Iraq: Saddam Hussein's Tribal Policies 1991–96," *International Journal of Middle East Studies* 29, no. 1 (February 1997: 1–31).

12. Haddad, *Sectarianism in Iraq*.

13. Fanar Haddad, "A Sectarian Awakening: Reinventing Sunni Identity in Iraq after 2003," *Current Trends in Islamist Ideology* (Washington, DC: Hudson Institute, 2014), https://hudson.org/research/10544-a-sectarian-awakening-reinventing-sunni-identity-in-iraq-after-2003.

14. Roel Meijer, "The Association of Muslim Scholars in Iraq," *Middle East International Report* 23, no. 237 (Winter 2005), https://www.merip.org/mer/mer237/association-muslim-scholars-iraq.

Chapter 7. Bahrain: The Legacy of a Conquest

1. Juan Cole, "Rival Empires of Trade and Imami Shiism in Eastern Arabia, 1300–1800," *International Journal of Middle East Studies* 19, no. 2 (1987): 178–80.

2. Like all Gulf monarchies, Bahrain contains a very large population of foreign workers. Since 2010 they have constituted a narrow majority of the population.

3. A status it held from 1820 until 1971.

4. Justin Gengler, *Group Conflict and Political Mobilization in Bahrain and the Arab Gulf* (Bloomington: Indiana University Press, 2015), 96.

5. Fuad I. Khuri, *Tribe and State in Bahrain: The Transformation of Social and Political Authority in an Arab State* (Chicago: University of Chicago Press, 1980), 35ff.

6. As we saw in chapter 2, Akhbarism is a doctrine that, in contrast to Usulism, confines itself to scriptural sources in the development of Muslim law. Bahrain is today one of the last bastions of Akhbarism.

7. Hasan Tariq al-Hasan, "Sectarianism Meets the Arab Spring: TGONU, a Broad-Based Sunni Movement Emerges in Bahrain," *Arabian Humanities* 4 (2015), https://cy.revues.org/2807.

Chapter 8. Pakistan: From Muslim State to Islamic State

1. Justin Jones, *Shi'a Islam in Colonial India: Religion, Community and Sectarianism* (Cambridge: Cambridge University Press, 2012), 52–53.

2. Cole, *Roots of North Indian Shi'ism*, 233–39.

3. Jones, *Shi'a Islam in Colonial India*, 41–51.

4. Jones, *Shi'a Islam in Colonial India*, 57.

5. Jones, *Shi'a Islam in Colonial India*, 100–105.

6. Christophe Jaffrelot, *Le Syndrome pakistanais* (Paris: Fayard, 2013), 481.

7. Stanley Wolpert, *Jinnah of Pakistan* (New York: Oxford University Press, 1984), 18.

8. Faisal Devji, *Muslim Zion: Pakistan as a Political Idea* (London: Hurst, 2013).

9. Khaled Ahmed, *Sectarian War: Pakistan's Sunni-Shia Violence and Its Link to the Middle East* (Oxford: Oxford University Press, 2011), 8.

10. Ahmed, *Sectarian War*, 22.

11. Jaffrelot, *Le Syndrome pakistanais*, 111–26.

12. Jaffrelot, *Le Syndrome pakistanais*, 445–50.

13. Jaffrelot, *Le Syndrome pakistanais*, 451.

14. Rieck, "The Struggle for Equal Rights," 275.

15. Jaffrelot, *Le Syndrome pakistanais*, 461–66.

16. Jaffrelot, *Le Syndrome pakistanais*, 467–72.

17. Andreas T. Rieck, *The Shias of Pakistan: An Assertive and Beleaguered Minority* (London: Hurst, 2015), 25–30.

18. Mohammad Saijad, *Muslim Politics in Bihar: Changing Contours* (London: Routledge, 2014), 204–6.

19. Ahmed, *Sectarian War*, 29.

20. Ahmed, *Sectarian War*, 29.

21. Mariam Abou-Zahab, "The Politicization of the Shia Community in Pakistan in the 1970s and 1980s," in *The Other Shiites: From the Mediterranean to Central Asia*, ed. Alessandro Monsutti, Silvia Naef, and Farian Sabahi (Berne: Peter Lang, 2007), 103.

22. Vali Nasr, "Islam, the State and the Rise of Sectarian Militancy in Pakistan," in *Pakistan: Nationalism without a Nation?*, ed. Christophe Jaffrelot (London: Zed Books, 2004), 100–105.

23. Mariam Abou-Zahab, "Le SSP, héraut du sunnisme militant au Pakistan," in *Milices armées d'Asie du Sud*, ed. Laurent Gayer and Christophe Jaffrelot (Paris: Presses de Sciences Po, 2008), 182.

24. Abou-Zahab, "Le SSP, héraut du sunnisme militant," 186–91.

25. Muhammad Qasim Zaman, "Sectarianism in Pakistan: The Radicalization of Shi'i and Sunni Identities," *Modern Asian Studies* 32, no. 3 (July 1998): 698.

26. Qasim Zaman, "Sectarianism in Pakistan," 702–3.

27. Abou Zahab, "The Regional Dimension," 118.

Chapter 9. Pragmatic Sectarianism? Sunnis and Shi'a in Saudi Arabia and Iran

1. Zoroastrianism was the religion of the Sasanian Empire, which in 651 came to an end with the Arabo-Muslim conquest. The religion of Bahaism derives from a nineteenth-century mystical current of Shi'a Islam. As a religion, Mandaeism has similarities to Judaism and ancient Christianity. Its followers claim to follow the teachings of Saint John the Baptist.

2. Stéphane A. Dudoignon, "Un tropisme indo-pakistanais? Le sunnisme en Iran aujourd'hui," *Outre-terre* 28, no. 2 (2011): 331.

3. Rosemary Stanfield Johnson, "The Tabarra'iyyan and the Early Safavids," *Iranian Studies* 37, no. 1 (March 2004).

4. Said Amir Arjomand, "Religious Extremism (Ghuluww), Sufism and Sunnism in Safavid Iran: 1501–1722," *Journal of Asian History* 15, no. 1 (1981): 10–33.

5. Dudoignon, "Un tropisme indo-pakistanais?," 329.

6. Gilles Riaux, "Téhéran et ses provinces," *Outre-terre* 28, no. 2 (2011): 320.

7. Gilles Riaux, "Enquête et frontières du politique dans la République islamique d'Iran: La cause azerbaïdjanaise," *Critique internationale* 67, no. 2 (2015).

8. Eliz Sanasarian, "Nationalism and Religion in Contemporary Iran," in *Religious Minorities in the Middle East: Domination, Self-Empowerment, Accommodation*, ed. Anh Nga Longva and Anne Sofie Roald (Leiden: Brill, 2012), 311.

9. Rasmus Christian Elling, *Minorities in Iran: Nationalism and Ethnicity after Khomeini* (New York: Palgrave Macmillan, 2013), 51.

10. Steinberg, "The Shiites in the Eastern Province," 243–45.

11. Toby Matthiesen, *The Other Saudis: Shiism, Dissent and Sectarianism* (Cambridge: Cambridge University Press, 2015), 65.

12. Abdulaziz H. Al-Fahad, "The 'Imama vs. the 'Iqal: Hadari-Bedouin Conflict and the Formation of the Saudi State," in *Counter-Narratives: History, Contemporary Society and Politics in Saudi Arabia and Yemen*, ed. Madawi al-Rasheed and Robert Vitalis (New York: Palgrave, 2004), 36.

13. Stéphane A. Dudoignon, "Iran, an Unexpected Sunni Hub between South Asia and the Gulf," in *Pan-Islamic Connections: Transnational Networks between South Asia and the Gulf*, ed. Christophe Jaffrelot and Laurence Louër (London: Hurst, 2017).

14. Dudoignon, "Un tropisme indo-pakistanais?," 339.

15. Stéphane A. Dudoignon, "Un mawlawi contre les pasdaran?," *La Pensée de midi* 27, no. 1 (2009): 97.

16. Dudoignon, "Iran, an Unexpected Sunni Hub."

17. Dudoignon, "Iran, an Unexpected Sunni Hub."

18. Dudoignon, "Un mawlawi contre les pasdaran?," 98.

19. Dudoignon, "Iran, an Unexpected Sunni Hub."

Chapter 10. Yemen: Zaydism between Sunnism and Shi'ism

1. Gabriel vom Bruck, "Regimes of Piety Revisited: Zaydi Political Moralities in Republican Yemen," *Die Welt des Islams*, no. 50 (2010): 186.

2. Wilferd Madelung, "Zaydiyya," *The Encyclopedia of Islam*, vol. 11, 2nd ed. (Leiden: Brill, 2002), 477–81. To express the noninfallible nature of the Zaydi imams, I have chosen to use a lowercase letter for *imam* in reference to the Zaydis. This better captures their human dimension, in contrast to the Shia Imams, who are the intimates of God.

3. Gerald J. Obermayer, "La formation de l'imamat et de l'État au Yémen: Islam et culture politique," in *La Péninsule arabique aujourd'hui*, vol. 2, ed. Paul Bonnenfant (Paris: CNRS, 1982), 33–34.

4. In regard to the status of reason, free will, the nature of the Koran, etc. (see chapter 2).

5. Laurent Bonnefoy, "Les identités religieuses contemporaines au Yémen: Convergence, résistances et instrumentalisations," *Revue des mondes musulmans et de la Méditerrannée*, no. 121–22 (April 2008: 199–213).

6. Bernard Haykel, *Revival and Reform in Islam: The Legacy of Muhammad Al-Shawkani* (Cambridge: Cambridge University Press, 2003), 47–75.

7. Michael Cook, *Commanding Right and Forbidding Wrong in Islamic Thought* (Cambridge: Cambridge University Press, 2000), 247, quoted in vom Bruck, "Regimes of Piety Revisited," 192.

8. Haykel, *Revival and Reform in Islam*, 84.

9. al-Abdin, "The Free Yemeni Movemen," 40–43.

10. A communist regime was created in the southern part of Yemen in 1967 and named the People's Democratic Republic of Yemen.

11. Bonnefoy, "Les identités religieuses contemporaines," 205.

12. Bonnefoy, "Les identités religieuses contemporaines," 203.

13. Samy Dorlian, *La Mouvance zaydite dans le Yémen contemporain: Une modernisation avortée* (Paris: Karthala, 2013), 154.

14. Dorlian, *La Mouvance zaydite*, 106–9.

15. Laurent Bonnefoy, *Salafism in Yemen: Transnationalism and Religious Identity* (London: Hurst, 2011), 54–60.

16. Abdullah Lux, "Yemen's Last Zaydī Imām: The Shabāb al-mu'min, the Malāzim and 'hizb allāh' in the Thought of Husayn Badr al-Dīn al-Hūthī," *Contemporary Arab Affairs* 2, no. 3 (July–September 2009): 376.

17. Laurent Bonnefoy, "La guerre de Saʿda: Des singularités yéménites à l'agenda international," *Critique internationale*, no. 48 (2010/3): 143.

18. Lux, "Yemen's Last Zaydī Imām," 393–96.

19. Dorlian, *La Mouvance zaydite*, 146.

20. Dorlian, *La Mouvance zaydite*, 169–80.

Chapter 11. Lebanon: The Search for a New Sectarian Pact

1. Bernard Rougier, *Le Jihad au quotidien* (Paris: PUF, 2004), 114–19.

2. Élisabeth Picard, "De la 'communauté-classe' à la résistance 'nationale': Pour une analyse du rôle des chi'ites dans le système politique libanais (1970–1985)," *Revue française de science politique* 35, no. 6 (1985): 1003.

3. Michael Johnson, *Class and Client in Beirut: The Sunni Muslim Community and the Lebanese State, 1840–1985* (London: Ithaca Press, 1986), 46–47.

4. Picard, "De la 'communauté-classe,'" 1005.

5. Daher, *Le Hezbollah*, 46.

6. Daher, *Le Hezbollah*, 52.

7. Rougier, *Le Jihad au quotidien*, 5–6.

8. Johnson, *Class and Client in Beirut*, 213.

9. As'ad Abu Khalil, "Druze, Sunni and Shiite Political Leadership in Present-Day Lebanon," *Arab Studies Quarterly* 7, no. 4 (Fall 1985): 35–43.

10. Rougier, *Le Jihad au quotidien*, 28.

11. Élisabeth Picard, "Unité et diversité de la communauté chiite libanaise à l'épreuve des urnes (2009–2010)," *Critique internationale*, no. 52 (2011/2): 41.

12. Picard, "Unité et diversité," 31.

13. Hannes Baumann, "The Ascent of Rafiq Hariri and Sunni Philanthropy," in *Leaders et partisans au Liban*, ed. Franck Mermier and Sabrina Mervin (Paris and Beirut: Karthala, IFPO, and IISMM, 2012), 81–104.

14. International Crisis Group, *Lebanon: Hizbollah's Weapons Turn Inward*, Middle East Briefing no. 23 (Paris: International Crisis Group, May 15, 2008), 2.

BIBLIOGRAPHY

A. Z. al-Abdin. "The Free Yemeni Movement (1940–48) and Its Ideas on Reform." *Middle Eastern Studies* 15, no. 1 (January 1979).

Mariam Abou-Zahab. "The Politicization of the Shia Community in Pakistan in the 1970s and 1980s." In *The Other Shiites: From the Mediterranean to Central Asia*, edited by Alessandro Monsutti, Silvia Naef, and Farian Sabahi. Bern: Peter Lang, 2007.

———. "The Regional Dimension of Sectarian Conflicts in Pakistan." In *Pakistan: Nationalism without a Nation?*, edited by Christophe Jaffrelot. London: Zed Books, 2004.

———. "Le SSP, héraut du sunnisme militant au Pakistan." In *Milices armées d'Asie du sud*, edited by Laurent Gayer and Christophe Jaffrelot. Paris: Presses de Sciences Po, 2008.

Ziad Abu Amr. *Islamic Fundamentalism in the West Bank and Gaza: Muslim Brotherhood and Islamic Jihad*. Bloomington: Indiana University Press, 1994.

As'ad Abu Khalil. "Druze, Sunni and Shiite Political Leadership in Present-Day Lebanon." *Arab Studies Quarterly* 7, no. 4 (Autumn 1985).

Khaled Ahmed. *Sectarian War: Pakistan's Sunni-Shia Violence and Its Link to the Middle East*. Oxford: Oxford University Press, 2011.

Muzaffar Alam. "The Pursuit of Persian: Language in Mughal Politics." *Modern Asian Studies* 32, no. 2 (1998).

Mohammed-Ali Amir-Moezzi. *Le guide divin dans le shî'isme original: Aux sources de l'ésotérisme en Islam*. Lagrasse: Verdier, 2007.

———. "Le shî'isme doctrinal et le fait politique." In *Le Grand Satan et la Tulipe. Iran: Une première république*, edited by Mortéza Kotobi. Paris: Institut supérieur de gestion, 1983.

Mohammad-Ali Amir-Moezzi and Christian Jambet. *Qu'est-ce que le shî'isme?* Paris: Les Éditions du Cerf, 2014.

Said Amir Arjomand. "The Crisis of the Imamate and the Institution of Occultation in Twelver Shiism: A Sociohistorical Perspective." *International Journal of Middle East Studies* 28, no. 4 (November 1996).

———. "Religious Extremism (Ghuluww), Sufism and Sunnism in Safavid Iran: 1501–1722." *Journal of Asian History* 15, no. 1 (1981).

Mohammed Arkoun. *La pensée arabe*. Paris: PUF Quadrige, 2015. First edition 1975.

Constance Arminjon Hachem. *Chiisme et État: Les clercs à l'épreuve de la modernité*. Paris: CNRS, 2013.

Basim al-Azami. "The Muslim Brotherhood: Genesis and Development." In *Ayatollahs, Sufis, and Ideologues*, edited by Abdul-Jabar. London: Saqi Books, 2002.

Fabrice Balanche. "Géographie de la révolte syrienne." *Outre-Terre* 29, no. 3 (2011).

Amatzia Baram. "Neo-Tribalism in Iraq: Saddam Hussein's Tribal Policies 1991–96." *International Journal of Middle East Studies* 29, no. 1 (February 1997).

Hanna Batatu. *The Old Social Classes and the Revolutionary Movement in Iraq: A Study of Iraq's Old Landed and Commercial Classes and of Its Communists, Ba'thists and Free Officers.* Princeton, NJ: Princeton University Press, 1978.

———. "Syria's Muslim Brethren." *MERIP* 12, no. 110 (November–December 1982). http://www.merip.org/mer/mer110/syrias-muslim-brethren.

Hannes Baumann. "The Ascent of Rafiq Hariri and the Sunni Philanthropy." In *Leaders et partisans au Liban,* edited by Franck Mermier and Sabrina Mervin. Paris and Beirut: Karthala, IFPO, and IISMM, 2012.

Myriam Benraad. "Irak: le double échec des Frères musulmans in un pays en voie de partition." In *Les Frères musulmans et le pouvoir,* edited by Pierre Puchot. Paris: Galaade éditions, 2015.

Laurent Bonnefoy. "La guerre de Sa'da: Des singularités yéménites à l'agenda international." *Critique internationale* 48, no. 3 (2010).

———. "Les identités religieuses contemporaines au Yémen: Convergence, résistances et instrumentalisations." *Revue des mondes musulmans et de la Méditerranée,* no. 121–22 (April 2008).

———. *Salafism in Yemen: Transnationalism and Religious Identity.* London: Hurst, 2011.

Laurent Bonnefoy and Marine Poirier. "The Yemeni Congregation for Reform (al-Islâh): The Difficult Process of Building a Project for Change." In *Returning to Political Parties: Partisan Logic and Political Transformations in the Arab World,* edited by Myriam Catusse and Karam Karam. Beirut: Lebanese Center for Policy Studies and Presses de l'IFPO, 2010.

Nathan Brown. "The Muslim Brotherhood." Congressional testimony, April 13, 2011. Washington, DC: Carnegie Endowment for International Peace, 11. http://carnegieendowment.org/files/0413_testimony_brown.pdf.

Gabriele vom Bruck. "Regimes of Piety Revisited: Zaydi Political Moralities in Republican Yemen." *Die Welt des Islams,* no. 50 (2010).

Rainer Brunner. *Islamic Ecumenism in the 20th Century.* Leiden: Brill, 2004.

Wilfried Buchta. "Tehran's Ecumenical Society (Majma' al-Taqrib): A Veritable Ecumenical Revival or a Trojan Horse of Iran?" In *The Twelver Shia in Modern Times: Religious Culture and Political History,* edited by Rainer Brunner and Werner Ende. Leiden: Brill, 2001.

François Burgat. "Le Yémen islamiste entre universalisme et insularité." In *Le Yémen contemporain,* edited by Rémy Leveau, Franck Mermier, and Udo Steinbach. Paris: Karthala, 1999.

Olivier Carré. *Mystique et politique: Lecture révolutionnaire du Coran par Sayyid Qutb, Frère musulman radical.* Paris: Presses de Sciences Po and Éditions du Cerf, 1984.

Olivier Carré and Gérard Michaud. *Les Frères musulmans: Égypte et Syrie (1928–1982).* Paris: Gallimard/Julliard, 1983.

Juan R. I. Cole. "Rival Empires of Trade and Imami Shiism in Eastern Arabia, 1300–1800." *International Journal of Middle East Studies* 19, no. 2 (1987).

———. *Roots of North Indian Shi'ism in Iraq and Iran: Religion and State in Awadh, 1722–1859.* Berkeley: University of California Press, 1989.

Michael Cook. *Commanding Right and Forbidding Wrong in Islamic Thought.* Cambridge: Cambridge University Press, 2000.

Patricia Crone and Martin Hinds. *God's Caliph: Religious Authority in the First Centuries of Islam.* Cambridge: Cambridge University Press, 2003.

Aurélie Daher. *Le Hezbollah: Mobilisation et pouvoir.* Paris: PUF, 2014.

Christian Décobert. "L'Autorité religieuse aux premiers siècles de l'islam." *Archives de sciences sociales des religions*, no. 125 (January–March 2004).

Faisal Devji. *Muslim Zion: Pakistan as a Political Idea*. London: Hurst, 2013.

Toby Dodge. *Inventing Iraq: The Failure of Nation Building and a History Denied*. New York: Columbia University Press, 2003.

Samy Dorlian. *La mouvance zaydite in le Yémen contemporain: Une modernisation avortée*. Paris: Karthala, 2013.

Stéphane A. Dudoignon. "Iran, an Unexpected Sunni Hub between South Asia and the Gulf." In *Pan-Islamic Connections: Transnational Networks between South Asia and the Gulf*, edited by Christophe Jaffrelot and Laurence Louër. London: Hurst, 2017.

———. "Un mawlawi contre les pasdaran?" *La pensée de midi* 27, no. 1 (2009).

———. "Un tropisme indo-pakistanais? Le sunnisme en Iran aujourd'hui." *Outre-terre* 28, no. 2 (2011).

Guillaume Dye. "Pourquoi et comment se fait un texte canonique? Quelques réflexions sur l'histoire du Coran." In *Hérésies: Une construction d'identités religieuses*, edited by Guillaume Dye, Anja Van Rompaey, and Christian Brouwer. Brussels: Éditions de l'Université de Bruxelles, 2015.

Rasmus Christian Elling. *Minorities in Iran: Nationalism and Ethnicity after Khomeini*. New York: Palgrave Macmillan, 2013.

Abdulaziz H. al-Fahad. "The 'Imama vs. the 'Iqal: Hadari-Bedouin Conflict and the Formation of the Saudi State." In *Counter-Narratives: History, Contemporary Society and Politics in Saudi Arabia and Yemen*, edited by Madawi al-Rasheed and Robert Vitalis. New York: Palgrave, 2004.

Kais M. Firro. *A History of the Druzes*. Leiden: Brill, 1992.

Yaron Friedman. *The Nusayris-Alawis: An Introduction to the Religion, History and Identity of a Leading Minority in Syria*. Leiden: Brill, 2010.

Justin Gengler. *Group Conflict and Political Mobilization in Bahrain and the Arab Gulf*. Bloomington: Indiana University Press, 2015.

Frank Griffel. "What Do We Mean by 'Salafi'?" Connecting Muhammad Abduh with Egypt's Nur Party in Islam's Contemporary Intellectual History." *Die Welt des Islam* 55 (2015).

Fanar Haddad. "A Sectarian Awakening: Reinventing Sunni Identity in Iraq after 2003." *Current Trends in Islamist Ideology*. Washington, DC: Hudson Institute, 2014. https://hudson.org/research/10544-a-sectarian-awakening-reinventing-sunni-identity-in-iraq-after-2003.

———. *Sectarianism in Iraq: Antagonistic Visions of Unity*. London: Hurst, 2011.

Masashi Haneda. "Emigration of Iranian Elites to India during the 16–18th Centuries." *Cahiers d'Asie centrale* 3/4 (1997).

Hasan Tariq al-Hasan. "Sectarianism Meets the Arab Spring: TGONU, a Broad-Based Sunni Movement Emerges in Bahrain." *Arabian Humanities* 4 (2015). https://cy.revues.org/2807.

Bernard Haykel. "Al-Qa'ida and Shiism." In *Fault Lines in Global Jihad: Organizational, Strategic and Ideological Fissures*, edited by Assaf Moghadam and Brian Fishman. London: Routledge, 2013.

———. "On the Nature of Salafi Thought and Action." In *Global Salafism: Islam's New Religious Movement*, edited by Roel Meijer. New York: Columbia University Press, 2009.

———. *Revival and Reform in Islam: The Legacy of Muhammad Al-Shawkani*. Cambridge: Cambridge University Press, 2003.

Thomas Hegghamer. "Abdallah Azzam, l'imam du jihad." In *Al-Qaida in le texte*, edited by Gilles Kepel et al. Paris: PUF, 2005.

Marshall G. S. Hodgson. "How Did the Early Shīʻa become Sectarian?" *Journal of the American Oriental Society* 75, no. 1 (January–March 1955).

International Crisis Group. *Lebanon: Hizbollah's Weapons Turn Inward*. Middle East Briefing no. 23. Paris: International Crisis Group, May 15, 2008.

Raihan Ismail. *Saudi Clerics and Shiʻa Islam*. New York: Oxford University Press, 2016.

Faleh A. Jabar. *The Shiʻite Movement in Iraq*. London: Saqi, 2003.

Christophe Jaffrelot. *Le syndrome pakistanais*. Paris: Fayard, 2013.

Michael Johnson. *Class and Client in Beirut: The Sunni Muslim Community and the Lebanese State 1840–1985*. London: Ithaca Press, 1986.

Rosemary Stanfield Johnson. "The Tabarraʻiyan and the Early Safavids." *Iranian Studies* 37, no. 1 (March 2004).

Justin Jones. *Shiʻa Islam in Colonial India: Religion, Community and Sectarianism*. Cambridge: Cambridge University Press, 2012.

Rula Jurdi Abisaad. *Converting Persia: Religion and Power in the Safavid Empire*. London: I. B. Tauris, 2004.

Gilles Kepel. *Le prophète et Pharaon: Aux sources des mouvements islamistes*. Paris: Seuil, 1993.

Malcolm H. Kerr. *The Arab Cold War: Gamel Abd al-Nasr and His Rivals, 1958–1970*. Oxford: Oxford University, 1965.

Fuad I. Khuri. *Tribe and State in Bahrain: The Transformation of Social and Political Authority in an Arab State*. Chicago: University of Chicago Press, 1980.

Gudrun Krämer. *Hasan al-Banna*. London: Oneworld, 2010.

Stéphane Lacroix. "Ayman al-Zawahiri, le vétéran du jihad." In *Al-Qaida in le texte*, edited by Gilles Kepel et al. Paris: PUF, 2005.

———. *Les islamistes saoudiens: Une insurrection manquée*. Paris: PUF, 2010.

———. "L'islamisme au prisme des Frères musulmans." In *Islams politiques: Courants, doctrines et ideologies*, edited by Sabrina Mervin and Nabil Mouline. Paris: CNRS, 2017.

———. "Sheikhs and Politicians. Inside the New Egyptian Salafism." Brookings Doha Center, *Policy Briefing*, June 11, 2012. https://www.brookings.edu/research/sheikhs-and-politicians -inside-the-new-egyptian-salafism/.

Carine Lahoud-Tatar. *Islam et politique au Koweït*. Paris: PUF, 2011.

Henri Lauzière. *The Making of Salafism: Islamic Reform in the Twentieth Century*. New York: Columbia University Press, 2016.

Laurence Louër. *Chiisme et politique au Moyen-Orient: Iran, Iraq, Liban, monarchies du Golfe*. Paris: Autrement, 2008. New edition Perrin, 2009.

———. "D'une *intifada* à l'autre: La dynamique des soulèvements au Bahreïn." In *Au cœur des révoltes arabes: Devenir révolutionnaires*, edited by Amin Allal and Thomas Pierret. Paris: Armand Colin, 2013.

———. *Transnational Shia Politics: Religious and Political Networks in the Gulf*. London: Hurst, 2008.

Pierre-Jean Luizard. *Histoire politique du clergé chiite*. Paris: Fayard, 2014.

———. "Le mandat britannique et la nouvelle citoyenneté irakienne in les années 1920." In *Le choc colonial et l'islam*, edited by Pierre-Jean Luizard. Paris: La Découverte, 2006.

———. *Le piège Daech: L'État islamique ou le retour de l'Histoire*. Paris: La Découverte, 2015.

———. *La question irakienne*. Paris: Fayard, 2002.

Abdullah Lux. "Yemen's last Zaydī Imām: The Dhabāb al-mu'min, the Malāzim, and 'Hizb Allāh' in the Thought of Ḥusayn Badr al-Dīn al-Ḥūthī." *Contemporary Arab Affairs* 2, no. 3 (July–September 2009).

Wilferd Madelung. "Zaydiyya." In *The Encyclopaedia of Islam*. Volume 11. 2nd edition. Leiden: Brill, 2002.

Toby Matthiesen. *The Other Saudis: Shiism, Dissent and Sectarianism*. Cambridge: Cambridge University Press, 2015.

Roel Meijer. "The Association of Muslim Scholars in Iraq." *Middle East International Report*, 23, no. 237 (Winter 2005). https://www.merip.org/mer/mer237/association-muslim-scholars-iraq.

Sabrina Mervin. *Un réformisme chiite: Oulémas et lettrés du Gabal 'Amil (actuel Liban-Sud) de la fin de l'Empire ottoman à l'indépendance du Liban*. Paris, Beirut, and Damascus: Karthala, CER-MOC, and IFEAD, 2000.

Jean-Pierre Mileli. "Abou Musab al-Zarqawi, le jihad en Mésopotamie." In *Al-Qaida in le texte*, edited by Gilles Kepel et al. Paris: PUF, 2005.

Richard Paul Mitchell. *The Society of the Muslim Brothers*. Oxford: Oxford University Press, 1993.

Moojen Momen. *An Introduction to Shi'i Islam: The History and Doctrines of Twelver Shi'ism*. New Haven, CT: Yale University Press.

Nabil Mouline. *Le califat*. Paris: Flammarion, 2016.

———. *Les clercs de l'islam. Autorité religieuse et pouvoir politique en Arabie saoudite, XVIIIème–XXIème siècle*. Paris: PUF, 2011.

Yitzhak Nakash. *Reaching for Power: The Shi'a in the Modern Arab World*. Princeton, NJ: Princeton University Press, 2006.

———. *The Shi'is of Iraq*. Princeton, NJ: Princeton University Press, 1994.

Seyyed Vali Nasr. "Islam, the State and the Rise of Sectarian Militancy in Pakistan." In *Pakistan: Nationalism without a Nation?*, edited by Christophe Jaffrelot. London: Zed Books, 2004.

———. *The Vanguard of the Islamic Revolution: The Jama'at-i Islami of Pakistan*. London: I. B. Tauris, 1994.

Gerald J. Obermayer. "La formation de l'imamat et de l'État au Yémen: Islam et culture politique." In *La Péninsule arabique aujourd'hui*, edited by Paul Bonnenfant. Volume 2. Paris: CNRS, 1982.

Elizabeth Picard. "De la 'communauté-classe' à la résistance 'nationale': Pour une analyse du rôle des Chi'ites in le système politique libanais (1970–1985)." *Revue française de science politique* 35, no. 6 (1985).

———. "Unité et diversité de la communauté chiite libanaise à l'épreuve des urnes (2009–2010)." *Critique internationale*, no. 52 (2011/2).

Thomas Pierret. "Syrie: l'islam in la revolution." *Politique étrangère* (2011/4).

Lawrence G. Potter. "Sufis and Sultans in Post-Mongol Iran." *Iranian Studies* 27, no. 1/4 (1994).

Gérard Prunier, with the collaboration of Marc Lavergne. "Les Frères musulmans au Soudan: Un islamisme tactician." In *Le Soudan contemporain*, edited by Marc Lavergne. Paris: Karthala/Amman, CERMOC, 1989.

Muhammad Qasim Zaman. "Sectarianism in Pakistan: The Radicalization of Shi'i and Sunni Identities." *Modern Asian Studies* 32, no. 3 (July 1998).

Gilles Riaux. "Enquête aux frontières du politique in la République islamique d'Iran: La cause azerbaïdjanaise." *Critique internationale* 67, no. 2 (2015).

———. "Téhéran et ses provinces." *Outre-terre* 28, no. 2 (2011).

Andreas T. Rieck. *The Shias of Pakistan: An Assertive and Beleaguered Minority.* London: Hurst, 2015.

———. "The Struggle for Equal Rights as a Minority: Shia Communal Organizations in Pakistan, 1948–1968." In *The Twelver Shia in Modern Times: Religious Culture and Political History,* edited by Rainer Brunner and Werner Ende. Leiden: Brill, 2001.

David B. Roberts. "Qatar, the Ikhwan, and Transnational Relations in the Gulf." *Project on Middle East Political Science,* March 9, 2014. https://pomeps.org/2014/03/18/qatar-the-ikhwan-and-transnational-relations-in-the-gulf/#fn2.

Bernard Rougier. *Le jihad au quotidien.* Paris: PUF, 2004.

Olivier Roy. "The Crisis of Religious Legitimacy in Iran." *Middle East Journal* 53, no. 2 (Spring 1989).

———. "Islamisme et nationalism." *Pouvoirs* 104/1 (2003).

———. *L'échec de l'Islam politique.* Paris: Seuil, 1992.

Mohammad Sajjad. *Muslim Politics in Bihar: Changing Contours.* London: Routledge, 2014.

Eliz Sanasarian. "Nationalism and Religion in Contemporary Iran." In *Religious Minorities in the Middle East: Domination, Self-Empowerment, Accommodation,* edited by Anh Nga Longva and Anne Sofie Roald. Leiden: Brill, 2012.

Michel Seurat. *L'État de barbarie.* Paris: PUF, 2012.

Emmanuel Sivan. "Sunni Radicalism in the Middle East and the Iranian Revolution." *International Journal of Middle East Studies* 21, no. 1 (February 1989).

Dominique Sourdel. "La politique religieuse du calife abbaside al-Ma'mun." *Revue des études islamiques,* no. 30 (1962).

Guido Steinberg. "Jihadi Salafism and the Shi'is." In *Global Salafism: Islam's New Religious Movement,* edited by Roel Meijer. New York: Columbia University Press, 2009.

———. "The Shiites in the Eastern Province of Saudi Arabia (al-Ahsa), 1913–1953." In *The Twelver Shia in Modern Times: Religious Culture and Political History,* edited by Rainer Brunner and Werner Ende. Cologne: Brill, 2001.

Liyakat N. Takim. *The Heirs of the Prophet: Charisma and Religious Authority in Shi'ite Islam.* Albany: State University of New York Press, 2006.

John P. Turner. *Inquisition in Early Islam: The Competition for Political and Religious Authority in the Abbasid Empire.* New York: I. B. Tauris, 2013

Marie Vannetzel. *Les Frères musulmans égyptiens: Enquête sur un secret public.* Paris: Karthala, 2016.

Gilles Veinstein. "La question du califat ottoman." In *Le choc colonial et l'islam,* edited by Pierre-Jean Luizard. Paris: La Découverte, 2006.

Stanley Wolpert. *Jinnah of Pakistan.* New York: Oxford University Press, 1984.

Sami Zubaida. "The Fragments Imagine the Nation: The Case of Iraq." *International Journal of Middle East Studies* 34, no. 2 (2002).

INDEX

❧ ❧ ❧

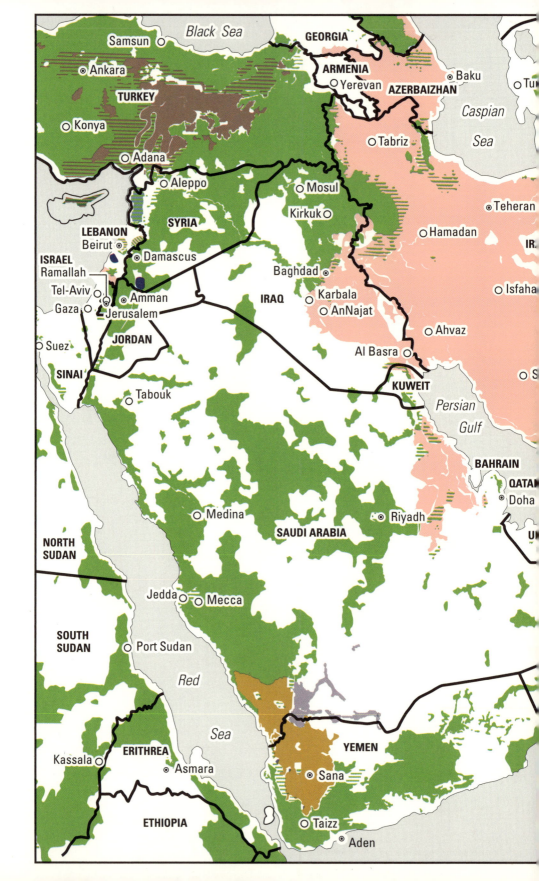